Demystifying Relationship Therapy

What happens when two therapists work together in extended sessions with couples in crisis? *Demystifying Relationship Therapy: A View from the Therapist's Chair* takes readers inside the therapy room to witness the Duo Coaching framework in action; a pioneering approach that challenges the limitations of traditional 50-minute sessions.

Through eight complete therapeutic journeys, from couples drowning in decades of silence to those navigating the aftermath of betrayal, Dr Neil Wilkie reveals the inner workings of co-therapy: the unspoken communication between therapists, the pivotal moments of breakthrough, and the delicate art of holding space for transformation. Interwoven with these case studies is the Relationship Paradigm framework, offering both theoretical grounding and practical insight into what makes relationships thrive.

This is relationship therapy with the curtain pulled back; essential reading for therapists and counsellors seeking alternatives to conventional models, and for anyone curious about how profound change actually happens between two people.

Dr Neil Wilkie is a relationship therapist, founder of Duo Coaching and creator of the Relationship Paradigm. Awarded his doctorate in the Phenomenology of Relationships, he is a Visiting Fellow at Middlesex University. His previous work includes *Reinventing Relationship Therapy through the Duo Coaching Framework.*

‘This groundbreaking book offers a new way to look at the complexity of human relationships and provides a roadmap towards clarity, potential and ultimately transformation for couples facing the challenges of modern living. Having wrestled with couples therapy over the years, this work is quite simply a breath of fresh air.’

Dr Keith Jones, *Psychotherapist and Organisational Development Consultant*

‘This book challenges conventional thinking and provides a powerful alternative that is proven to make a sustainable difference in couples’ relationships — a must-have resource for anyone working in this field.’

Nikki Owen, *Author and Transformationalist*

‘Relationship therapy has been slow to evolve to meet the challenges of contemporary times. This work is notably generous in spirit, inviting practitioners across diverse modalities to expand their practice through collaboration, and it draws a clear link between the interventions it offers and the wider benefits of reparative relationships for social cohesion, health and wellbeing.’

Professor Kate Maguire, *Social Anthropologist, Trauma Psychotherapist, Head of Transdisciplinary Research Programmes, Middlesex University*

Demystifying Relationship Therapy

A View from the Therapist's Chair

Neil Wilkie

Routledge
Taylor & Francis Group
LONDON AND NEW YORK

Designed cover image: Getty images

First published 2027
by Routledge
4 Park Square, Milton Park, Abingdon, Oxon OX14 4RN

and by Routledge
605 Third Avenue, New York, NY 10158

Routledge is an imprint of the Taylor & Francis Group, an informa business

British Library Cataloguing-in-Publication Data
A catalogue record for this book is available from the British Library

ISBN: 9781041271239 (hbk)
ISBN: 9781041271222 (pbk)
ISBN: 9781003752776 (ebk)

DOI: 10.4324/9781003752776

Typeset in Times New Roman
by Newgen Publishing UK

Contents

About the Author

Some therapists study relationships from a distance. Dr Neil Wilkie has lived them – in all their messy, beautiful, heartbreaking, and transcendent complexity. Now seventy, Neil brings to his work as a relationship therapist the kind of wisdom that only comes from walking through fire: marriage, divorce, remarriage, widowhood, and the courage to keep opening his heart despite knowing intimately what love costs.

But Neil's journey to the therapy room took an unexpected path. He started work life as a chartered accountant, moved into running large businesses, and spent years as a strategy consultant – achieving success by conventional measures while sensing something essential was missing. In his late forties, he made a radical choice: to leave the boardroom behind and discover what would truly give him fulfilment. That search led him to helping others navigate their relationship journeys, marking the beginning of both his professional calling and his own deeper learning about love's expression. What had been a successful career became preparation for something more meaningful – using his understanding of systems, strategy, and human dynamics to help couples transform their most intimate connections.

This personal and professional journey led Neil to create Duo Coaching, an innovative approach that pairs two therapists in extended sessions, drawing from multiple therapeutic modalities to help couples achieve breakthroughs that traditional therapy often cannot reach. His Relationship Paradigm framework, born from both rigorous training and lived experience, offers couples a practical roadmap toward the kind of connection that sustains.

Neil holds a doctorate in the Phenomenology of Relationships and serves as Visiting Fellow at Middlesex University, bringing academic rigour to work that remains profoundly human.

Perhaps his most important credential, though, is his willingness to remain a student of relationships even after fifteen years of professional practice. Some of his most profound insights have arrived in unexpected places – standing on a beach in South Georgia watching penguins navigate partnership with enviable clarity, or adjusting course aboard Moon River, the sailing yacht he shares with his wife Gwen.

Gwen, a recent doctoral graduate in the Future of Work, shares Neil's commitment to both professional excellence and personal balance. Ten days each month, they leave behind emails and appointments to sail wherever winds and tides take them – practising what Neil preaches about the necessity of protecting time for connection. Together with their two adopted daughters, they've created a family that honours both complexity and joy.

At an age when many contemplate retirement, Neil describes himself as getting his 'second wind' in this work. His love of travel, sailing, and 'unexpected and challenging situations' reflects a life philosophy that shapes his therapeutic approach: growth happens when we lean into discomfort rather than avoid it. Though he misses his Golden Retrievers of previous chapters of life, he's learned that every stage offers its own gifts – if we're willing to receive them.

After witnessing hundreds of couples transform their relationships, Neil remains convinced that connection is humanity's greatest untapped resource. This book represents his invitation to join what he calls the 'relationship revolution' – not through grand gestures, but through the daily choice to show up, speak truth, and nurture the bonds that make life meaningful.

Acknowledgements

Some books emerge from solitary contemplation. This one was forged in collaboration, refined through countless conversations, and shaped by the generous wisdom of people who believed in work that challenges convention.

Writing a practical guide feels different from writing theory. Theory can hide behind abstraction, but implementation demands specificity – and that specificity was only possible because of the practitioners, colleagues, and partners who've walked this path alongside me.

My deepest gratitude goes to Maria, my co-therapist and co-pilot in this work. Every protocol in these pages has been tested in the crucible of real sessions, and Maria's calmness, insight, and ability to hold space for both couples and for me has been invaluable.

I remain grateful to Cathy, whose early partnership planted seeds that grew into everything that followed. Her vision and collaboration gave Duo Coaching its initial foundation – without which none of this would exist.

The transdisciplinary team at Middlesex University deserves special acknowledgement. They taught me to think beyond single modalities, to honour complexity without drowning in it, and to remain intellectually rigorous while staying grounded in human experience. Their encouragement to look not just at couples but within myself transformed both my practice and my understanding of what relationship work requires.

To the hundreds of couples who've trusted us with their most intimate struggles – thank you for your courage. You've taught me more about relationships than any textbook ever could. Your willingness to be vulnerable, to risk change, to show up even when hope felt distant – this is what makes the work meaningful. Every technique in this book was refined because you showed me what actually helps and what merely sounds good on paper.

To my fellow relationship therapists who work within traditional frameworks – I honour your commitment even as I challenge some conventions. This book isn't a rejection of what came before but an invitation to consider what else might be possible. The field grows through respectful dialogue, not dogmatic certainty.

My wife Gwen deserves acknowledgement that goes beyond words. She's lived with a man who's simultaneously writing about relationships while figuring out his own. Her patience with my absences – both physical when I'm in sessions and mental when I'm lost in writing – has been extraordinary. More than that, she's shown me what partnership looks like when two people choose each other daily, even when winds aren't favourable. Our ten days each month sailing together aren't an escape from life but a return to what matters most. She keeps me honest, calls me on my blind spots, and reminds me that expertise doesn't exempt anyone from the hard work of showing up.

To my adopted daughters – thank you for teaching me that family takes many forms and that love's expression isn't limited by convention. You've each shaped my understanding of connection in ways that inform this work.

I acknowledge the relationships that preceded this one – the marriages, widowhood, partnerships, and connections that taught me about love through both joy and heartbreak. Every ending held lessons. Every beginning required courage. The man who writes this book was shaped by all of it.

Finally, to readers holding these pages – whether you're a therapist seeking deeper understanding of this work or someone navigating your own relationship journey: you're the reason this book exists. If you're a practitioner, watching real couples transform through these approaches will deepen your own practice in ways theory alone cannot. If you're in a relationship yourself, seeing how others have walked through fire and emerged stronger may illuminate your own path. My hope is that these stories don't remain abstract case studies but become mirrors in which you recognise something of your own experience, your own struggles, your own possibilities.

The relationship revolution we need won't happen through grand manifestos but through daily choices – therapists choosing to truly see the couples before them, partners choosing vulnerability over self-protection, all of us choosing connection even when isolation feels safer.

Thank you for joining this journey. Whether you're offering help or seeking it, these pages hold stories that matter – because every relationship matters.

With gratitude and respect
Neil

Chapter 1

Introduction

The silence in my therapy room was so thick I could almost touch it. Hazel sat frozen on the left side of the sofa, her hands clenched in her lap, knuckles white. Roger occupied the far-right corner, as far from her as the furniture would allow, his jaw working as he stared at a spot on the carpet between them. The space separating them – no more than two feet – might as well have been an ocean.

'So', I said gently, 'what brings you both here today?'

Hazel's breath caught. Roger's eyes flickered briefly to her face, then away. Neither spoke.

I'd witnessed this moment hundreds of times – the terrible weight of unsaid words, the fear of what might happen if the dam finally broke, the hope and dread mingled in equal measure. This couple, like so many before them, had arrived at my door carrying years of accumulated pain, standing at a crossroads they never imagined they'd reach.

'Take your time', I assured them. 'This is often the hardest part – beginning'.

It was Roger who finally spoke, his voice rough. 'We had an affair. I mean ... she did. Two years ago'. He swallowed hard. 'We're trying to move past it, but I don't think ... I don't know if we can'.

Hazel's eyes filled with tears. 'I've said I'm sorry a thousand times. I don't know what else to do'.

'Saying it and meaning it are different things', Roger shot back, still not looking at her.

'I do mean it. God, Roger, I do. But you won't let me–'

'This is good', I interrupted gently, seeing the familiar spiral about to begin. 'You're both here. You're both speaking. That's more than many couples manage when they first arrive'.

Later, after they'd left – Hazel tearful but composed, Roger rigid with controlled emotion – I stood at my window watching the rain tap against the glass. Steam rose from my cup of peppermint tea as I reflected on what I'd just witnessed. Another couple taking their first tentative steps on a journey that might save them or finally give them permission to let go.

My name is Neil Wilkie, and for the past fifteen years, I have had the extraordinary privilege of witnessing the most intimate moments of hundreds of couples'

DOI: 10.4324/9781003752776-1

lives. As a relationship therapist, I have become a keeper of secrets, a witness to pain, and a guide toward healing.

This book is an invitation to join me on the other side of the therapy room, to see relationships through my eyes – not as abstract concepts, but as living, breathing entities that grow, falter, and sometimes flourish against all odds.

An Unexpected Journey

This is not the career I had planned for myself decades ago. My path to becoming a relationship expert was circuitous, marked by my own failed relationships, heartbreaks, and eventual discovery of profound love. It was those personal experiences – the darkness of disconnection and the light of genuine intimacy – that ultimately led me to develop Duo Coaching and the Relationship Paradigm, approaches that have helped countless couples find their way back to each other.

I believe that one of the greatest gifts in life is a loving and fulfilling relationship. Yet for many, this remains elusive. We are not taught how to create and maintain healthy relationships. Most of us learn by trial and error, often repeating patterns we observed in our childhoods, wondering why we keep arriving at the same painful destinations despite taking what seem to be different paths.

Through the stories in this book – all based on real couples whose identities have been carefully disguised – I hope to demystify the therapeutic process and offer insights into the complex dynamics that shape our most important relationships. I will take you through the journeys of eight couples; starting with their first session and, later in the book, where this journey took them. I have interleaved this with my thoughts on relationships as well as some vignettes of other couples.

The Couples You'll Meet

You will meet:

Rebecca and James – struggling with an affair and its lingering aftermath
Stuart and Clare – who drifted apart over many years and are trying to resolve cultural differences, a blended family, and protective children
Thomas and Eleanor – dreading retirement as they were strangers with no shared purpose
Sarah and John – who had been living different lives for many years with constant arguments
Sam and Suzy – their love under attack from a toxic ex
Barry and Edith – the pain of betrayal still causing misery after thirty years
Jon and Sophia – trying to come to terms with life-changing illness
Richard and Kaye – dealing with irreconcilable differences

These narratives are not merely case studies. They are windows into the human heart, into our universal need for connection, our fear of vulnerability, our capacity for growth, and our remarkable resilience. Between these stories, I will share the frameworks and approaches I've developed throughout my career, Duo Coaching, and explaining the elements of the Relationship Paradigm: Communication, Connection, Commitment, Fun, Growth, and Trust.

I will also take you on my own journey – from a boy growing up in post-war Scotland, where emotions were rarely expressed, to a man who has found purpose in helping others express and understand their deepest feelings. My personal story is woven throughout these pages because I believe that as therapists, we cannot separate ourselves from our work. Our own wounds and healing inform how we guide others.

The world of relationship therapy has high walls and can be a scary place to enter. It requires couples to be open, honest, and prepared to accept that their partner may have very different perceptions. It demands bravery to face what many see as failure or embarrassment. My hope is that this book will take down those walls, making relationship therapy more accessible and less intimidating.

Whether you are a therapist, someone in a relationship seeking understanding, or simply curious about the complex dance of human connection, I invite you to step into my world. Together, we will explore the full spectrum of relationship experiences; the joys, the sorrows, the challenges, and the profound moments of transformation that I have been privileged to witness.

As you read these stories, you may recognise aspects of your own relationships. You may find comfort in knowing that your struggles are not unique. You may discover new perspectives or tools that help you navigate your own journey. And perhaps most importantly, you may find hope; hope that even relationships that seem irreparably broken can be healed with the right guidance, commitment, and understanding.

So let us begin this journey together; a journey into the heart of what it means to love and be loved, to hurt and to heal, to connect and to grow. Welcome to a view from the therapist's chair.

Chapter 2

Rebecca and James – The Price of Silence

A Modern Love Story

It was early morning when Maria, my colleague and co-therapist, and I greeted our newest couple. In our years of practising Duo Coaching, we've learned to read the unspoken language of couples in crisis. The moment Rebecca and James walked through the door, the tension between them was palpable – like a glass wall, transparent but impenetrable.

Rebecca, a successful executive with piercing eyes that couldn't quite mask her exhaustion, sat rigidly in her chair. Her fingers constantly fidgeted with her wedding ring – the symbol that had lately begun to feel more like a question mark than a statement of commitment. Beside her, James, a distinguished academic whose polished exterior betrayed none of the nightmares that would later be revealed, kept stealing glances at his wife of twenty-five years.

'I feel hollow', Rebecca whispered, her voice carrying the weight of recent discovery. As therapists, we've learned that affairs often create what we call a Toxic Triangle – a complex dynamic between the betrayed partner, the partner who had the affair, and the person with whom the affair occurred. But in Rebecca and James's case, we would discover layers of complexity that went far beyond the usual patterns.

Their love story had begun like many great romances – on a hiking expedition in the Lake District, with shared adventures and intellectual debates. Young James had been immediately drawn to Rebecca's sharp mind and vitality, and she to his thoughtful perspective and quiet confidence. For three years, they built their relationship weekend by weekend, until it blossomed into marriage. The foundation seemed solid, built on shared passions and mutual respect.

But life, as it often does, had other plans. While they built their dream life – successful careers, a beautiful home, enviable social status – something else was quietly unravelling. Many nights, in their Tudor-style home, James would wake up in cold sweats from nightmares he couldn't explain, carrying the crushing weight of his hidden learning disability. Every day at the prestigious university where he lectured, he lived in fear that someone would discover his secret, even after decades in academia.

Meanwhile, Rebecca was fighting her own battles. She had faced a serious health crisis five years ago which changed her view of life. At work, she shouldered the

DOI: 10.4324/9781003752776-2

burden of being understaffed whilst trying to meet challenging targets; all while doubting her own self-worth. She sought validation in extreme physical challenges – mountain climbing, ultra-marathons – pushing her body to extremes perhaps to feel something beyond the growing numbness.

Their lives had become a carefully choreographed dance of avoidance – James immersed in his research, Rebecca with her outdoor pursuits. The space between them grew wider until someone else stepped into it: a colleague, with whom James began an affair. This is where the Toxic Triangle began to form – that complex three-way relationship between the betrayed partner, the unfaithful partner, and the affair partner; but with a twist we often see in long-term relationships. The affair was less about passion and more about escape from the suffocating silence that had enveloped their marriage. In this triangle, the colleague represented not primarily a romantic alternative but rather an emotional refuge where James could feel competent and accepted, free from the pressure of maintaining his carefully constructed professional facade. Meanwhile, Rebecca sensed the energetic shift in their relationship even before discovering the affair, intensifying her feelings of disconnection and inadequacy without understanding their true source.

When Rebecca discovered the truth, it wasn't anger that consumed her, but a deep, resonating sadness. 'Will I be enough?' she asked during our session, her voice barely above a whisper. This question revealed the heart of their struggle – both partners had been asking versions of this same question for years, but neither had found the courage to voice it.

As therapists, we've seen many couples devastated by infidelity, but something about Rebecca and James felt different. We introduced them to our pebble constellation exercise – a technique we use to help couples visualise their relationship dynamics. Perhaps it was the way they both created nearly identical representations of their relationship, showing that somewhere, beneath the pain and fear, they still shared the same vision of their future.

We explained to them the four stages of healing from betrayal, using our Toxic Triangle framework:

1. The Initial Stage – where the affair creates intense emotions and complex dynamics
2. The Discovery Stage – where the betrayal comes to light and trust is shattered
3. The Recovery Stage – where both partners decide whether to rebuild
4. The Resolution Stage – where the triangle dissolves and a new relationship can form

James, despite his academic achievements, sat before us like a student again, finally sharing his terror of being 'found out'. His affair, we came to understand, was less about desire and more about finding someone who didn't expect him to be perfect. Rebecca, the ultra-marathoner who had overcome a life-threatening illness, allowed herself to appear vulnerable, acknowledging that her strength had become a wall between them.

By the end of our first session, something had shifted. The glass wall wasn't gone, but hairline cracks had appeared. James spoke of 'trusting the process', while Rebecca admitted her mind felt quieter. As they left, walking slightly closer together than when they arrived, Maria and I shared a knowing look. In their brokenness, we saw the potential for something new to grow – a relationship built not on the polished surface of success, but on the solid ground of shared vulnerability and truth.

Their story exemplifies why relationship therapy can be so transformative. It's not just about healing from betrayal or improving communication – it's about creating a space where long-held secrets can finally be spoken, the unconscious mind brought into the open, where strength can coexist with vulnerability, and where two people can rediscover each other through their shared willingness to change.

Sometimes it takes breaking apart to build something stronger, as in the Japanese art of Kintsugi where broken pottery is repaired using very visible gold. In the shattered pieces of their past, we could already see the glimmers of a more authentic future taking shape. Their story wasn't over; in many ways, it was just beginning. The affair that threatened to end their marriage might become the catalyst that saves it, not because of the pain it caused, but because it finally broke the silence that had been slowly suffocating their love.

As they continue their journey through the stages of healing, Rebecca and James's story reminds us that real love isn't about perfection; it's about having the courage to be imperfect together. Sometimes the price of silence is too high to pay, and only by finding our voice can we find our way back to each other.

I head out into the sunshine; their words still echo and I release them with each step, returning with a clear mind ready for the next challenges.

We will return to Rebecca and James in Chapter 22.

Chapter 3

Relationships

As a therapist, I've observed that we often use the word 'relationship' without truly examining what it means. We speak of 'being in a relationship' or 'working on our relationship' as if we all share the same definition. Yet in my years of practice, I've come to understand that relationships are far more complex, nuanced, and multidimensional than our everyday language suggests.

At its most fundamental level, a relationship is a connection between two people. But this simple definition belies the intricate dance of emotions, expectations, histories, and hopes that constitutes a true relationship. Relationships are living entities; they breathe, grow, stumble, evolve, and sometimes wither. They exist not just between two individuals but in the invisible space between them, what I often call the 'relationship field'.

Beyond the Dictionary

The Oxford Dictionary defines a relationship as 'the way in which two or more people or things are connected, or the state of being connected'. But this clinical definition captures none of the richness, none of the messy beauty that characterises human connections.

In my therapy room, I've witnessed relationships in all their forms, from the passionate beginnings of new love to the comfortable silences of decades-long marriages, from the raw pain of betrayal to the tentative hope of reconciliation. What I've learned is that relationships are not static states but dynamic processes. They are not things we have but things we do, continuously, day after day.

When Tanya and Frank first sat in my office, their definition of their relationship bore little resemblance to each other's. For Frank, their relationship was a vital, living connection that had simply lost its way. For Tanya, it had become a business arrangement, a practical partnership devoid of emotional intimacy. Neither was wrong; they were simply experiencing different aspects of the same relationship, like the proverbial blind men describing different parts of an elephant.

DOI: 10.4324/9781003752776-3

Relationships as Mirrors

Perhaps one of the most profound aspects of intimate relationships is their capacity to serve as mirrors, reflecting back to us parts of ourselves we might not otherwise see. Our partners trigger our deepest wounds and our greatest joys, often without realising it.

I remember Clare saying of Stuart, 'He brings out a childish part of me I don't like'. This insight revealed not just something about Stuart, but something about Clare herself, a vulnerability she'd rather not acknowledge. Similarly, Stuart's dominant behaviour in their relationship reflected his own early experiences of feeling powerless.

This mirroring quality of relationships offers us extraordinary opportunities for growth if we're brave enough to look at what's being reflected. When we react strongly to our partner, with anger, hurt, or even overwhelming love, it's often because they've touched something deep within us, something that belongs to our own story.

The Many Dimensions of Connection

In my work, I've found it helpful to conceptualise relationships along multiple dimensions:

Emotional Connection: This is the feeling of being emotionally attuned to another person, the sense that they see you, understand you, and respond to your inner world. When Harriet described the moment Ed truly listened to her fears about not being 'enough', she was describing a moment of profound emotional connection.

Physical Connection: Beyond just sexuality, this encompasses all forms of physical touch and presence, from passionate lovemaking to the simple comfort of holding hands, from the electric excitement of a new lover's touch to the familiar warmth of an aging partner's embrace.

Intellectual Connection: The sharing of ideas, the stimulation of conversation, the respect for each other's minds; these form the basis of intellectual connection. John and Sarah had lost this dimension amid their struggles, no longer seeing each other as thinking beings with valuable perspectives.

Spiritual Connection: This transcends religious beliefs, though it can include them. It's about shared values, a sense of purpose, and the feeling of being connected to something larger than ourselves through our bond with another.

Practical Connection: The day-to-day logistics of shared lives, managing households, raising children, navigating finances, making decisions; these form the practical dimension that many couples underestimate until it becomes problematic.

A thriving relationship doesn't require perfect alignment across all these dimensions at all times. Rather, it requires awareness of them, attention to them, and a willingness to nurture them over time.

The Dance of Autonomy and Connection

One of the most common paradoxes I observe in relationships is the tension between our need for connection and our need for autonomy. We desire closeness, yet we also require independence. We want to be fully known, yet we fear being fully seen. We seek security in our bonds, yet we crave freedom within them.

This tension lies at the heart of many relationship struggles. When Clare spoke of feeling 'controlled' in her relationship with Stuart, she was expressing his thwarted need for autonomy. When Rebecca worried she 'wouldn't be enough', she was voicing her fear that their connection wasn't secure.

Healthy relationships aren't those that eliminate this tension; they're those that dance with it gracefully. They allow space for individual growth while maintaining the bonds of intimacy. They recognise that sometimes we need to move apart to come together more fully.

Relationships as Systems

One of the most important shifts in my understanding of relationships came when I began to view them not just as connections between two individuals but as systems in themselves. A relationship system has its own patterns, rules, feedback loops, and homeostasis, its tendency to maintain equilibrium even when that equilibrium is dysfunctional.

This systems perspective helps explain why change can be so difficult in relationships. When one partner begins to change, the entire system must reorganise itself. This creates instability, which the system naturally resists. That's why, when Clare began to express emotions after years of emotional withdrawal, Stuart initially found it destabilising rather than welcome; their system was designed around her silence, however unhealthy that might have been.

Understanding relationships as systems also helps us see why individual therapy sometimes isn't enough. We may gain personal insights and growth, but when we return to our relationship system, its patterns pull us back into familiar roles. This is why I developed Duo Coaching, to work with the relationship system as a whole.

The Three Levels of Relationship

In my work with couples, I often describe three levels of relationship that exist simultaneously:

The 'Me' Level: This encompasses everything we bring to the relationship as individuals, our histories, wounds, expectations, dreams, fears, and patterns.

The 'You' Level: This is our perception and experience of our partner, who we believe them to be, how we interpret their behaviours, and what we expect from them.

The 'Us' Level: This is the relationship itself, the shared identity, the co-created patterns, the unique culture that emerges between two specific people.

Problems arise when we confuse these levels or focus exclusively on one while neglecting the others. Many couples come to therapy focusing entirely on the 'You' level: 'If only my partner would change, everything would be fine'. True healing requires attention to all three levels. It also requires each to understand that 'in a relationship there is no reality, there is only perception. Each can have very different perceptions and be equally right'.

Cultural Narratives and Relationships

Our understanding of relationships doesn't develop in a vacuum. We're influenced by cultural narratives about love and connection, from fairy tales promising 'happily ever after' to romantic comedies suggesting that finding the right person solves all problems, from religious teachings about commitment to contemporary notions of self-fulfilment.

These narratives shape our expectations, often without our awareness. They lead us to believe relationships should be a certain way, should follow a particular path, should feel a particular way. When our lived experience doesn't match these narratives, we may feel something is wrong with our relationship rather than questioning the narrative itself.

Stuart and Clare's relationship was profoundly influenced by cultural narratives from their respective upbringings, South African and French, creating subtle but significant differences in their expectations about gender roles, communication, and the nature of commitment.

Relationship Role Models

One of the most profound insights I've gained through years of working with couples is that we don't enter relationships as blank slates. Long before we meet our partners, we've been absorbing messages about what relationships should look like, how they should function, and what we should expect from them. These relationship role models shape our expectations, behaviours, and patterns – often without our conscious awareness.

At the heart of how we learn to relate to others lies attachment theory – a framework first developed by John Bowlby and later expanded by Mary Ainsworth and others. This theory illuminates how our earliest relationships with caregivers create internal 'working models' of what relationships are and how they function. These models become the template upon which we build all future connections.

Parents: Our First and Most Powerful Models

For most of us, our parents or primary caregivers provide our first and most influential relationship template. Not only do we observe their interactions with each other, but our direct experiences with them form our attachment style; the particular way we connect with others and manage emotional intimacy.

Attachment theory identifies several patterns that develop in early childhood and often persist into adulthood. Those fortunate enough to experience consistent, responsive caregiving typically develop secure attachment; characterised by comfort with both intimacy and autonomy. Others might develop anxious attachment (preoccupied with fears of abandonment), avoidant attachment (uncomfortable with closeness), or disorganized attachment (exhibiting contradictory behaviours in relationships) based on less consistent or responsive caregiving experiences.

I recall working with Derek and Alison, a couple whose arguments followed a predictable pattern: Derek would withdraw into stony silence when tensions rose, while Alison would pursue with increasing intensity, demanding engagement. This classic 'pursue–withdraw' dynamic often reflects attachment patterns from the past being activated. Derek's avoidant attachment style led him to disconnect when emotional intensity increased, while Alison's anxious attachment triggered escalating efforts to reestablish connection.

When we explored their family backgrounds, Derek described a father who retreated to his garage whenever conflicts arose at home, and a mother who eventually stopped trying to engage him. He had learned early that emotional needs were overwhelming and best managed through distance. Alison, meanwhile, grew up with parents who had explosive arguments that always ended in tearful reconciliations, teaching her that emotional intensity was necessary to maintain connection.

Neither consciously chose these patterns, yet they were faithfully reproducing both what they had witnessed and what they had experienced. As Derek put it when the realisation dawned: 'I'm becoming my father, aren't I? I always swore I wouldn't do that'.

What's particularly powerful about parental role models is that we absorb them during our formative years, before we've developed the critical thinking skills to evaluate what we're seeing. A child doesn't think, 'My parents have an unhealthy communication style that I should avoid replicating'. Instead, they simply internalise: 'This is what relationships are'.

Even when we consciously reject our parents' relationship model, we may unconsciously reproduce it or swing to the opposite extreme, which brings its own problems. I've worked with many couples where one partner is determined to be 'nothing like my parents', only to discover they've created a relationship with different but equally challenging dynamics.

Siblings: The Practice Ground

For those who grew up with siblings, these relationships often provided a first experience of navigating conflicts, sharing resources, and handling complicated emotions with peers. The negotiation skills (or lack thereof) developed with siblings frequently transfer to adult romantic relationships.

Hannah and Tom sought therapy because Hannah felt Tom never truly engaged with conflict in their marriage. During our exploration, Tom revealed he was the youngest of five brothers in a household where disagreements were settled through physical dominance. Having always been the smallest, he'd learned that the safest strategy was avoidance and appeasement. This pattern, which had protected him in childhood, was now undermining his marriage.

Sibling relationships can also model positive patterns. Those lucky enough to witness healthy conflict resolution, mutual support, and respectful boundaries between siblings often carry these skills forward into their adult relationships.

Friends and Peer Relationships

As we move through adolescence and early adulthood, our friends' relationships increasingly influence our expectations. We observe their dating experiences, listen to their relationship stories, and absorb their advice (whether sound or misguided).

These peer role models can be particularly influential during formative relationship years. The friend who tolerates disrespectful behaviour from partners may normalise such treatment for their entire social circle. Conversely, friends who demonstrate healthy boundaries and mutual respect can inspire others to expect the same.

I've noticed how frequently couples in therapy reference their social circles when discussing relationship expectations: 'None of our friends seem to have these problems' or 'My best friend says all couples go through this'. These comparisons, often based on limited information about what truly happens in others' private lives, significantly shape how people evaluate their own relationships.

Teachers, Mentors, and Community Leaders

Beyond family and friends, authority figures like teachers, religious leaders, and mentors provide relationship templates that can be equally influential. These adults often explicitly discuss or implicitly model values around commitment, gender roles, conflict resolution, and partnership.

In communities with strong religious or cultural traditions, these figures may be the primary source of relationship education. Their teachings – whether progressive or traditional, empowering or restrictive – often carry the weight of moral authority.

Raj and Surya came to therapy struggling with expectations around gender roles in their marriage. Both had been raised in a religious community where male leadership and female submission were explicitly taught as divine principles. Despite their conscious desire for a more equal partnership, they found themselves unconsciously reproducing these patterns and feeling guilty when they attempted to establish more balanced dynamics.

Media Representations: The Pervasive Influence

Perhaps no influence on our relationship expectations has grown more powerful in recent decades than media. From childhood fairy tales to romantic comedies, from advertising to social media, we are continuously bombarded with images and narratives about what relationships should look like.

These portrayals are often deeply problematic, emphasising romantic myths that can lead to unrealistic expectations:

- The 'soulmate' myth that suggests there is one perfect person for everyone
- The belief that love should be effortless if it's 'meant to be'
- The idea that passion should remain as intense as in the early stages
- The narrative that jealousy and possessiveness are signs of true love
- The expectation that a partner should intuitively know our needs without communication

When Cathy and William came to therapy, Cathy expressed profound disappointment that their relationship didn't match her vision of true love. 'I thought when I found "the one", everything would just fall into place', she explained. 'We wouldn't need to work at it. We'd just understand each other completely'. This expectation, largely shaped by the romantic media she had consumed, had prevented her from engaging with the normal challenges of a long-term relationship.

Social media has intensified these effects by presenting carefully curated glimpses into others' seemingly perfect relationships. The #RelationshipGoals phenomenon creates the impression that other couples experience constant romance, adventure, and harmony – making normal relationship challenges seem like evidence of failure.

Celebrity and Influencer Relationships

In today's digital age, celebrities and influencers have emerged as a new category of relationship role models. Their partnerships are publicly documented, celebrated, and analysed, creating new templates for what relationships should look like.

While some public figures provide positive examples by openly discussing the work they put into their relationships, many present highly idealised versions that bear little resemblance to most people's lived experiences. The recent trend of 'relationship content' on platforms like TikTok and Instagram often presents performative displays of affection or material demonstrations of love (elaborate proposals, expensive gifts) as standards to aspire to.

These influences can be particularly powerful for younger generations who have grown up in a media-saturated environment. I've noted an increase in couples whose expectations have been shaped more by these public displays than by witnessing actual relationships in their immediate community.

Breaking the Pattern: Creating Conscious Relationship Models

Becoming aware of our relationship role models and attachment patterns is the first step toward evaluating which serve us and which we might want to change. This awareness allows us to make conscious choices rather than unconsciously repeating what we've observed and experienced.

The good news from attachment research is that while our early experiences create powerful templates, they are not our destiny. What researchers call 'earned secure attachment' can develop through meaningful relationships later in life, whether with partners, friends, therapists, or mentors. These relationships can provide corrective emotional experiences that gradually reshape our internal working models.

In my work with couples, I often suggest creating an explicit 'relationship genealogy' that maps the models they've been exposed to and identifies the patterns they've absorbed. Alongside this, we explore their attachment histories; the specific experiences that formed their comfort with intimacy, trust, and dependency. This dual exploration can be revelatory, helping partners understand both their own behaviour and their reactions to their partner's approaches.

For couples with children, this awareness carries additional importance. They are now creating the relationship template that their children will carry forward. This perspective often motivates couples to work through difficulties they might otherwise avoid. As one father told me, 'I realised I'm not just fixing our marriage for us; I'm showing my son what marriage should be'.

The Possibility of New Models

What gives me hope is that relationship patterns can be changed. While our early role models and attachment experiences create powerful templates, neuroplasticity – the brain's ability to form new neural connections throughout life – means we can intentionally seek out and incorporate healthier models at any stage.

Attachment researchers have demonstrated how emotionally focused therapy can help couples create a 'secure base' for each other, gradually healing attachment wounds through new experiences of emotional availability and responsiveness. When partners can consistently be there for each other during vulnerable moments, they essentially rewrite each other's relationship expectations at the neurobiological level.

I've worked with many couples who have transformed their relationships by:

- understanding and modifying unhelpful patterns
- deliberately practising new forms of communication and conflict resolution
- creating 'secure base' experiences where they respond to each other's attachment needs in healing ways

These efforts can gradually replace unhealthy internalised models with more constructive approaches. The couples who succeed in this transformation often become powerful role models themselves, breaking intergenerational patterns and creating ripple effects through their families and communities.

Expanding Our Relationship Vision

Perhaps the most important thing to understand about relationship role models is that their influence is neither deterministic nor permanent. While we may begin with the templates we absorbed in childhood, we have the capacity to critically evaluate these models, retain what's valuable, and consciously develop new approaches when needed.

This process requires both awareness and intention. We must be willing to examine our assumptions about what relationships should look like, consider where these assumptions came from, and ask ourselves whether they truly serve our well-being and connection.

When couples engage in this reflective process together, they often discover the possibility of creating a relationship that transcends the models they inherited; one that incorporates the best of what they've witnessed while avoiding the patterns that caused pain or disconnection. This co-creation of a unique relationship model, tailored to their specific values, needs, and aspirations, represents one of the most meaningful aspects of partnership.

As one client beautifully expressed after working through this process: 'We realised we weren't doomed to repeat our parents' mistakes, nor did we have to swing to the opposite extreme. We could take the pieces that worked from all the relationships we'd observed and create something that was uniquely ours. That was incredibly liberating'.

In this possibility lies great hope for the future of relationships. Each couple that breaks unhealthy patterns and heals attachment wounds creates new neural pathways not just within their own relationship but potentially across generations. When securely attached children grow from witnessing healthy attachment between their parents, the intergenerational transmission of relationship patterns can shift from a cycle of dysfunction to one of connection and security.

What Makes a Relationship 'Good'?

After working with hundreds of couples, I'm often asked what makes a 'good' or 'successful' relationship. My answer may surprise some: there is no universal standard. A relationship that works beautifully for one couple might be intolerable for another.

What matters is not whether a relationship matches some external ideal, but whether it supports the growth, well-being, and authenticity of both partners. A relationship isn't an achievement to be unlocked or a destination to be reached; it's a continuous journey of co-creation.

That said, certain qualities tend to characterise relationships that thrive over time. These are the elements I've integrated into my Relationship Paradigm framework: Communication, Connection, Commitment, Fun, Growth, and Trust. When these elements are fulfilling the needs of both, relationships tend to flourish. When they're absent, relationships tend to struggle.

Relationships as Journeys, Not Destinations

One of the most liberating perspectives I try to share with couples is the idea that relationships are journeys without a final destination. There is no point at which we can say, 'We've arrived. Our relationship is complete'. There is only the continuing journey of deepening understanding, renewed connection, fresh challenges, and new discoveries.

This perspective frees us from the pressure of perfection. It allows us to see disagreements, miscommunications, and challenges not as failures but as inevitable terrain on the relationship landscape. It invites us to approach our relationships with curiosity rather than judgement, with a spirit of exploration rather than evaluation.

When Harriet and Ed began to see their relationship this way, as a journey they were on together rather than a problem to be fixed, something shifted. Their focus moved from what had gone wrong to what they were creating together, from the pain of the past to the possibilities of the future.

The Cardiovascular System of Relationships

Just as a heart needs constant, healthy blood flow to thrive, relationships require a continuous stream of positive interactions to remain vital and strong. Micro connections and disconnections are the small, seemingly insignificant moments that can either nourish or gradually diminish the health of our relationships.

Imagine your relationship as a living, beating heart. Each positive interaction, no matter how small, represents fresh, oxygen-rich blood flowing through healthy arteries. These micro connections keep the relationship strong, resilient, and full of life. However, just as cardiovascular disease often begins with small changes in the arteries, relationship deterioration frequently starts with minor negative interactions or missed opportunities for connection.

Relationships as Choices

Finally, and perhaps most importantly, relationships are choices, not just the initial choice to be together, but the thousands of small choices we make each day to turn toward or away from our partner, to open or close our hearts, to risk vulnerability or retreat into safety.

These choices aren't always conscious. They're influenced by our past experiences, our attachment patterns, our fears, and our hopes. But becoming aware of them, bringing them into consciousness, is one of the most powerful steps we can take toward creating the relationships we truly desire.

I've seen couples transform seemingly hopeless situations through the simple but profound choice to see their relationship differently, to approach their partner with curiosity instead of criticism and to take responsibility for their part in co-created patterns.

Conclusion

So, what are relationships? They are connections and systems. They are mirrors and dances. They are choices and journeys. They are the spaces between us where we discover not just each other, but ourselves.

In the chapters that follow, we'll explore how these understandings translate into practical approaches for healing and strengthening relationships. We'll see how real couples have navigated the complexities of connection, and how the elements of the Relationship Paradigm can guide us toward more fulfilling ways of being together.

For now, I invite you to consider your own definition of relationship. What does it mean to you to be in relationship with another? What expectations, hopes, and fears colour your understanding? What narratives influence your perspective? As we continue this journey together, these reflections will provide fertile ground for deeper understanding and growth.

Chapter 4

Stuart and Clare

When Love Gets Lost in Translation

From the moment Stuart and Clare's consultation forms landed in my inbox, I knew we were facing an uphill battle. The preliminary phone conversations and intake forms revealed layers of complexity that made me question whether reconciliation was even possible. Yet, as with all couples who reach out for help, they deserved the chance to try.

Their story began like a romantic comedy – two people falling in love over bandages during a first aid course. But thirty years later, sitting in my office, that lighthearted beginning felt like ancient history. Stuart, a South African businessman in his sixties, cut an imposing figure with his large frame and dusty boots that seemed oddly out of place for a corporate executive. Beside him sat Clare, a petite French designer, her body language speaking volumes about years of feeling diminished.

The cultural differences between them might have once added spice to their relationship, but now they seemed to underscore a deeper divide. Their family structure was equally complex: two children together, plus four from Clare's previous marriage. Though all were grown, two still lived at home, creating an intricate web of loyalties and resentments.

'From the outside, we looked enormously successful', Stuart explained, his voice carrying a weight of resignation. 'But on the inside, it was empty. Has been for twenty years, though the last five have been particularly tough'.

Clare's perspective painted an even darker picture. 'I don't feel safe', she admitted, her words barely above a whisper. 'Stuart's anger, his ranting, the contempt, the physical eruptions ...' She paused, gathering strength. 'I haven't felt loved, valued, supported, or respected for years. I've been living in fight-or-flight mode for two decades, and now I've just settled into numb resignation'.

The intimacy between them had died a decade ago, leaving both partners with unanswered questions. Clare had even wondered if Stuart might be gay, searching for any explanation for their 'mechanical rather than proper' physical relationship. When she had unexpectedly become pregnant years ago, what should have been joyous news felt to her like another chain binding her to an unfulfilling marriage.

'I feel controlled', Stuart stated firmly, while Clare countered that she felt ignored and repressed. When conflicts arose, both admitted to regressing to childlike behaviours, unable to communicate effectively as adults.

DOI: 10.4324/9781003752776-4

Using my constellation exercise – where couples represent their relationship using stones – revealed telling insights. Stuart chose an enormous stone to represent himself, placing it far from Clare's, with their two shared children positioned between them. Clare's arrangement was similar, but she surrounded herself with all four of her children, creating a protective barrier.

The future she envisioned was telling: Stuart's stone became smaller, less dominating. 'If he could be loving, gentle, listening, understanding, not competitive or scornful – then I could get close to him', she explained.

Stuart's response surprised me. 'I can be that smaller stone', he said softly. 'As human beings, I feel we're equal'. He shared about surviving a difficult childhood, being sensitive and developing late. 'I want to be loving and gentle, listening and understanding, treating people fairly'.

But the elephant in the room was the blended family dynamic. Clare's grown children from her previous marriage clearly harboured negative feelings toward Stuart, creating an invisible barrier between the couple. With her ex-husband's continued negative influence and her strong sense of maternal duty, Clare seemed caught between her roles as mother and wife.

Working with blended families presents unique challenges, particularly when adult children maintain influence over their parents' relationships. A few carefully chosen words from a child can poison a partnership, and that sense of parental duty often overshadows what might be best for the couple themselves.

As our first session drew to a close, Stuart expressed his hope: 'I want to reset our relationship, to rejoin for this next stage of our lives and truly love and nurture each other'. Clare's goal was more individual: 'I want to better understand myself and walk out of this physical and emotional desert'.

The question remained: Could these different objectives find common ground? Could Stuart's dominating presence shrink enough to make Clare feel safe? Could Clare's loyalty to her children make space for a renewed connection with Stuart? Most importantly, after thirty years of ingrained patterns, was change still possible?

As they left my office that day, I couldn't help but notice Stuart's dusty boots again. They seemed to symbolise the long, difficult journey ahead – if they chose to take it together. In the hour between clients, I let go completely to become empty enough to receive and notice again.

We will explore more of their journey in Chapter 24.

Chapter 5

My Own Journey

A Path to Love and Understanding

The Search for Love

My journey to becoming a relationship therapist began long before I understood what relationships truly were. As I reflect on the path that led me here, I recognise that my life's work has been shaped by my own quest for love and connection – a quest that started in my earliest childhood memories.

I was born into a post-war Scottish family where love was a foreign word, never mentioned and rarely demonstrated. My parents, David and Kathleen, carried the emotional restraint of their generation, shaped by the hardships of World War II. In this environment of unspoken affection, I found myself longing for something I couldn't name but instinctively knew was missing. Perhaps my earliest vivid memory captures this longing: being locked in a dark cellar at the age of two or three, listening to scampering feet that my imagination transformed into rats, feeling an intense sense of rejection and isolation. Those very intense feelings of a very young Neil became locked away in my subconscious, only to emerge many years later.

School offered little solace. At grammar school, I was a year younger than everyone else because I was considered intelligent – a gap that felt like a chasm at that age. The physical, emotional, and psychological differences created a profound sense of separation from my peers. While other boys my age were beginning to explore relationships and sexuality, these remained territories completely unfamiliar to me. I had no concept of what I was missing or how it might shape my future.

The emotional climate at home reinforced this disconnect. My father, often absorbed in his accounting work with his thirteen-column analysis pads, embodied the stoic provider. From him came subtle pressure to follow his path and the unspoken messages that 'big boys don't cry' and that emotional expression was a form of weakness. My mother, who had been uprooted from her Welsh farming family at a young age, seemed to live with her own unmet expectations of marriage.

In this atmosphere, I developed a deep, unconscious yearning that would echo through decades of my life: 'I just want to be loved'. This simple yet profound desire would become the invisible compass guiding my personal and professional journey.

DOI: 10.4324/9781003752776-5

Relationships as Learning Grounds

My early romantic relationships reflect the pattern of someone searching without knowing what they were looking for. After university and a transformative year sailing across the Atlantic, I met Thelma, my first significant relationship. She was caring and tender, qualities I was drawn to instinctively. Our relationship felt connected and growing, but when I proudly introduced her to my parents, their thinly veiled racism – 'Of course, son, we are not racist, but what would the neighbours think?' – created an insurmountable barrier. Whether from cowardice or pragmatism, I took what seemed the path of least resistance.

Soon after, I married Fiona, the neighbour's daughter, someone socially acceptable to my parents. Was this love? Looking back, I don't think so. It wasn't the intense feeling of connection I secretly longed for, but rather a sense of fulfilling expectations. The marriage lasted only three years, ending when I discovered her numerous affairs.

My third significant relationship was with Kate, an ex-colleague who represented safety after betrayal. Our marriage provided security, a ready-made family with her two children, and later, our two adopted daughters, Alisia and Michelle. But over the twenty years we spent together, what began as a reasonably satisfying relationship slowly deteriorated. Without the foundation of deep love, the relationship gradually eroded. Kate found escape in alcohol, and I found myself sitting in our living room watching her fall asleep after dinner, wondering if this was all there was to connection.

After Kate came Diana, with whom I experienced physical connection but little intellectual or emotional depth. A few short relationships followed, each teaching me what I didn't want, but not yet revealing what I truly needed.

Then came Debbie in 2012, and for the first time, I felt authentic love – as if Cupid's arrow had finally found its mark. We enjoyed a wonderful year of courtship before marrying in November 2013. Just months later, in February 2014, came the devastating diagnosis of a glioblastoma, a brain tumour with a grim prognosis of fourteen months with treatment.

The journey through Debbie's illness transformed my understanding of love. It became about total dedication – putting all my attention, focus, and energy on her, trying everything possible to extend her life while making each day as joyful as possible. Despite our efforts and twenty-seven months of struggle, Debbie passed away. Yet even in this profound loss, I was learning about the depths of love and commitment.

The Turning Point

Grief could have become my companion for years, following socially accepted patterns of mourning. Instead, a Buddhist retreat shortly after Debbie's death became a pivotal moment. There, I experienced three powerful realisations: first, that I had already been grieving for twenty-seven months since her diagnosis and could now release that grief; second, that I deserved a good future not defined by loss; and third, that I could love and be loved again, perhaps even more deeply.

This spiritual awakening prepared me for what came next. On July 2, 2017, at precisely 11:17 am, I saw Gwen walking up the stairs at The Haven in Lymington. Her strong, confident shoulders spoke of someone who knew herself completely. Our scheduled thirty-minute coffee stretched into five and a half hours of conversation that felt like reuniting with a soul I'd always known. We discovered our lives had run in parallel for years, with similar work and interests, sometimes being inches from meeting but never connecting until that perfect moment.

As I said goodbye that day, I felt an unusual sensation of love washing through me – an epiphany that this was what I had been seeking my entire life. This profound connection with Gwen transformed my understanding of love. For the first time in sixty-three years, I experienced being valued completely for who I was, without the sense that I needed to be 'better' to be worthy of love. This unconditional acceptance created a foundation from which I could take risks, explore possibilities, and discover deeper joy than I had known possible.

From Business to Relationships

My professional journey paralleled this emotional evolution. After years in corporate roles – chartered accountancy, retail management, strategy consultancy, and business ownership – I found myself successful by conventional standards but deeply unfulfilled. The pivotal moment came on Mount Aconcagua in Argentina, one of the Seven Summits. On the night before we were to reach the summit, I had a dream in which my much loved but long-deceased Golden Retriever, Kirsty, appeared on the path, barking and snarling, refusing to let me pass. Heeding this warning, I descended the next day and was examined by the doctor at base camp. He told me that I had developed pulmonary oedema and would have died had I continued upward.

This near-death experience crystallised a profound truth: life is about the journey, not the destination. It prompted me to reassess everything, eventually leading me to sell my businesses, divorce Kate, and retrain as a psychotherapist. I discovered that what truly fulfilled me was talking to people, helping them understand their world and themselves. I began working with successful but unhappy business owners, using my own journey as a touchstone to help them reconnect with their authentic desires and find genuine fulfilment.

The culmination of this professional transformation came with the creation of Duo Coaching. Born from my own disappointing experiences with traditional relationship counselling during the breakdown of my marriage to Kate, this approach represented a complete reimagining of how to help couples in distress. Working alongside Cathy, and later Maria, I developed a framework that broke away from the conventional fifty-minute session model, the power imbalance of a single therapist, and the directionless approach I had experienced as a client.

The results were transformative. As I witnessed couples reconnect, fall back in love, and rebuild their relationships, I experienced a profound sense of purpose. There is nothing more rewarding than working with a couple who have been together for many years and have drifted apart, helping them reconnect and experience that moment in the room where they fall in love once again. This work finally aligned my professional life with my deepest values of love, fun, and fulfilment.

The Birth of the Relationship Paradigm

Despite the success of Duo Coaching, I felt compelled to reach more people than I could see face-to-face. In September 2017, shortly after marrying Gwen, we were honeymooning in the Caribbean aboard a forty-foot boat. In this liminal space, Gwen asked what seemed a simple question: 'Why do you want to write a book?' This prompted deep reflection on my motivations. Was it ego? A desire to impress my father? Or something more meaningful?

I concluded that the only worthy reason would be to help others and make the world a slightly better place. Given my experience with couples, relationships seemed the natural subject. Gwen pressed further: 'How can you distil what you have learnt from all the couples you have worked with, and what are the key elements of a good relationship?'

In that moment, sailing south from St Vincent under clear skies, everything I had learned through years of personal experience and professional practice crystallised into a coherent framework. I identified six essential elements of thriving relationships: Communication, Connection, Commitment, Fun, Growth, and Trust. Alongside these elements, I recognised the importance of three key players in every relationship: 'Me', 'You', and 'Us'.

This framework, which I named the Relationship Paradigm, differed from other models in its simplicity, flexibility, and accessibility. It provided couples with clear components they could understand and work with, while allowing for personalisation based on their unique circumstances and values.

With this framework as my foundation, I began writing *Reset*, the first book of what would become a series. Beginning during a stormy North Atlantic crossing, heading east through a hurricane, aboard the Queen Mary, the writing process evolved as I found ways to inhabit the characters' perspectives. The novel tells the story of John and Rachel, a couple who have drifted apart over sixteen years and are on the brink of separation but find their way back to love through the principles of the Relationship Paradigm.

Following the success of *Reset*, I wrote *Recover*, focusing on the challenge of rebuilding trust after betrayal, told through the story of Andy and Susan. This second book expanded my framework to address the specific trauma of infidelity, creating concepts like the Toxic Triangle to help couples navigate the complicated emotional terrain of affair recovery.

As my writing reached more people, media outlets began approaching me for commentary on relationship issues. Over two years, I authored more than 370 articles, reaching 4.8 million readers in print and 2.8 billion online. Publications from *The Times* and *Sunday Times* to *The Independent* and *The Sun* dubbed me 'the relationship expert' or 'the relationship guru'. During the COVID-19 pandemic and subsequent lockdowns, I produced additional content to help couples navigate the unprecedented pressures of 'isolationship'.

A Life's Purpose Discovered

Looking back at the rough seas that led me here, I see how every relationship, every professional role, every moment of joy and heartbreak contributed to my development as a relationship expert. The boy who once whispered 'I just want to be loved' to himself in a dark cellar has grown into a man who not only found love but developed the tools to help others find it too.

In January 2022, life took another unexpected turn when I suffered a heart attack leading to quadruple bypass surgery. In a two-day coma after the operation, I experienced what felt like a near-death moment, encouraged back to life by my long-dead mother who told me I still had work to do. This brush with mortality only strengthened my resolve to focus on what truly matters: love, connection, and helping others.

I have spent the last two years immersed in academia and research, pulling together all my learning and writing and have been awarded a doctorate in the Phenomenology of Relationships.

Today, at seventy, I feel a sense of purpose and fulfilment that would have been unimaginable to my younger self. My ambitious goal – 'to impact and improve ten million relationships around the world in this decade' – guides my ongoing work. Three years into this journey, with nearly five million people reached, the target seems challenging but achievable.

The Relationship Paradigm represents both my professional legacy and my contribution to a world where relationships often struggle under unprecedented pressures. My framework serves as a chart by which couples can navigate their journey together – identifying the essential elements of thriving relationships and possible routes to connection, while maintaining the freedom to discover their own unique path to love.

As I continue this work, I am not looking backward from a rocking chair wearing a beige cardigan but forward with excitement and purpose. There may be fewer years ahead than behind, but the depth of meaning I find in helping others discover the profound joy and growth that come from healthy, thriving relationships makes every day a new adventure.

The journey from that little boy seeking love to becoming 'the relationship expert' has been long and often difficult, but it has led me to a place of authentic purpose. I have found what love truly is for me, and I am privileged to help others discover it for themselves. In a world where meaningful connection grows increasingly precious, my life's work offers both a map and a compass for those seeking to navigate the sometimes turbulent but ultimately rewarding waters of intimate partnership.

Chapter 6

Thomas and Eleanor – Empty Orbits

Finding Each Other after Years Apart

The January light filtered softly through the windows of our therapy room as Maria and I prepared for our next couple. Outside, winter had stripped the trees bare, revealing the essential architecture beneath; a fitting metaphor, I thought, for the work we were about to begin.

When I'd first spoken with Eleanor on the phone several weeks earlier, her voice had carried a complex mixture of determination and uncertainty. 'We need help to reconnect', she had explained. 'Thomas is retiring in six months, and I'm afraid we've been living parallel lives for so long, we don't know how to be together anymore'.

Her words had stayed with me; that quiet acknowledgement of distance grown over years, the hope that something might still bridge it, and beneath both, the unspoken fear that perhaps it was too late.

At precisely two o'clock, they arrived. Thomas entered first; tall, trim, with the purposeful stride of someone accustomed to making decisions. Eleanor followed a half-step behind, elegant in a simple navy dress, her silver-streaked hair pulled back in a loose knot. What struck me immediately was the careful space they maintained between them; not the awkward distance of a couple in active conflict, but the practised gap of two people who had grown accustomed to orbiting each other without touching.

'Welcome', I said, extending my hand to each in turn. 'I'm Neil, and this is my colleague, Maria'.

As we settled into our seats, I noticed Thomas glance at his watch; a habitual gesture rather than an impatient one. Eleanor's eyes, meanwhile, darted around the room, taking in the arrangement of chairs, the artwork on the walls, perhaps seeking clues about what would happen next.

'Before we begin', I explained, 'I'd like to share a bit about how Duo Coaching works. Unlike traditional therapy where you might meet weekly for months or even years, we typically work with couples over five or six intensive sessions spread across a few months. Maria and I work as a team, which gives you the benefit of both male and female perspectives'.

DOI: 10.4324/9781003752776-6

They nodded, Thomas with the brisk efficiency of someone evaluating a business proposal, Eleanor with cautious hope.

'Today', I continued, 'is about understanding how you've arrived at this point in your relationship. We'll explore your journey together from when you first met to now, and we'll also look at your individual backgrounds; how your childhood experiences and previous relationships might be influencing your current patterns'.

'I'm willing to try anything at this point', Eleanor said, her hands folded tightly in her lap.

I began where we always do, with the fundamentals. 'Tell me about how you two met'.

There was a moment of hesitation, each seemingly waiting for the other to begin. Then Thomas cleared his throat.

'It was at a colleague's birthday celebration', he said. 'Thirty-five years ago, now. I was working at Barclays then, in their international division. Eleanor was friends with Richard's wife; Richard was the colleague'.

'I remember you were wearing a ridiculous bow tie', Eleanor added, a faint smile softening her features.

Thomas looked at her, surprised. 'Was I? I don't recall that'.

'Red with little blue boats on it. You told me later your sister had given it to you'.

He shook his head, but there was warmth in his eyes that hadn't been there a moment before. 'You remember the strangest details'.

'What drew you to each other?' Maria asked.

Another pause, longer this time.

'Eleanor was ... different from the women I typically met through work', Thomas finally said. 'More thoughtful. Less impressed by title or status. I found that refreshing'.

Eleanor's expression softened further. 'Thomas was so confident, but not in an arrogant way. He listened, really listened, when I spoke about my interests in art and literature. Most men I'd dated seemed to be waiting for me to finish talking so they could impress me with their own knowledge'.

'How quickly did the relationship become serious?' I asked.

'Rather rapidly', Thomas replied. 'We were married within eighteen months of meeting'.

'It felt right', Eleanor added. 'We wanted the same things: a home, children, stability but also adventure'.

As they continued to separately recount the early years of their relationship, I observed how their bodies shifted subtly. They had arrived sitting stiffly, oriented slightly away from each other. Now, as they recalled their beginnings, they had turned fractionally toward one another, the space between them no longer quite so pronounced.

'And when did things begin to change?' I asked after they'd each described their early married life and the birth of their two children.

The warming atmosphere cooled immediately. Eleanor glanced at Thomas, who had returned to his earlier, more formal posture.

'I suppose it was when Thomas began taking international assignments', she said carefully. 'About twenty-five years ago. The children were still young'.

Thomas nodded. 'My career was advancing. The opportunities were too significant to decline'.

'You were gone for months at a time', Eleanor added, her voice now holding a thin edge. 'When you were home, you were distracted, already planning the next trip'.

'I was providing for our family', Thomas replied, a defensive note entering his voice. 'Those years built the financial security we enjoy now'.

'Yes, we have a lovely house and healthy investment accounts', Eleanor said. 'And a marriage that's been conducted largely via telephone for the past two decades'.

The familiar pattern emerged as clearly as if it had been scripted: his focus on provision and security, her longing for presence and connection, neither fully understanding the other's perspective.

'Let me ask you both', Maria interjected gently, 'what has kept you together through these years of distance?'

This question seemed to surprise them both. They looked at each other, perhaps realising they'd never explicitly considered it.

'I've always believed in commitment', Thomas said after a moment. 'When I make a promise, I keep it'.

I noticed how Eleanor's shoulders dropped slightly at his words, a response to their inadequacy rather than their insincerity.

'Eleanor?' I prompted.

She took a deep breath. 'There's always been ... something between us, even at our most distant. A foundation. I've never doubted that Thomas cares for me, even when he's been impossible to reach emotionally'.

Thomas looked at her with genuine surprise. 'I didn't know you felt that way'.

'You never asked', she said simply.

As our session continued, they traced the contours of their gradually diverging lives: his increasing responsibilities at work taking him around the globe, her raising their children and eventually returning to university to complete a degree in art history, then finding fulfilling work at a small gallery. When their children left home, the scaffolding that had given their marriage structure had gone with them, leaving them facing each other across an expanse neither knew how to cross.

'And now?' I asked. 'What's brought you here today, specifically?'

'Thomas is retiring in June', Eleanor explained. 'Suddenly we're facing the prospect of being together full-time for the first time in decades. I realised I don't know how to do that; how to be with him day in and day out. And more importantly, I don't know if we want the same things for this next stage'.

'Eleanor wants to sell our home', Thomas added. 'I've only just begun to enjoy it, now that my travel has decreased'.

'It's too large for us', she countered. 'Echoing rooms, we never use, a garden that requires constant maintenance ...'

'It's where we raised our family', he said, a rare note of emotion breaking through his controlled facade.

I nodded, understanding now the immediate practical issue bringing their long-simmering disconnection to a crisis point. 'Before we explore that specific decision further, I'd like to step back and understand more about each of your backgrounds; the families you grew up in and how they might have shaped your expectations of marriage'.

Over the next hour, a clearer picture emerged. Thomas had grown up in a household where his father, a naval officer, was frequently absent. His mother had managed the home with stoic efficiency, never complaining about her husband's deployments. Expressions of emotion had been discouraged; duty and responsibility were paramount.

'My father taught me that a man's primary obligation is to provide', Thomas explained. 'When he was home, he was physically present but emotionally ... elsewhere. I never questioned that arrangement until now'.

Eleanor, by contrast, had been raised in a home rich with expressiveness. Her father, a teacher, had been deeply involved in family life. Her mother, though managing the household, had maintained her own interests and friendships.

'My parents talked constantly', she recalled. 'Sometimes they argued passionately, but they always found their way back to each other. There was never any doubt they were deeply connected'.

As they spoke about their childhoods, I could see them making connections they'd never articulated before; how Thomas had recreated his father's distant provision without questioning it, how Eleanor had measured their marriage against her parents' emotional intimacy and found it wanting.

'Now', I said, gesturing to the collection of pebbles in the baskets, 'I'd like us to try something different. These stones will help us visualise your relationship in a new way'.

I explained the constellation exercise, asking each of them to select pebbles to represent themselves, each other, important people in their lives, and significant elements like work, home, and future aspirations. They would arrange these pebbles to show their current reality, then create a second arrangement showing their ideal future.

Thomas approached the task methodically, selecting stones of similar size for himself and Eleanor, positioning them perhaps an arm's length apart on the floor. Between them, he placed smaller stones representing their two children and four grandchildren. To his right, he positioned a large, angular stone.

'My work', he explained. 'Though I suppose it will be smaller after June'.

Eleanor's arrangement showed a different perspective. The stone representing herself was modest in size, while Thomas's was substantially larger. The distance between them was greater than in his arrangement. Her children and grandchildren clustered close to her stone, while a collection of smaller pebbles, representing her friends, her work at the gallery, her volunteer activities, created a semicircle around her.

'What do you notice about each other's arrangements?' Maria asked after they had both completed the task.

'Eleanor sees me as ... dominant', Thomas observed, surprise evident in his voice. 'And she feels we're further apart than I perceive us to be'.

'You've placed work so prominently', Eleanor noted. 'Even with retirement looming, it's still a massive presence in your conception of your life'.

They studied each other's stone arrangements with genuine curiosity, perhaps seeing their relationship through the other's eyes for the first time in years.

'Now', I suggested, 'create an arrangement showing not your current reality, but your ideal future; how you would like things to be'.

This second task proved more revealing still. In both of their ideal arrangements, the stones representing themselves moved closer together. The work stone in Thomas's configuration shrank dramatically. In Eleanor's arrangement, the stone representing their home changed position, moving from a peripheral location to a more central one, though smaller than their current residence.

'It seems you both desire greater closeness', Maria observed. 'And Thomas, you see your work receding in importance, which aligns with your approaching retirement'.

'I notice that in your ideal arrangement, Eleanor, you've changed the home stone', I added. 'Not eliminated it but transformed it'.

Eleanor nodded. 'I don't want to erase our history or the place where we raised our children. I just want something more manageable, more suited to who we are now rather than who we were'.

'I hadn't realised you felt so overwhelmed by the house', Thomas said quietly. 'I've always seen it as a symbol of what I've provided for us'.

'It was a wonderful family home', Eleanor acknowledged. 'But now it feels like it's consuming time we could be using to actually live our lives. I want to travel, take classes, see our grandchildren; not spend every weekend maintaining a property too large for us'.

For perhaps the first time in our session, they were truly looking at each other, beginning to glimpse the unspoken hopes and fears that had been driving their disconnection.

As our three-hour session ended, I asked them what they hoped to achieve through our work together. Their answers revealed both the distance they needed to bridge and the foundation that might make it possible.

'I want to understand what will make Eleanor happy in this next phase', Thomas said. 'I've spent my career making decisions, directing teams. But I realise I don't know how to collaborate on creating a shared vision for our retirement'.

'I want to feel that we're partners again', Eleanor added. 'Not just occupants of the same house, but two people building something meaningful together. I want to rediscover joy with Thomas; to laugh together, to make plans that excite us both'.

As they prepared to leave, I gave them their first homework assignments: a journal to record their thoughts between sessions, the Bids for Connection questionnaire to help them understand how they reached out to each other and how they responded to each other's overtures, and the Hunt the Good Stuff exercise to help them notice and share positive moments each day.

'Also', I suggested, 'take some time this week to write freely about your hopes for the future. Don't edit or censor yourselves; just explore what you each truly want from this next chapter'.

They gathered their things, the space between them as they walked to the door still present but perhaps fractionally reduced. I felt the familiar mixture of concern and hope that accompanies the beginning of any therapeutic journey: concern for the work ahead, hope for the possibilities I could already glimpse beneath the accumulated distance of years.

As the door closed behind them, Maria turned to me. 'Thirty-five years is a long time to be moving gradually apart'.

'And yet', I replied, 'there's still something there; something they both want to rediscover. Did you notice how they looked at each other when they spoke about their early days?'

She nodded. 'The question is whether they can build a new connection based on who they are now, not who they were then'.

'That', I agreed, 'is exactly the question'.

Outside, the winter afternoon was fading toward evening, the bare trees silhouetted against a darkening sky. Thomas and Eleanor would drive home separately: he to his office in the city, she from our session to the too-large house that had become both symbol and battleground. But perhaps tonight, with the stone constellations fresh in their minds, they might begin a different kind of conversation about the future stretching before them: a future that, despite decades of growing distance, they still hoped to navigate together.

We will find what has unfolded in their story in Chapter 26.

Chapter 7

From Experience to Expertise – My Journey as a Relationship Therapist

My path to becoming a relationship therapist was far from conventional. It was a journey born out of personal experiences, professional insights, and a deep-seated desire to help others navigate the complex terrain of love and relationships that I had struggled with for so long.

For much of my life, I was a successful businessman, climbing the corporate ladder and focusing on financial success. But beneath the surface of professional achievements, I grappled with my own relationship challenges. Each failed relationship, each heartbreak, and each moment of confusion about love was unknowingly preparing me for my future role as a therapist.

The turning point came with my relationship with Debbie. As I navigated the painful journey of her decline and eventual passing, I found myself delving deeper into understanding the nature of love, commitment, and the human capacity for connection. This personal tragedy became the catalyst for my professional transformation.

I experienced a profound shift in my perspective. A Buddhist retreat opened my eyes to new possibilities, not just for myself, but for how I could contribute to the world. It was then that I made the decision to retrain as a psychotherapist, specialising in relationships.

My training was rigorous, but I approached it with the same determination and focus that had served me well in the business world. However, I quickly realised

DOI: 10.4324/9781003752776-7

that traditional therapeutic approaches often fell short when it came to addressing the complex dynamics of couple relationships. I found myself questioning the established norms, particularly the standard fifty-minute session model and the practice of seeing only one partner at a time.

It was during this period of questioning and exploration that the idea for Duo Coaching began to take shape. I envisioned a new approach to relationship therapy – one that involved two therapists working simultaneously with a couple. This method, I believed, could provide a more balanced, comprehensive, and effective form of support for couples in distress.

Developing Duo Coaching was not without its challenges. It required a complete rethinking of the therapeutic process, from the length and structure of sessions to the dynamics between therapists and clients. But with each hurdle overcome, I grew more convinced of its potential to transform lives.

As I began implementing Duo Coaching, I saw remarkable results. Couples who had been stuck in destructive patterns for years were finding new ways to communicate and connect. The presence of two therapists allowed for a more nuanced understanding of each couple's dynamics and provided a model for healthy communication and problem-solving.

My own relationship with Gwen, which blossomed during this period of professional growth, became a source of both personal joy and professional inspiration. Our connection reinforced my belief in the power of love and the importance of continual growth and communication in relationships.

As my practice grew, so did my understanding of the wider implications of relationship health. I began to see how improving couple relationships could have a ripple effect, positively impacting families, communities, and society as a whole. This realisation fuelled my passion for not just helping individual couples, but advocating for better relationship education and support at a societal level.

My journey as a relationship therapist has been one of continuous learning and evolution. I've come to understand that effective therapy is not just about applying techniques or following a set protocol. It's about creating a safe space for vulnerability, fostering genuine connection, and helping couples rediscover the love that brought them together in the first place.

The development of my Relationship Paradigm model, with its six key elements of Communication, Connection, Commitment, Fun, Growth, and Trust, emerged from this ongoing process of learning and reflection. This model has become a cornerstone of my work, providing a practical framework for couples to understand and improve their relationships.

Looking to the future, I'm excited about the potential of new technologies to enhance relationship therapy. While I believe in the irreplaceable value of human connection in therapy, I'm exploring how tools like AI and virtual reality might be integrated to provide additional support and resources for couples.

My journey from a struggling individual to a relationship therapist has been transformative. It's a path that has taught me the true meaning of resilience, the power of love, and the incredible capacity for human growth and change. Every day, as I work with couples, I'm reminded of my own journey and the possibility of transformation that exists within each of us.

As I continue in this field, my goal remains clear: to help as many couples as possible discover the joy, fulfilment, and growth that a healthy relationship can bring. I believe that by improving relationships, we can create a ripple effect of positive change in the world. And in doing so, I find that I continue to grow and learn, both as a therapist and as a human being in my own loving relationship.

This journey has shown me that love, in its purest form, is not just an emotion, but a skill that can be learned and a gift that can transform lives. As a relationship therapist, I am privileged to be a guide on this journey for others, helping them navigate the sometimes turbulent waters of love toward a horizon of understanding, connection, and lasting happiness.

Chapter 8

John and Sarah – Parallel Lives

They arrive seven minutes late, a flurry of apologies and quick glances at their phones. Sarah leads the way, her movements precise and efficient. John follows a half-step behind, his shoulders slightly hunched as if perpetually bracing for impact. Their entrance carries a charged energy, not the quiet, measured distance of some couples, but something more volatile, crackling just beneath the surface.

The room welcomes them with its calm simplicity. Sarah's eyes sweep the space, taking inventory, while John's gaze remains fixed somewhere near the floor. They settle onto the three-seater couch with Sarah perched at the edge of the right cushion, her handbag placed carefully beside her like a shield. John sinks into the left side, creating a valley of space between them. Their bodies seem to speak entirely different languages, hers alert and forward-leaning, his collapsed inward as if trying to occupy less space.

'Thank you for coming in today', I begin, noting the way Sarah checks her watch. 'I know finding time can be challenging'.

'We've been meaning to do this for ages', Sarah replies, her voice carrying a crisp, professional tone that suggests she approaches all problems with the same methodical efficiency. 'Things just never seem to slow down enough'.

John nods but offers nothing. Already, the dynamic between them reveals itself, her readiness to speak for both of them, his quiet acquiescence. Maria catches my eye briefly; we've seen this pattern before, this subtle imbalance of verbal presence.

'Before we begin exploring your history together', I say, 'I'd like to ask each of you a simple but important question. What would you like to have happen in our sessions together?'

Sarah crosses her legs and straightens her back, as if preparing for an interview. 'I want to understand why John has become so ... absent. Physically he's there, but mentally ...' She gestures vaguely toward him. 'It's like living with a ghost sometimes'.

John looks at his hands. 'I'd like to feel like I matter again', he says quietly, surprising us all with the directness of his admission. 'Like what I say and do actually makes a difference'.

DOI: 10.4324/9781003752776-8

The rawness of his statement hangs in the air between them. Sarah blinks rapidly, perhaps taken aback by his candour. For the briefest moment, her composed facade falters.

'Those are both important aspirations', Maria says gently. 'Would it be alright if we learn more about how you arrived at this point in your relationship?'

What unfolds over the next hour is the story of two ambitious people who once shared a common vision. John and Sarah met at university, he studying engineering, she pursuing business management. Their courtship was a whirlwind of shared goals and complementary strengths. They married young, determined to build their careers in tandem. For the first few years, they moved in perfect synchronicity, her strategic thinking and his technical creativity forming a powerful alliance.

The fractures began when their first child, Emma, was born. While they had intellectually prepared for parenthood, discussing childcare arrangements and career adjustments with characteristic thoroughness, the emotional reality caught them both unprepared. Sarah's maternity leave stretched uncomfortably, her identity as a rising corporate star suddenly eclipsed by the demands of a colicky baby. John worked longer hours, partly from necessity to compensate for her reduced income, partly as refuge from the unfamiliar chaos at home.

'I felt like I was drowning', Sarah admits, her voice losing some of its practised smoothness. 'Everything I was good at suddenly didn't matter. And John seemed to just ... carry on with his life'.

'I didn't know what to do', John responds, his voice so low we must lean forward to hear him. 'Nothing I tried seemed to help. Eventually, it felt easier to just stay away'.

Their second child, Jacob, arrived three years later, deepening the patterns already established. Sarah became the primary parent by default, managing the household with the same exacting standards she had once applied to her corporate projects. John retreated further into work, earning promotions and accolades while his presence at home grew increasingly peripheral.

Now, with Emma ten and Jacob seven, they find themselves living essentially parallel lives, connected primarily through the logistics of parenting rather than any genuine intimacy.

'We don't fight', Sarah explains, as if this were conclusive evidence of relationship health. 'We're very efficient at managing our responsibilities'.

'But we don't really talk anymore', John adds. 'Not about anything that matters'.

As they speak, the architecture of their relationship emerges, built on competence rather than connection, achievements rather than affection. There is respect between them, certainly, but little warmth. They have become excellent co-managers of a family enterprise, but somewhere along the way, they ceased being partners in any deeper sense.

After gathering this history, I move to the next stage of our session. 'I'd like to try something different now', I explain, lifting the lid on two wicker baskets filled with pebbles of various sizes, shapes, and colours. 'These stones will help us understand your relationship in a way that sometimes words alone cannot'.

Sarah eyes the baskets with polite scepticism. John leans forward slightly, the first sign of genuine curiosity I've seen from him.

'There's no right or wrong way to do this', I assure them. 'I'd like each of you, starting with John, to choose one pebble to represent yourself, and place it where it needs to be'.

John considers the stones thoughtfully, then selects a smooth, flat grey pebble with flecks of darker material embedded within it. He places it carefully on the floor, just slightly left of centre.

Sarah chooses next, her fingers moving purposefully through the basket before selecting a polished, reddish stone with sharp edges. She places it a considerable distance to the right of John's stone, creating an expanse of empty carpet between them.

'Now', I continue, 'please select other pebbles to represent important people or elements in your lives and place them where they need to be'.

What emerges over the next fifteen minutes is revealing. John places smaller stones representing Emma and Jacob much closer to Sarah's stone than to his own. His parents are represented by two similar-sized pebbles positioned at some distance behind him. His work is symbolised by a large, imposing stone placed directly in front of him, while his few close friends are scattered in a loose semicircle to his left.

Sarah's constellation tells its own story. The children are also placed close to her stone, but in front rather than beside her, as if she is propelling them forward. Her mother is represented by a small stone almost touching her own, while her father is positioned far away, nearly off the edge of their working space. Her work, represented by several small, precisely arranged stones rather than a single one, forms a neat line leading away from her position.

'I notice that your stones are quite far apart', Maria observes gently. 'And John, you've placed the children much closer to Sarah than to yourself'.

John nods, his eyes fixed on the arrangement. 'That's how it feels', he says simply.

'And Sarah, I notice you've positioned work in a very organised line leading away from you', I add. 'Can you tell us about that placement?'

She glances at the stones, then back at me. 'It's my way forward', she says after a moment. 'My path back to myself'.

The room grows quiet as these revelations settle around us. Both John and Sarah stare at the constellation they've created, perhaps seeing the physical representation of their emotional distance for the first time.

'I'd like to try something else', I say after allowing this moment to breathe. 'Could each of you now create a constellation that represents your ideal future? What would you like your arrangement to look like if things were exactly as you wished?'

This second exercise brings unexpected insights. John rebuilds his constellation with his and Sarah's stones much closer together, with the children's pebbles arranged in a small semicircle near both of them. Most significantly, he adds a new stone, a small, rounded blue pebble that he places between their two stones.

'This represents connection', he explains quietly, not meeting Sarah's eyes. 'Something just for us, not about the children or work or anything practical'.

Sarah's ideal arrangement is more measured. She moves her stone somewhat closer to John's, though still maintaining a distinct space between them. The children remain in similar positions, though she adds several new stones representing activities and interests she wishes to develop. Notably, she also places a smooth green stone between her and John's pebbles.

'What does this stone represent for you, Sarah?' Maria asks.

Sarah studies it for a moment. 'Time', she says finally. 'Protected time that doesn't get swallowed up by everything else'.

As our first session moves into its final hour, we explore the significance of these arrangements. John speaks with growing animation about his desire for genuine reconnection, while Sarah acknowledges her tendency to manage emotions like projects, efficiently but without true engagement. They begin to identify patterns that have calcified over the years: his retreat into passive silence when feeling dismissed, her acceleration into hyper-efficiency when feeling vulnerable, their shared habit of prioritising practicalities over emotional needs.

I decided to address an area couples often find difficult to discuss. 'I'd like to ask about intimacy in your relationship', I said, intentionally using a word that could encompass both emotional and physical connection.

The shift in the room was palpable. John's gaze dropped to his hands, while Sarah's posture stiffened almost imperceptibly. The silence stretched for several seconds before Sarah spoke, her efficient tone now carefully measured.

'If you mean physical intimacy, there isn't any', she stated with a practised neutrality that suggested she'd cordoned off this topic emotionally. 'Not since Jacob was born. Seven years ago'.

John nodded, his expression a complex mixture of resignation and unspoken longing. 'It just ... stopped being a priority', he offered quietly. 'There were always more pressing matters – children's needs, work deadlines, household logistics'.

'We became excellent managers of a family enterprise', Sarah added, a hint of sadness briefly cracking through her composed exterior. 'But somewhere along the way, we stopped being partners in any other sense'.

When I asked how this absence of physical connection affected them, another telling silence filled the room. John finally spoke, his voice lower than before. 'It's like living with a colleague rather than a wife. We coordinate schedules, divide responsibilities, resolve practical issues, but there's no ... warmth. No sense of being special to each other'.

Sarah's response revealed the self-protective wall she'd constructed around this vulnerability. 'I learned to stop noticing the absence', she said. 'When you're constantly running between work commitments and children's activities, it's easier to pretend those needs don't exist than to acknowledge something that seems impossible to address'.

What struck me was not just the absence of physical intimacy, but how this symptom reflected their broader pattern of disconnection. Their bodies, like their lives, operated in carefully managed parallel tracks, never truly intersecting. The efficiency they'd developed in running their household had become a substitute for genuine connection, a way to maintain the appearance of partnership while avoiding the vulnerability that true intimacy requires.

This revelation illuminated the architecture of their estrangement more clearly than anything else they'd shared. The careful distance they maintained on the couch was not circumstantial but emblematic of the emotional moat they'd constructed between them – wide enough to prevent genuine connection yet narrow enough to maintain the illusion of a functioning partnership.

'For our next session', I explain as our three and a half hours together draw to a close, 'we'd like you to complete a few exercises that will help us go deeper'. I hand them each a folder containing materials on Bids for Connection and Love Languages.

'We'd also like you to keep track of moments when you feel most connected to each other, however brief or seemingly insignificant', Maria adds. 'Just notice them, without trying to force them'.

As they prepare to leave, I observe subtle shifts in their physical bearing. John stands slightly taller, his gaze more direct. Sarah's movements have lost some of their brittle efficiency, becoming more fluid. They gather their belongings without speaking, yet something in the air between them has changed, a quiet acknowledgement of truths long unspoken.

'Remember', I say as they reach the door, 'we're available by phone or email between sessions if anything comes up that feels important to discuss'.

Sarah nods, slipping her folder into her bag with characteristic precision. 'Thank you', she says, and the simple words carry unexpected weight.

They walk out together, still maintaining their separate rhythms but perhaps with a new awareness of the space between them, no longer just empty distance but a field of possibility. As the door closes behind them, Maria and I exchange a glance of cautious optimism. Beneath the polished exterior of their efficient partnership, something more vital still pulses, waiting to be remembered.

The moment between seeing couples is sacred; a clearing of mind that honours who has left and who will arrive.

John and Sarah's journey continues in Chapter 28.

Chapter 9

Breaking the Mould – Why Duo Coaching Works

Introduction

The Duo Coaching Framework represents a paradigm shift in relationship therapy, born from both personal experience and professional insight. This innovative approach emerged from recognising fundamental limitations in traditional relationship counselling methodologies and developing a more effective, client-centred alternative.

Genesis of Duo Coaching

My journey toward creating Duo Coaching began with personal disappointment in traditional relationship counselling. During the breakdown of my second marriage, I reluctantly agreed to try relationship counselling, not with hope for reconciliation but to ensure I had exhausted all possibilities. What followed were three separate attempts at conventional therapy, each more disappointing than the last.

The first attempt featured a depressing environment and a rigid fifty-minute session in a small, claustrophobic counselling room with minimal time for both partners to speak. The second attempt was similarly dispiriting, with my wife dominating the conversation and the counsellor showing clear bias. The third ended abruptly when I mentioned experiencing physical abuse from my wife, and the counsellor stated we couldn't continue because they couldn't work with couples experiencing any form of violence.

These experiences crystallised several critical insights that would shape the Duo Coaching framework: the importance of the therapeutic environment, the insufficiency of brief sessions for deep exploration, the problematic power dynamics with a single therapist, the absence of clear outcomes in traditional approaches, and the lack of tools for creating sustainable change.

Core Principles of the Duo Coaching Framework

The Co-Therapist Dynamic

The cornerstone of Duo Coaching is the presence of two therapists working collaboratively with the couple. This creates a balanced power dynamic that eliminates

DOI: 10.4324/9781003752776-9

the perception of the therapist taking sides. With Maria and myself, a male and female therapist, this arrangement provides diverse perspectives and models healthy communication. While one therapist leads a particular segment, the other can observe subtle dynamics between the couple, catching nuances that might otherwise be missed. This dual perspective provides much richer insights than a single counsellor could offer.

Time and Space Reimagined

The framework deliberately breaks from the traditional fifty-minute session model, which I found woefully inadequate for addressing complex relationship issues. Instead, we create a spacious temporal environment that allows for depth exploration and genuine transformation.

Central to this approach is the creation of what anthropologists call a 'liminal space' – a transitional threshold between one state and another, where transformation becomes possible. In traditional cultures, liminal spaces were sacred grounds where initiations and rites of passage occurred, places neither here nor there, where ordinary rules and limitations were temporarily suspended. In our therapy room, we consciously cultivate this liminality, creating a space that exists outside the constraints and patterns of couples' everyday lives.

The first session typically lasts about three and a half hours, providing ample time to explore the couple's history, patterns, and desired outcomes. This extended duration allows couples to move through different emotional states within a single session – from initial defensiveness, through vulnerability, to new understanding – rather than being sent home just as deeper material begins to emerge. Subsequent sessions run approximately two and a half hours each, giving space for substantive work rather than rushing through superficial discussions. Unlike conventional approaches, sessions conclude when reaching a natural stopping point, not when the clock dictates it's time to end.

The physical environment reflects this philosophy of spaciousness and liminality. Couples enter a comfortable, professional setting deliberately designed to feel both safe and slightly separate from ordinary reality – a transitional space where new possibilities can emerge. There are no visible clocks to create time pressure, allowing clients to relax into the process without constantly monitoring the passing minutes. The room itself becomes a container for transformation, a bounded space where couples can experiment with new ways of being together without the intrusion of daily distractions and entrenched patterns.

Sessions are thoughtfully spaced over three to four months, allowing couples to integrate insights and practise new skills between meetings. This rhythm creates a pulsation between intensive therapeutic work and real-world application that honours both the need for deep exploration and the time required for neural pathways to reorganise. The liminal quality extends beyond individual sessions to encompass the entire therapeutic journey – a designated period where the relationship is in an acknowledged state of transformation.

As one client described it: 'When we stepped into your room, it felt like entering a different dimension – not quite therapy in the traditional sense, not quite coaching, not quite spiritual guidance, yet somehow all of these. It was as if the normal rules were suspended, and we could see each other and our relationship with new eyes'.

This approach addresses a key insight from my experience: 'Temporality seems to shift and bend when in an emotional state. When in a good state a moment can last forever because we want it to. When in a bad place we want it to end, now'. By creating a flexible, expansive approach to time and space, the framework accommodates the emotional reality of therapeutic work, allowing couples to fully inhabit their experience without the artificial constraints of conventional session structures.

Outcome-Focused Methodology

Unlike open-ended traditional therapy, the Duo Coaching framework is structured around clear outcomes established from the beginning. During the initial consultation and first session, we work with couples to define specific goals that will guide the therapeutic process. The framework typically encompasses six sessions, creating focus and a sense of urgency that motivates couples to engage fully in the process.

Transdisciplinary Therapeutic Approach

Perhaps the most distinctive aspect of the Duo Coaching framework is its transdisciplinary approach to therapeutic intervention. Rather than adhering to a single methodology, we integrate multiple therapeutic modalities tailored to each couple's specific needs, including elements from psychodynamic theory, client-centred therapy, coaching techniques, neuro-linguistic programming, Gestalt approaches, clean language, timeline therapy, transactional analysis, clinical hypnotherapy, and various personality profiling tools.

The Triad Approach: Me, You, and Us

The framework addresses relationships at three critical levels, recognising that relationship dynamics cannot be understood or transformed without attending to both individual and systemic patterns. We explore each person's patterns, history, and unconscious behaviours – the 'Me' and 'You' dimensions. We examine interaction patterns, communication styles, and joint goals that constitute the 'Us' dimension. Finally, we integrate these understandings to reveal how individual patterns affect the relationship system as a whole.

Comprehensive Support System

The framework extends beyond session time to create continuous support through unlimited telephone and email access between sessions 24/7. Before the first session, couples complete an extensive intake form that explores their background, relationship history, and goals. The professional environment supports this work, providing a comfortable, dedicated space where couples feel welcomed and valued.

The Duo Coaching Process

The therapeutic journey begins before the first session with an initial telephone conversation and comprehensive consultation form. The first session creates the foundation for the work to follow, establishing safety, clarifying outcomes, exploring the couple's history, and assessing individual patterns and needs. Subsequent sessions build on this foundation, reviewing changes, refining outcomes, addressing emerging dynamics, and teaching techniques couples can implement in daily interactions.

Results and Impacts

The evidence for the framework's effectiveness comes from over fifteen years of practice with hundreds of couples, yielding consistent patterns of transformation and healing. Most couples achieve their desired outcomes within six sessions, demonstrating the effectiveness of this focused approach. Many report a dramatic rekindling of connection and intimacy that had seemed permanently lost. The framework's effectiveness leads clients to frequently refer others after experiencing transformation in their own relationships.

Notably, many clients have previously tried traditional therapy without success, finding in Duo Coaching an approach that finally addresses their deeper needs and creates lasting change. The framework's reputation has attracted clients willing to travel internationally to access this unique methodology.

Distinctive Features and Innovations

Several unique aspects distinguish the Duo Coaching framework from conventional approaches to relationship therapy. Rather than positioning ourselves as experts or passive listeners, we serve as guides on the couple's journey. As I explain: 'We positioned ourselves as the guides rather than the "experts" and made it clear in the introductions that we were there to understand how they had got to where they were now. We were not there to judge so that their openness and honesty would help us to understand and to plot together the course forward'. This creates partnership rather than dependency or authority dynamics.

A foundational insight of the framework is my view that 'in a relationship there is no reality, there is only perception, and those perceptions can be very different but equally correct'. This principle allows both partners to feel validated while building understanding of different perspectives, moving beyond the unhelpful dynamic of trying to establish who is 'right' in conflicts.

The framework deliberately creates what anthropologists call a 'liminal space' – a transformative environment between established states. As I describe it: 'The space needed to be liminal, to be a place where people felt safe, where they felt there was room physically and emotionally for them to occupy'. This liminal quality enables deeper change than conventional therapeutic environments by creating a space where transformation becomes possible outside the constraints of everyday life.

I conceptualise the process as guiding couples through their own Hero's Journey (as described by Joseph Campbell): 'Our clients are the Heroes of their own story going on an important and perilous journey and that we are the guides. This feels to be a very different relationship than exists in most forms of relationship therapy where the therapist can often be seen as the wailing wall, to help the clients to offload and create their own learning, or the mountain top guru, dispensing wisdom'. This narrative structure gives meaning to the challenges and transformation couples experience.

The framework attends to what Nora Bateson calls 'Warm Data' – the qualitative, contextual information beyond mere facts: 'Warm Data captures the qualitative dynamics and offers another dimension of understanding to what is learned through quantitative (cold) data. Warm Data is a specific kind of information about the way a couple come together to give vitality to that system'. This holistic awareness allows for a deeper understanding of relationship dynamics than conventional approaches that focus primarily on verbal exchanges and visible behaviours.

The complexity of human relationships demands a rich tapestry of therapeutic modalities: approaches that deal with both the unconscious and conscious mind and the ability to weave all of these together to meet the unique needs of each couple. When a relationship has become stuck in destructive patterns, purely cognitive techniques may prove insufficient, as the unconscious mind continues to operate according to its own deeply embedded templates. Similarly, approaches focused solely on emotional catharsis or past wounds may fail to provide the practical tools needed for daily interaction. The effective therapist must move fluidly between different modalities – at times using clean language to explore metaphors, at others employing constellation work to illuminate systemic patterns, sometimes utilising cognitive reframing to interrupt negative thought cycles, and occasionally accessing somatic awareness to reconnect partners with embodied wisdom.

This transdisciplinary approach allows for addressing both conscious behaviours and choices while also accessing the unconscious processes that often drive relationship dynamics beneath awareness. The integration of these varied approaches, tailored specifically to each couple's unique situation, creates a comprehensive therapeutic environment where transformation becomes possible at multiple levels simultaneously.

Necessary Conditions for Effective Relationship Therapy

Based on extensive experience and my doctoral research, I believe that several conditions appear necessary for truly effective relationship therapy. From the clients' perspective, both partners must be present and committed to the process, have clarity about desired outcomes, and be willing to be open and honest. Understanding each other's perspectives and accepting shared responsibility for the relationship's current state are essential starting points for meaningful change.

From the therapists' side, establishing clear boundaries and expectations, providing clarity about the process, maintaining an outcome focus, creating a safe space for vulnerability, and facilitating perspective-sharing are crucial. Challenging assumptions, addressing both individual and couple issues, avoiding dependency, and employing varied techniques all contribute to successful outcomes.

The Duo Coaching Client Experience

The client experience differs dramatically from traditional therapy in numerous ways. Couples enter a professional yet warm setting with a dedicated, depersonalised counselling room designed specifically for therapeutic work. Water, refreshments, and healthy snacks are available throughout the session, creating a sense of hospitality and care. The absence of visible clocks removes time pressure, while comfortable seating with space for movement allows for various therapeutic activities. The environment is professional but welcoming, establishing a sense of safety and respect from the moment couples arrive.

The therapeutic relationship itself has unique qualities. Clients engage with two therapists who provide balanced attention to both partners, preventing feelings of bias or neglect that can arise with a single therapist. We position ourselves as guides rather than experts, empowering couples to discover their own solutions with our support. The interaction between the male and female therapists models healthy communication across gender lines, providing a living example of the dynamics we encourage. Our approach is non-judgemental but directive when needed, offering clear guidance while respecting the couple's autonomy. Our committed availability between sessions demonstrates our investment in their progress and provides security during difficult moments.

Clients typically highlight several elements as particularly transformative. Many describe the profound experience of being truly heard by both their partner and the therapists, often for the first time in years. Understanding each other's perspectives without judgement creates new bridges of empathy and connection. Recognising unconscious patterns from their past helps couples depersonalise conflicts and see how historical experiences shape current reactions. Learning practical communication techniques provides concrete tools for navigating future challenges, while many experience a rekindling of connection and intimacy that had seemed lost forever. Perhaps most importantly, couples gain tools for ongoing relationship maintenance, enabling them to continue their growth long after therapy concludes.

Conclusion

The Duo Coaching framework represents a fundamental reimagining of relationship therapy based on direct experience, client needs, and integrative therapeutic approaches. Its success demonstrates that relationship therapy need not be a prolonged, indeterminate process but can instead be a focused, transformative journey with clear outcomes and lasting change.

In a world where relationships continue to face increasing pressures, the Duo Coaching framework offers a more effective, efficient alternative to help couples navigate their challenges and rediscover connection.

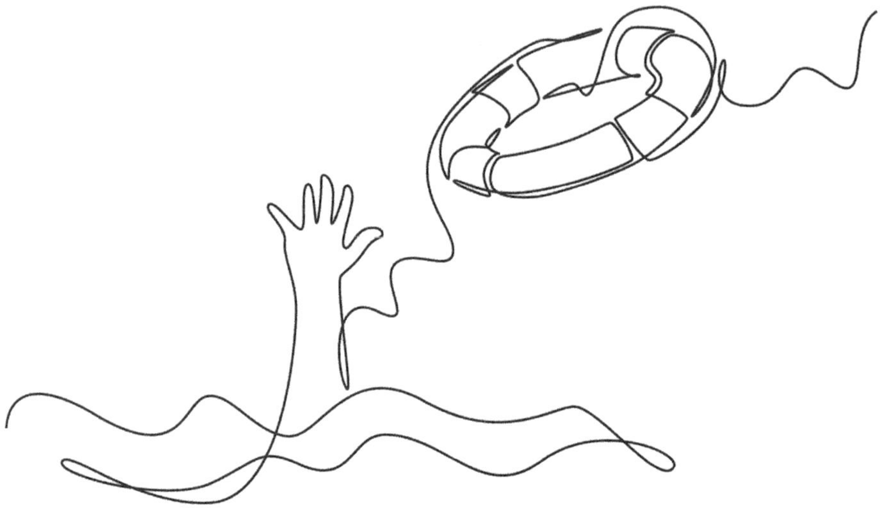

Chapter 10

Sam and Suzy – Fractured Foundations

First Steps to Healing

They arrive together yet somehow apart, inhabiting the same physical space while emotionally miles distant. Sam enters first, holding the door with mechanical courtesy rather than genuine attentiveness. Suzy follows, her smile polite but never reaching her eyes. There is a weariness about them both that speaks of battles fought too long without reinforcements or rest.

Sam is tall with the slight stoop of someone perpetually accommodating the world around him. Suzy moves with the careful precision of a person who has learned to navigate minefields, both literal and emotional. They settle onto the three-seater couch with practised coordination: she on the right, he on the left, the middle cushion between them empty yet somehow cluttered with unspoken grievances.

'Thank you for coming in today', I begin, noting the way they both straighten slightly, as if preparing for evaluation. 'I know finding the time must have been challenging with your complex family schedule'.

'We rearranged some pickups', Sam explains, his voice level and pragmatic. 'My mother is helping with Maya today, and Suzy's sister has taken Noah for the afternoon'.

Already, the logistics of their blended family emerge: Maya, Sam's daughter from his previous marriage, and Noah, Suzy's son from hers, forming the complicated foundation of their shared life.

'Before we begin exploring your history together', I say, 'I'd like to ask each of you a simple but important question. What would you like to have happen in our sessions together?'

Suzy glances at Sam, a habit suggesting she often calibrates her responses based on his reaction. 'I want to find us again', she says finally, her voice soft but determined. 'Sometimes I feel like we're just crisis managers living in the same house, not partners anymore'.

Sam nods slightly. 'I want peace', he says after a moment, the word heavy with meaning. 'In our home, in our relationship. Just ... peace'. The weariness in his voice suggests this simple wish feels increasingly unattainable.

'Those are both meaningful aspirations', Maria says gently. 'Would it be alright if we learn more about how you arrived at this point in your relationship?'

DOI: 10.4324/9781003752776-10

What unfolds over the next hour is the story of two people who found each other after individual disappointments, only to discover that blending lives carries its own profound challenges. Sam and Suzy met four years ago; both newly divorced, both single parents determined to create something more stable for their children. Their connection was immediate and based on mutual understanding of past pain and hope for a different future.

'It felt like finding a fellow survivor', Suzy explains, something softening in her face with the memory. 'Someone who understood the particular grief of a marriage ending, who didn't need everything explained'.

'We were careful at first', Sam adds. 'Introduced the children slowly, didn't rush anything. It all seemed so thoughtful and measured compared to our previous relationships'.

They married two years ago, creating a household with Sam's daughter Maya (now eleven) and Suzy's son Noah (now eight). The early days were challenging but hopeful; two children adjusting to new stepparents, new routines, new expectations. They approached these challenges as a team, united in their determination to create the stable, loving family both had lacked in their first marriages.

The fractures began appearing about eighteen months ago, coinciding with a significant escalation in hostility from Sam's ex-wife, Glenda.

'She'd always been difficult', Sam explains, tension evident in his jaw. 'But when Maya started talking about how much she enjoyed spending time with Suzy, something ... shifted. Glenda became explicitly hostile, not just to me but to our entire household'.

'It's been systematic', Suzy adds, her voice tightening. 'Using Maya as a weapon, scheduling conflicts with our family plans, sending Maya to us without necessary medications or school materials, calling constantly during our time with her, undermining our household rules, encouraging Maya to report back on every detail of our lives ...'

'And the allegations', Sam continues, his voice dropping almost to a whisper. 'Unfounded reports to social services, claims of neglect, suggestions that Maya isn't safe in our home. Each one investigated and dismissed, but the damage is done every time'.

As they speak, the toll of this sustained campaign becomes evident; not just in their relationship with Maya, whose loyalty is constantly tested, but in the fabric of their marriage itself. Sam has become increasingly defensive and withdrawn, perpetually braced for the next attack. Suzy feels increasingly isolated as the target of Glenda's particular venom, yet unable to disengage for the sake of both children. The constant state of siege has left little energy for nurturing their connection as partners.

'And Noah is caught in the crossfire', Suzy explains, genuine pain in her voice. 'He's exposed to this toxicity that has nothing to do with him. He's becoming anxious, walking on eggshells, afraid of doing anything that might become ammunition'.

'I feel responsible for bringing this into his life', Sam admits, the first crack appearing in his composed facade. 'Into both their lives'.

As their story unfolds, the weight they carry becomes palpable; not just ordinary marital adjustments but the extraordinary burden of parenting under siege, of loving children caught in adult conflicts they didn't create and cannot resolve.

After a thoughtful pause, I decide to address another dimension often left unspoken. 'I'd like to ask about something that couples often find difficult to discuss', I say. 'Can you tell me about the intimacy in your relationship?'

The question lands as intended; a gentle disruption in the narrative they've been crafting. Suzy glances at Sam, then looks away. Sam studies his hands. The silence speaks volumes.

'It's ... been a while', Suzy finally admits, colour rising in her cheeks despite her evident desire to be matter-of-fact. 'With everything else happening, it just ...'

'It doesn't feel like a priority anymore', Sam finishes for her. 'By the time we get through each day, manage the crisis du jour from Glenda, tend to the children's needs, we're just ... depleted'.

'When was the last time you were physically intimate?' Maria asks gently.

They exchange another glance, this one carrying surprise at their mutual uncertainty.

'Three months? Maybe four?' Suzy ventures.

'Longer', Sam says quietly. 'I think it was before Christmas'.

The realisation lands heavily between them; nearly six months without this fundamental form of connection. As they begin to discuss this aspect of their relationship, more nuances emerge. It isn't simply exhaustion, though that plays a significant role. Sam reveals a growing fear of rejection, choosing pre-emptive withdrawal over risking Suzy's potential refusal. Suzy admits that the constant spillover of parenting stress has made it difficult to transition mentally into seeing Sam as a lover rather than a co-administrator.

'Sometimes I feel like we're running a small, dysfunctional country together', she says with a sad smile. 'Managing borders, negotiating with hostile neighbours, putting out fires. It doesn't exactly set the mood'.

'And there's always the fear of being interrupted', Sam adds. 'Or worse, having something we do become fodder for Glenda's next allegation. The walls feel very thin'.

This candid discussion about their intimate life reveals how thoroughly external pressures have invaded their private space; not just practically in terms of time and energy, but psychologically, with Glenda's presence hovering like a spectre even in their most personal moments.

After gathering this history, I move to the next stage of our session. 'I'd like to try something different now', I explain, bringing forward two wicker baskets filled with pebbles of various sizes, shapes, and colours. 'These stones will help us understand your relationship in a way that sometimes words alone cannot'.

Sam regards the baskets with cautious interest, while Suzy leans forward with more open curiosity.

'There's no right or wrong way to do this', I assure them. 'I'd like each of you, starting with Sam, to choose one pebble to represent yourself, and place it where it needs to be'.

Sam considers the stones carefully before selecting a solid, dark-grey pebble with smooth edges. He places it on the floor slightly left of centre, his movements deliberate and measured.

Suzy explores the basket more spontaneously, her fingers moving through the stones before selecting a smaller, light-coloured pebble with streaks of pink running through it. She places it on the floor at a moderate distance from Sam's stone; not the vast separation we've seen with some couples, but a definite space between them.

'Now', I continue, 'please select other pebbles to represent important people or elements in your lives and place them where they need to be'.

What emerges over the next few minutes is revealing. Sam places a bright, multi-coloured stone representing Maya very close to his own, but notably positioned between his stone and Suzy's, as if simultaneously connecting and separating them. His parents are represented by two similar stones placed at a comfortable distance behind him. His work, a source of both stress and escape, is symbolised by a substantial stone placed to his right.

Most strikingly, he selects a jagged, dark stone and places it at the edge of the arrangement, explaining quietly, 'This is Glenda'. Its position on the periphery cannot disguise its outsized presence in the constellation.

Suzy's arrangement tells its complementary story. Noah is represented by a smooth river stone placed very close to her but slightly angled toward Sam's stone. Her sister, a crucial support, is symbolised by a stone positioned just behind her own. Various small stones represent her part-time work, her volunteer commitments, her friends; all arranged in a loose semicircle that suggests connection but not central focus.

She too acknowledges Glenda's presence, not with a separate stone but by placing her finger near Sam's dark, jagged pebble and saying simply, 'What he said. She affects everything'.

Neither of them initially includes any stone specifically representing their relationship itself, a telling omission. When gently prompted about this, they exchange a glance of recognition.

'I suppose that's part of the problem', Suzy says softly. 'It's got lost among everything else'.

Sam nods in silent agreement, then reaches for a small, unremarkable stone and places it in the space between their pebbles. 'It's there', he says. 'Just ... buried sometimes'.

'I notice that the children are placed quite centrally in both your arrangements', Maria observes. 'And Sam, you've positioned Maya between yourself and Suzy'.

Sam studies the placement thoughtfully. 'That's how it feels', he acknowledges. 'Not because I want it that way, but because that's how circumstances have forced it to be. Maya needs extra protection, extra care, because of everything happening with Glenda'.

'And I notice, Suzy, that while Noah is very close to you, he's angled toward Sam', I add. 'Can you tell us about that placement?'

Suzy looks at the arrangement with a soft smile. 'Noah adores Sam', she says. 'It's been one of the few uncomplicated blessings in all this, how quickly and completely they bonded. Sam is the father figure Noah's been craving'.

This simple statement carries significant weight. Amid all the challenges of their blended family, this genuine connection between stepfather and stepson represents a real achievement; one perhaps not fully appreciated amid the more dramatic struggles.

'And I'd like to ask you both about Glenda's stone', Maria says gently. 'It's placed at the edge, yet both of you immediately identified it as a powerful presence'.

'She should be even further away', Sam says with a flash of frustration. 'But her influence doesn't respect boundaries'.

'It feels like she's always there', Suzy adds, fatigue evident in her voice. 'A third party in our marriage, an unwelcome ghost in our home'.

The room grows quiet as these revelations settle around us. Both Sam and Suzy stare at the constellation they've created, perhaps seeing the physical representation of their complex reality from a new perspective.

'Could each of you now create a constellation that represents your ideal future? What would you like your arrangement to look like in your ideal future?'

This second exercise brings hopeful insights. In his ideal arrangement, Sam brings his and Suzy's stones much closer together, placing them side by side at the centre of the constellation. The children's stones are positioned nearby but in a way that creates a clear family unit rather than barriers between the adults. Most significantly, he moves Glenda's stone much further away, almost beyond the edge of their working space.

'I can't make her disappear entirely', he explains with resignation born of realism. 'But I need her influence to be contained, manageable, not the central force it's become'.

Suzy's ideal arrangement mirrors Sam's in key ways. She too brings their stones closer together, though with a subtle difference: she places them at a slight angle toward each other, creating a sense of engagement rather than simply parallel positioning. The children remain close but are arranged as part of a family circle rather than between the adults. Her work and other commitments remain present but in more balanced proportion.

She doesn't move Glenda's stone, looking at it with a complicated expression before saying, 'I can't control where she positions herself. I can only control how we respond, how much power we give her presence'.

As they contemplated the stark difference between their current constellations and their ideal arrangements, I asked the question that would help bridge the gap between reality and aspiration.

'What do you need to have happen to get you from your current constellation to your ideal future? What journey would take you there?'

Sam studied the arrangements thoughtfully, his gaze moving between the two versions – particularly the positioning of the jagged stone representing Glenda. After a moment, he looked up with newfound clarity in his expression.

'I need to develop stronger boundaries', he said, his voice more decisive than I'd heard before. 'Not just with Glenda, but with the whole situation. I've been reacting to every crisis, every allegation, every manipulation as if it's an emergency that requires my immediate attention. That's exactly what she wants – to keep us in constant turmoil'. He glanced at Suzy with a look of gentle recognition. 'And in doing that, I've been making Suzy carry too much of this burden with me, as if her role is to help manage my ex-wife. That's not fair or right'.

Suzy's reaction was subtle but evident – a small release of tension in her shoulders, a softening around her eyes. When she spoke, her words carried the weight of hard-earned insight.

'I need to stop taking Glenda's attacks personally', she said, touching the spot where she'd indicated Glenda's influence. 'I've been treating her hostility as if it's a referendum on my worthiness as a parent, as a partner to Sam. But it's not about me – it never has been. She'd behave this way toward anyone in my position'. She paused, gathering her thoughts. 'I also need to build a stronger identity for our family unit that isn't defined by this conflict. Right now, so much of our energy and conversation revolves around managing the latest crisis. We need to create experiences and memories that are just ours, especially for the children'.

Sam nodded emphatically at this. 'That's it exactly. We've let Glenda become the organising principle of our family life – everything revolves around anticipating her next move or recovering from her last one'.

'And what about that small stone representing your relationship?' Maria asked gently, pointing to the unremarkable pebble Sam had placed between them. 'How does that need to change?'

Sam and Suzy exchanged a look of shared understanding before Suzy responded.

'It needs to become central again, not peripheral', she said simply. 'Not just physically in the arrangement, but in our priorities. We need to remember that our connection is what gives us the strength to handle everything else'.

'And it needs to be more distinctive', Sam added, picking up the small, plain stone he'd chosen. 'Something with more character, more presence. Something that doesn't get lost among all the other elements of our lives'.

This exchange represented a significant shift – from seeing themselves primarily as co-managers of a crisis to recognising the need to reclaim their identity as partners first, co-parents second, and crisis responders third. Their recognition that Glenda's influence had become disproportionate, and that they had agency in how they responded to it, suggested the beginning of a new perspective that could transform their experience, even if their external circumstances remained challenging.

As our first session moved into its final hour, we explore the significance of these arrangements. Sam speaks with growing emotion about his desire to prioritise his marriage without abandoning his responsibilities to Maya. Suzy acknowledges the resentment she sometimes feels toward Glenda's intrusions, while emphasising her commitment to creating a safe space for both children despite these challenges. They begin to identify patterns that have developed under pressure: his tendency to emotionally withdraw when feeling helpless to resolve conflicts, her habit of taking on protective responsibilities that leave her depleted, their mutual struggle to maintain connection amid constant crisis management.

'For our next session', I explain as our three and a half hours together draw to a close, 'we'd like you to complete a few exercises that will help us go deeper'. I hand them each a folder containing materials on Love Languages, Talking Meaningfully to Your Partner, and exercises about rebuilding intimacy.

'We'd also like you to pay attention to the moments when you feel most connected to each other, however brief or seemingly insignificant', Maria adds. 'Just notice them, without trying to force them'.

As they prepare to leave, I observe subtle shifts in their physical bearing. Sam stands slightly straighter, as if some invisible weight has begun to lift. Suzy moves with a touch more ease, less of the hypervigilance that marked her arrival. They gather their belongings in companionable silence, the quality of their shared space somehow altered by the simple act of seeing their challenges laid out before them.

'Remember', I say as they reach the door, 'we're available by phone or email between sessions if anything comes up that feels important to discuss'.

They walk out together, their steps not perfectly synchronised but more harmonious than when they arrived. As the door closes behind them, Maria and I exchange a glance of cautious hope. Despite the extraordinary pressures on their relationship, genuine care and commitment remain visible beneath the layers of stress and strategic survival.

'They're still fighting for each other', Maria observes quietly.

'Yes', I agree. 'And now perhaps they can start fighting alongside each other rather than merely in parallel'.

We will find out the next stages for Sam and Suzy in Chapter 29.

Chapter 11

The Birth of the Relationship Paradigm

Genesis of a Framework

The Relationship Paradigm emerged not in a moment of academic contemplation, but rather in the open waters of the Caribbean, with the wind filling the sails and the endless horizon stretching before us. It was September 2017, and my new wife Gwen and I were honeymooning aboard a forty-foot boat, just the two of us navigating both the sea and the beginnings of our married life together. In that liminal space between our past and future, Gwen posed a question that would alter the course of my professional journey: 'Why do you want to write a book?'

The question caught me off guard. I had mentioned writing a book as one of my future dreams, but I hadn't deeply examined my motivations. Was it ego – to point at a bookshelf and claim ownership of a volume? Was it an unconscious attempt to win approval from my father? As I reflected in the gentle rocking of the boat, I concluded that the only worthy reason would be to help others and make the world a slightly better place.

My life experiences and professional practice had led me to relationships as the natural subject. After years of working with couples through Duo Coaching, I had accumulated insights that I felt compelled to share beyond the confines of my consulting room. But Gwen, ever the coach, pressed further: 'How can you distil what you have learnt from all the couples you have worked with, and what are the key elements of a good relationship?'

This question sparked a moment of synthesis that had perhaps been brewing beneath the surface of my consciousness for years. As we sailed south from St Vincent under clear skies with favourable winds, I found myself unwrapping fifteen years of learning in a matter of minutes. I reflected on the relationship books I had read – each offering an identikit model with prescribed steps – and felt they missed something essential. None provided a simple yet comprehensive framework that captured the essence of a great relationship while honouring the unique reality of each couple.

What emerged in those moments of reflection were six elements that I had observed consistently in thriving relationships. Interestingly, I deliberately avoided using the word 'love' as a central concept – not because it isn't important, but because its meaning varies so profoundly between individuals, contexts, and time

DOI: 10.4324/9781003752776-11

periods. Instead, I sought elements that were both universal and practical, components that couples could actually work with rather than abstract ideals.

The Six Elements

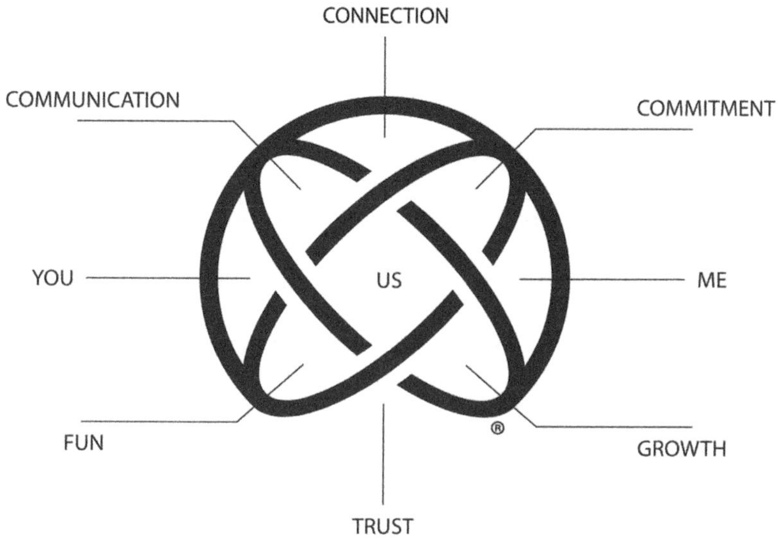

The framework crystallised around six interconnected elements, each essential to a flourishing relationship:

Communication emerged as the foundational element – the ability to express how you truly feel and to be truly listened to and understood. In my years of therapy, I had witnessed how communication breakdowns often marked the first stage of a relationship drifting apart. Couples who could maintain open, honest dialogue even through difficulties showed remarkable resilience.

Connection represented those profound moments of intimacy that sustain a relationship through challenges. This could manifest as a meaningful glance across a crowded room, a tender touch, or physical intimacy. I coined the phrase 'moments of intimacy' to describe those few seconds where connection happens and, in that moment, nothing else matters except the two people involved – a temporal space where the rest of the world falls away.

Commitment reflected the mutual dedication to nurturing the relationship actively. I had observed that relationships never simply maintain themselves – they require ongoing investment from both partners. Without this commitment to keep improving and flourishing together, relationships inevitably wither. This wasn't about a one-time promise but a daily choice to prioritise the partnership.

Fun emerged as an element that couples often overlooked but that proved vital for relationship health. One of my standard questions to couples in their first session was, 'When did the two of you last have fun together?' The common response – embarrassed looks and admission of 'a long time ago' – revealed how easily this essential component slips away. Fun allows couples to access their inner child, laugh together, be silly, and experience joy in one another's company.

Growth acknowledged the dynamic nature of both individuals and relationships. Stagnation, I had found, led to dissatisfaction and disconnection. Each person needed to continue evolving, and the relationship itself needed to adapt and develop with them. Without growth, relationships plateau and gradually fade.

Trust formed the bedrock upon which everything else stood. Without trust, no amount of communication, connection, commitment, fun, or growth could sustain a relationship. I had witnessed how mistrust could creep in insidiously when relationships faltered – questions about a partner's whereabouts, suspicion about phone messages, anxiety about late arrivals home. These unanswered questions fester and grow, undermining the entire relationship.

These six elements seemed to materialise almost magically in that moment on the boat, but they represented the distillation of countless hours working with couples, observing patterns, and facilitating transformation. As I reflected on them, I felt confident that I had captured the essential framework that could guide couples toward more fulfilling relationships.

The Triadic Foundation: Me, You, and Us

Beyond these six elements, another crucial insight informed the framework: the recognition of three key players in every relationship – 'Me', 'You', and 'Us'. I had observed that relationships cannot thrive when couples become joined at the hip, losing their individual identities. Each person needs to maintain their own life and selfhood while simultaneously building a fulfilling shared existence.

This triadic understanding became integral to the Relationship Paradigm. It acknowledged that individual well-being directly impacts relationship health, and that the relationship itself becomes a third entity requiring care and attention. A truly balanced relationship honours both individual autonomy and shared connection – neither sacrificing self for togetherness nor independence for intimacy.

Looking back at that moment of creation, I still feel it represented a beautiful confluence – where my professional experience, personal journey, and the open possibilities of a new marriage came together to create something of lasting value. Six years later, the framework remains as relevant and powerful as when it first emerged on that Caribbean voyage.

A Framework, Not a Model

An important realisation in my doctoral journey has been that what I created is not a model but a framework. This distinction proves significant. While models tend to be fixed and prescriptive, frameworks offer flexible structures that can adapt to different contexts and evolve over time. The Relationship Paradigm does not impose a rigid template but rather provides navigational markers that couples can use to chart their own course.

As creator of this framework, I recognise that it emerges from various influences – including other writers and thinkers – representing a synthesis rather than an entirely novel invention. This acknowledgement opens the framework to continued evolution and refinement rather than freezing it as an inviolable doctrine. The framework welcomes growth, just as it encourages growth within relationships themselves.

Standing Apart: The Distinctiveness of the Relationship Paradigm

In developing the Relationship Paradigm, I sought to create something distinct from existing approaches. My research into other relationship models confirmed both overlaps and significant differences. John Gottman's seven principles, Gary Chapman's five love languages, Esther Perel's concepts around desire and security, John Alan Lee's six love styles, and the frameworks proposed by organisations like BACP and Relate all offer valuable insights. However, the Relationship Paradigm distinguishes itself in several crucial ways.

Perhaps most importantly, it offers remarkable simplicity without sacrificing depth. The six elements provide an accessible entry point for couples, easy to remember and discuss. Yet each element opens into profound territories of relationship dynamics. This combination of accessibility and depth makes the framework particularly practical for couples at various stages of their journey.

The framework also emphasises flexibility and personalisation. Unlike prescriptive approaches that suggest all relationships should follow identical patterns, the Relationship Paradigm acknowledges that each couple must define what communication, connection, commitment, fun, growth, and trust mean within their unique context. Cultural differences, individual personalities, and relationship histories all influence how these elements manifest.

Additionally, the framework incorporates calibration as an essential component. Couples can assess their current state across the six elements, identifying areas of strength and opportunity. This measurement aspect encourages ongoing awareness and intentional development rather than a one-time application of principles.

The visual representation of the framework – with its distinctive logo showing interlocking circles and the placement of 'Me', 'You', and 'Us' – adds another dimension of accessibility. This graphic element helps couples visualise the interconnected nature of relationship components and serves as a mnemonic device for remembering the framework.

Embodiment through Narrative

While the framework provided a conceptual structure, I recognised that abstract concepts alone rarely inspire transformation. People connect with stories, with lived experiences that resonate with their own challenges and hopes. This understanding led to the creation of *Reset*, a novel that would embody the Relationship Paradigm through the journey of a couple named John and Rachel.

Reset tells the story of a couple who had been together for sixteen years and gradually drifted apart under the pressures of work, children, and unmet expectations. Standing at the brink of separation, they find their way back to love through a process guided by the principles of the Relationship Paradigm. The novel alternates between their perspectives, highlighting how differently they perceive their shared reality – reinforcing my core belief that in relationships, there is no objective reality, only perception.

Through this narrative approach, I could invite readers into the consulting room, allowing them to witness the pain, joy, and transformation of John and Rachel. The story offers a safe mirror in which readers might recognise their own relationship patterns without the defensiveness that direct confrontation might provoke. In crafting the novel, I drew from both my clients' experiences and my own, creating a bricolage that felt authentic while maintaining confidentiality.

The writing process itself proved transformative. Beginning aboard the Queen Mary during a hurricane on an eastbound North Atlantic crossing – while my wife Gwen suffered from seasickness – I found inspiration in watching the majestic waves from the ocean-facing library. After several false starts and methodological adjustments, I discovered that inhabiting the characters' worlds through dictation allowed their voices to flow more naturally. When my editor's first response was tears followed by praise, I knew the story had captured something essential about the human experience of relationship struggle and renewal.

Expanding the Vision: Recover

The success of *Reset* confirmed my belief in the power of narrative to convey complex relationship dynamics. It also highlighted a particular need among my readership and therapy clients – guidance for couples facing the devastating impact of betrayal. This led to my second book, *Recover: Rebuilding Trust after the Shock of Betrayal*, published in February 2021.

Recover follows the same narrative structure as *Reset*, alternating perspectives between characters to reveal the multifaceted nature of relationship betrayal. The story centres on Andy and Susan, whose marriage faces the trauma of infidelity, and introduces a third perspective through Diana, the woman with whom Andy had an affair. This triadic approach allows readers to witness the complex emotional terrain of what I term the Toxic Triangle – the interconnected relationships between the betrayed partner, the affair partner, and the illicit partner.

Through this narrative, I explore how betrayal creates profound ruptures in trust – perhaps the most fundamental element of the Relationship Paradigm framework. When trust is shattered, all other elements (communication, connection, commitment, fun, and growth) become compromised. Yet paradoxically, this crisis can create an opportunity for transformation. As I've witnessed repeatedly in my clinical practice, couples who successfully navigate betrayal often build relationships stronger than they had before – not despite the trauma, but because of how it forced them to address long-ignored issues.

In *Recover*, I introduce a structured framework for understanding the stages of affair recovery, from discovery through resolution. The Toxic Triangle model illustrates how emotional energies shift through four distinct phases, providing readers with a map for their own healing journey. This visual representation helps demystify what often feels like emotional chaos, offering clarity during a profoundly disorienting experience.

Research supports this approach. Studies on post-traumatic growth suggest that some individuals not only recover from trauma but experience significant positive psychological change as a result of their struggle. The work of Tedeschi and Calhoun particularly resonates with my observations – that growth commonly occurs in appreciation of life, relationships with others, recognition of new possibilities, personal strength, and spiritual dimensions.

Writing *Recover* felt different from my first book. The novelty had worn off, and I faced the classic 'second album syndrome'. Yet the importance of the message drove me forward. With approximately 20% of British adults admitting to affairs and most divorce stemming from infidelity, I recognised how essential this guidance was. The book needed to exist not just for those currently in crisis, but as preventive wisdom for all relationships.

Beyond the Page: Creating an Ecosystem

I soon realised that a book does not stand alone but requires an ecosystem to reach its full potential. This understanding led to the development of a website, videos, articles, and an online programme – all designed to extend the framework's reach and deepen its impact.

Working with professional filmmakers, we created videos bringing scenes from the book to life and exploring each element of the Relationship Paradigm. These visual pieces offered another medium through which people could engage with the concepts, watching actors portray the relationship dynamics described in the text. Even after hundreds of viewings, these videos still move me to tears as they capture the essence of relationship struggles and transformation.

The Relationship Paradigm program emerged as an online resource allowing individuals and couples worldwide to access my teachings through a structured approach including webinars, assessments, and downloadable resources. This programme follows what we called 'The Relationship Success Path', guiding participants through sequential stages of relationship development.

Perhaps most surprisingly, I found myself drawn into the world of media commentary. What began as tentative outreach for publicity evolved into over 370 articles reaching 4.8 million readers in print and 2.8 billion online. Various publications dubbed me 'the relationship expert', 'the relationship guru', and even – somewhat mysteriously – 'the royal relationship expert'. This media presence, while sometimes surreal, significantly amplified the framework's reach.

The COVID-19 pandemic and subsequent lockdowns created a moment when relationship support became more crucial than ever. Couples suddenly found themselves confined together without the usual escape valves of work and socialisation. In response, I produced articles, blogs, and videos addressing the unique pressures of 'isolationship', trying to offer guidance through an unprecedented relationship challenge.

Charting the Future Course

The journey of the Relationship Paradigm continues to unfold. What began as a framework has expanded into a multifaceted approach to relationship health, with *Reset* and *Recover* as the first two instalments in a projected series of books addressing different relationship challenges. While *Reset* addresses couples who have drifted apart and *Recover* helps those navigating betrayal, future volumes will explore workplace relationships, coping with illness, ending relationships well, starting new ones, navigating family dynamics, dealing with loss, living with teenagers, selling a business, and creating a happy retirement.

What you are now reading is my third book and takes a different approach. It offers readers insight into the transformative work that happens in relationship therapy. Following in the tradition of powerful clinical narratives by practitioners like Susanna Abse, Stephen Gross, and Oliver Sacks, this book will invite readers to witness the journey of transformation from the therapist's perspective, further demystifying the therapeutic process and potentially reducing barriers to seeking help.

My ambitious goal – 'to impact and improve ten million relationships around the world in this decade' – guides this ongoing work. Four years into this journey, with nearly five million people reached, the target seems challenging but achievable. Each article, video, or chapter represents an opportunity to address a fundamental gap in our social education. After all, who teaches us how to have great relationships? For many, parental models prove inadequate, yet relationship skills remain absent from formal education. The Relationship Paradigm aims to fill this void, providing accessible guidance for a fundamental human need.

Looking ahead, I will expand the framework's application to younger audiences, helping children and teenagers develop healthy relationship templates before problematic patterns become entrenched. I'm also intrigued by the potential of AI and avatars to provide relationship training and support, making guidance available to those who might never seek traditional therapy.

The Relationship Paradigm represents both my professional legacy and my contribution to a world where relationships often struggle under unprecedented pressures. The framework serves as a chart by which couples can navigate their journey together – identifying the islands they need to visit and possible routes to take, while maintaining the freedom to discover their own unique path to connection.

A significant milestone in this journey was the completion of my doctorate in the Phenomenology of Relationships in 2024. This academic pursuit wasn't motivated by a desire for credentials, but by a deep curiosity about the philosophical underpinnings of human connection. The rigorous research process allowed me to examine relationship dynamics through multiple lenses – from the neurobiology of attachment to the existential dimensions of intimacy. Drawing on phenomenological methodology, I explored how couples co-create their shared reality, how meaning emerges through interaction, and how relationship patterns become embodied over time. The doctoral journey deepened the theoretical foundation of my practical work, bringing together diverse disciplines including philosophy, psychology, systems theory, and communication studies. This transdisciplinary approach validated empirically what I had observed clinically: that relationships operate simultaneously at multiple levels of experience – cognitive, emotional, physical, and even spiritual. The insights from this research have further refined the Relationship Paradigm, ensuring that its practical accessibility remains grounded in sound theoretical understanding. Perhaps most importantly, the doctorate strengthened my conviction that relationship healing is not merely a personal good but a societal imperative, with ripple effects extending far beyond the couple themselves.

As I reflect on this journey, I see myself as captain of two vessels – Duo Coaching, an exclusive superyacht offering bespoke itineraries for individual couples, and the Relationship Paradigm, a cruise ship carrying countless passengers to transformative destinations. These complementary vessels serve different purposes but share a common mission: helping people discover the profound joy and growth that come from healthy, thriving relationships.

The Relationship Paradigm continues to evolve as I gather new insights from clients, readers, and my own relationship journey. What began as a moment of clarity on Caribbean waters has become a framework touching millions of lives – a testament to the power of distilling complex relationship dynamics into accessible wisdom that couples can actually use. In a world where meaningful connection grows increasingly precious, the Relationship Paradigm offers both a map and a compass for those seeking to navigate the sometimes turbulent but ultimately rewarding waters of intimate partnership.

Chapter 12

Communication

In my years of sitting with couples like Rebecca and James, Barry and Edith, and Sam and Suzy, I've witnessed the same pattern repeatedly: relationships don't typically fail from lack of love – they fail from lack of communication. James couldn't tell Rebecca about his growing loneliness before it drove him to seek connection elsewhere. Barry and Edith spent thirty years unable to speak the words that might have healed their wound. Suzy struggled to help Sam understand the impact of his ex-wife's intrusions without sounding controlling. The first of the six elements of the Relationship Paradigm – Communication – emerged as foundational precisely because I've seen so clearly what happens when it breaks down.

If relationships are gardens, then communication is both the water that nourishes growth and the pruning that shapes it. In my years of working with couples through Duo Coaching, I've observed that while many relationship issues present themselves as disagreements about finances, parenting, or intimacy, at their core lies a more fundamental challenge: the ability to truly communicate.

The Communication element of the Relationship Paradigm isn't simply about talking more. Many couples in distress talk constantly – about logistics, grievances, and surface-level concerns. Yet they remain profoundly disconnected. True communication encompasses not just the exchange of information but the sharing of meaning – the ability to express oneself authentically and to receive one's partner with openness and understanding.

The Anatomy of Effective Communication

Effective communication in relationships requires a delicate balance of several components:

Clarity: The ability to express one's thoughts, feelings, and needs in a way that can be understood by one's partner.

Active listening: Receiving one's partner's communication with full attention, seeking to understand rather than simply waiting to respond.

Emotional honesty: Sharing one's authentic emotional experience rather than disguising or diluting it.

DOI: 10.4324/9781003752776-12

Nonverbal attunement: Being aware of and responsive to the body language, facial expressions, and tone that often convey more than words alone.
Timing: Recognising when a conversation is likely to be productive versus when one or both partners are too stressed, tired, or emotional to engage constructively.
Repair: The ability to acknowledge communication missteps and restore connection when interactions go awry.

When these elements are present, communication serves as a bridge between partners, allowing them to navigate everything from daily coordination to life's deepest questions together. When they're absent, couples often find themselves talking past each other, trapped in cycles of misunderstanding and hurt.

Rosie and Don: The Silence between Words

I recall Rosie and Don, who came to Duo Coaching after fifteen years of marriage. They presented with what they called 'communication problems' – a term I've found often serves as shorthand for a complex web of relationship challenges.

'We just don't talk anymore', Rosie explained in their first session, her voice tight with frustration. 'Don comes home from work, grunts a hello, and disappears into his study until dinner'.

Don sighed heavily. 'That's not fair. I ask how your day was, and you always say "fine". What am I supposed to do with that?'

As Maria and I worked with them, it became clear that their surface complaint – not talking – masked deeper communication issues. Don, raised in a family where emotions were rarely discussed, struggled to engage with Rosie's desire for emotional disclosure. Rosie, sensing his discomfort, had stopped sharing her inner world, offering only perfunctory responses to his questions.

In our third session, I asked them to try a structured communication exercise. Each would take turns as speaker and listener, with the listener repeating back what they'd heard before responding. The exercise initially felt awkward to them both, but it created a container for a different kind of interaction.

'I feel lonely in our marriage', Rosie said, her voice barely above a whisper. 'Sometimes I wonder if you still love me'.

Don looked stricken. After repeating her words back to her, he responded: 'I had no idea you felt that way. I thought you were disappointed in me for not being more successful in my career. I've been working extra hours trying to get that promotion I thought would make you proud'.

'Do you see what's happening here?' Maria gently interjected. 'You've been having two completely different conversations for years – Rosie about emotional connection, Don about professional achievement – and neither of you realised it'.

This moment of clarity marked a turning point. Over the following sessions, we helped them develop new communication habits: daily check-ins with real emotional sharing, a weekly deeper conversation about their relationship, and agreements about how to raise difficult topics.

By our final session, their interaction had visibly transformed. They sat closer together, made eye contact more frequently, and had developed a kind of shorthand that reflected their renewed understanding of each other.

'The other night', Rosie told us, 'I could see Don was stressed about something at work. Before, I would have either ignored it or pushed him to talk when he wasn't ready. Instead, I just said, "Green, yellow, or red?" It's our new code for how ready someone is to talk. He said "yellow", which meant "I need a little time, but then I'd like to share". And later that evening, we had the most honest conversation about his work anxieties that we've had in years'.

Don nodded, adding, 'It's not that we never talked before. We just weren't talking about what mattered'.

Michael and David: The Words beneath the Words

Another couple, Michael and David, came to us with a different communication challenge. Unlike Rosie and Don, they talked constantly – but their communication had become a battlefield rather than a meeting ground.

'We can't have a simple conversation about what to have for dinner without it turning into World War III', Michael explained, while David nodded vigorously beside him.

'He takes everything as criticism', David added, with Michael immediately responding, 'Because everything you say is a criticism!'

As Maria and I observed their interaction, we noticed a pattern. Each would make statements that on the surface appeared to be about practical matters but contained hidden emotional content. When David said, 'I think we should eat at home more', what he was really expressing was anxiety about their finances and a desire for more intimate time together. When Michael heard this as criticism of his cooking or his desire to socialise, he was actually feeling shame about not contributing more financially to their household.

'Let's try something', I suggested midway through our second session, after a particularly heated exchange about household chores. 'Instead of responding to each other's surface statements, I'd like you to pause and consider what might be beneath the words. What is your partner really trying to tell you?'

This simple shift – looking for the message beneath the message – transformed their communication. They began to recognise that many of their arguments weren't really about the topics they appeared to be discussing, but about deeper needs for respect, security, and acknowledgement.

In our fourth session, David shared a breakthrough: 'Last night, Michael mentioned that the kitchen was a mess. In the past, I would have instantly defended myself and reminded him that he'd cooked last and left things everywhere. Instead, I took a breath and thought about what he might really be saying. I asked, "Are you feeling overwhelmed with everything you have to do?" And he just burst into tears. It turned out his mother had called with some health concerns, and he was worried but didn't know how to bring it up'.

'That's the thing about communication', Maria observed. 'Often, the words we speak are just the tip of the iceberg. True communication means being curious about all that lies beneath'.

The Technology Paradox

One communication challenge I've observed affecting many contemporary couples involves technology. We live in the most connected era in human history, with countless ways to stay in constant contact. Yet many couples report feeling more disconnected than ever.

Sophie and William exemplified this modern dilemma. Both professionals in their thirties, they managed a household with two young children and demanding careers. Their days were filled with texts arranging childcare handoffs, calendar invites for family events, and quick calls about logistics. Yet when they arrived in our therapy room, they could barely articulate what was happening in each other's inner lives.

'We communicate all day', Sophie insisted. 'I always know where he is and what he's doing'.

'But when was the last time you had a conversation that wasn't about scheduling or the children?' I asked.

The silence that followed spoke volumes.

'Digital communication tools are wonderful for coordination', Maria explained to them, 'but they can create an illusion of connection. Knowing your partner's location or schedule isn't the same as knowing their heart'.

We worked with Sophie and William to establish 'technology-free zones' in their relationship – times and spaces where devices were set aside in favour of face-to-face interaction. Their nightly ritual became placing their phones in a drawer after the children were in bed, giving themselves at least thirty minutes of undistracted time together before sleep.

'It's not always deep conversation', William reported in our fifth session. 'Sometimes we just laugh about something silly one of the kids did. But it feels like we're actually with each other, not just occupying the same space'.

Sophie added, 'I realised we were so focused on micro-coordination that we'd stopped having macro-conversations about our dreams, our fears, where we're headed as a family. Those short conversations before bed have reminded me why I fell in love with him in the first place'.

The Communication Toolbox

Through these and countless other cases, Maria and I have developed what we call The Communication Toolbox – practical approaches that couples can use to enhance this vital element of their relationship:

The Daily Check-In: A brief but focused time each day to connect beyond logistics. We encourage couples to ask three simple questions: 'How are you feeling right now? What's on your mind? How can I support you today?'

The Speaker–Listener Technique: A structured approach where each partner takes turns speaking uninterrupted for fifteen minutes with the listener validating what they've heard before responding.

Emotion Words Vocabulary: Many people, particularly those raised in families where emotional expression was limited, benefit from expanding their emotional vocabulary beyond basic terms like 'OK', 'angry', 'sad', or 'happy'.

The Soft Start-Up: This technique involves beginning difficult conversations with 'I' statements and expressions of need rather than criticism or blame.

Technology Boundaries: Clear agreements about when and how digital devices will be used, creating space for undistracted communication.

Communication Weather Report: A metaphorical way for couples to signal their emotional state and capacity for discussion (sunny, partly cloudy, stormy, etc.).

These tools aren't magic solutions, but they provide scaffolding for couples developing new communication patterns. The goal isn't perfect communication – such a thing doesn't exist – but rather a shared commitment to understanding and being understood.

The Bridge to Other Elements

While I've focused on Communication as a distinct element of the Relationship Paradigm, it's important to recognise its interconnection with the other five elements. Effective communication enables deeper Connection, demonstrates Commitment, facilitates Fun, supports Growth, and builds Trust.

Consider it the foundation upon which these other elements rest. Without clear, honest, attuned communication, couples struggle to achieve the emotional intimacy, security, playfulness, development, and reliability that characterise flourishing relationships.

Yet the relationship is also circular. As Trust grows, for instance, communication often becomes more honest and vulnerable. As Connection deepens, partners become more attuned to each other's nonverbal cues. Each element reinforces and enhances the others.

In my work with couples, I've found that improvements in communication often create a positive cascade effect, with benefits flowing into all aspects of the relationship. A couple who learns to truly hear each other discovers not just better problem-solving abilities but a renewed sense of being truly known and valued by their partner – perhaps the deepest human longing of all.

When I see a couple like Rosie and Don or Michael and David transform their communication patterns, I'm witnessing more than just a technical skill improvement. I'm observing a fundamental shift in how they experience each other and themselves within the relationship. In learning to speak and listen with greater presence, clarity, and compassion, they're rediscovering what drew them together in the first place: the profound joy of being fully seen and accepted by another human being.

Chapter 13

Barry and Edith – Half a Century of Silence

The Weight of Betrayal

They arrive together, moving with the synchronised rhythm of people who have shared daily routines for five decades. Barry holds the door for Edith not as a conscious courtesy but as an automatic gesture, worn smooth by fifty years of repetition. There is something both deeply familiar and strangely distant in how they navigate the space together; two dancers who know every step of their choreography yet seem to perform it without looking at each other.

Barry is tall and dignified, his seventy-four years evident in the silver of his hair and the careful deliberation of his movements, but there remains something youthful in his eyes; a kind of hopeful wariness that seems at odds with his age. Edith, seventy-two, moves with compact precision, her posture perfect, her silver-streaked dark hair cut in a neat bob that frames a face whose beauty has weathered rather than faded with time. Her expression carries a vigilance that never quite relaxes, even as she smiles politely in greeting.

They settle onto the couch with the practised coordination of countless similar actions over half a century. Barry takes the left cushion, Edith the right, leaving the middle section vacant between them, not the vast empty space of active estrangement but the careful buffer zone of a long-established accommodation.

'Thank you for coming today', I begin, noting how they both nod in acknowledgement yet somehow seem to be responding to different statements. 'Before we explore your history together, I'd like to start with a simple but important question for each of you. What would you like to have happen in our sessions together?'

Edith glances briefly at Barry, a quick assessment that carries decades of expectations. 'I want to understand if I can ever truly forgive', she says, her voice carrying both clarity and a faint tremor beneath its surface. 'Or if I am simply condemned to relive this betrayal every day for the rest of my life'.

Barry's shoulders tense slightly at her words, a reaction so subtle it would be imperceptible to anyone not watching closely. 'I want to know if there's a way forward that isn't defined by something that happened thirty years ago', he says, his voice gentle yet carrying an undercurrent of profound weariness. 'If there can ever be a day when we wake up and it isn't the first thing between us'.

The words 'betrayal' and 'thirty years ago' hang in the air, immediately providing the framework for their struggle; not the ordinary drifting apart of a long marriage,

DOI: 10.4324/9781003752776-13

but the specific, unhealed wound of infidelity that has somehow remained as raw as if it were inflicted yesterday rather than three decades past.

'These are deeply important questions', Maria says with gentle acknowledgement. 'Would it be alright if we learn more about your relationship, both before and since the affair?'

What unfolds over the next hour is the story of a marriage that spans half a century, with a clear dividing line running through its timeline. Barry and Edith met in their early twenties, introduced by mutual friends at a university social function in 1970. Their courtship was steady and earnest; both serious students with clear aspirations, both drawn to each other's intelligence and quiet determination. They married after graduation, building a life founded on shared values of hard work, family commitment, and creating security neither had fully known in childhood.

The early decades of their marriage followed a conventional but satisfying trajectory. Two children arrived: Catherine and James, now in their forties with families of their own. Barry built a successful career in engineering while Edith worked as a primary school teacher before taking several years away to focus on their young children, then returning to a career she found deeply fulfilling. They weathered the ordinary challenges of young parenthood, career setbacks, and financial pressures with mutual support and practical resilience.

'We were a good team', Barry says, a hint of nostalgia softening his voice. 'Not perfect, certainly, but solid. We faced things together'.

'Yes, that's what I thought as well', Edith responds, the pointed emphasis on 'thought' carrying volumes of retrospective reassessment.

The fracture occurred when they were in their early forties. Barry had an affair with a colleague during a period when work pressures had created significant strain in their marriage. The relationship lasted four months before Barry ended it, overwhelmed by guilt and the realisation of what he stood to lose. He confessed to Edith, who was devastated but ultimately chose to remain in the marriage for multiple reasons: their children, then teenagers; their shared history and assets; her religious convictions about marriage; and, she acknowledges, her continued love for Barry despite her profound sense of betrayal.

'I thought we were working through it', Barry explains, his voice carrying the confusion of someone still trying to understand what went wrong with the healing process. 'We had counselling. I answered every question Edith asked. I changed jobs to avoid any contact with ... the other person. I did everything I could think of to rebuild trust'.

'For a while, it seemed we might find our way forward', Edith admits, her hands clasped tightly in her lap. 'The first few years after were terrible, of course, but there were periods when it wasn't the centre of everything'.

Yet somehow, the wound never fully healed. Instead of gradually diminishing with time, Edith's pain and anger seemed to move in cycles; periods of apparent recovery followed by fresh waves of questioning, accusation, and distress. As the years passed, these cycles did not fade but instead became an integrated feature of their relationship, a chronic condition rather than an acute crisis.

'It can be triggered by anything', Edith explains, tension evident in her precisely controlled voice. 'A place that reminds me of that time. A certain expression on Barry's face. A scene in a film. Suddenly it's as immediate as if it happened yesterday, and I'm drowning in it all over again; the images in my head, the questions, the sense of being utterly deceived by the person I trusted most'.

'And there's nothing I can say or do that helps in those moments', Barry adds, genuine pain evident beneath his measured tone. 'The apologies, the reassurances; they've all been said thousands of times over thirty years. Sometimes I wonder if Edith actually wants to move past this, or if the anger has become ... necessary to her somehow'.

Edith's face tightens at this suggestion. 'How convenient to frame my pain as a choice', she says, the first flash of direct anger showing through her composed exterior. 'As if I enjoy living this way. As if I wouldn't give anything to be free of these thoughts'.

As they continue, the architecture of their impasse becomes increasingly clear. Edith experiences her recurring distress not as a choice but as an involuntary response she cannot control or predict. Barry experiences her ongoing anger as increasingly disconnected from his actual actions; both the affair itself and his three decades of subsequent efforts to make amends. They are locked in a pattern where her pain triggers his defensiveness, which she then interprets as minimising the significance of his betrayal, creating a self-perpetuating cycle that neither knows how to interrupt.

After a thoughtful pause, I decide to address another dimension that often becomes complicated in the aftermath of infidelity. 'I'd like to ask about something that couples sometimes find difficult to discuss', I say. 'Can you tell me about the intimacy in your relationship, both before the affair and in the years since?'

The question creates a subtle shift in the atmosphere. Barry's gaze drops briefly to his hands, while Edith's posture becomes, if possible, even more contained.

'We had a good physical relationship before', Edith says after a moment, her voice carefully neutral. 'Afterwards ... it was difficult, of course. For a long time'.

'There was a period of about two years when Edith couldn't bear for me to touch her at all', Barry adds quietly. 'Which I understood completely. Over time, physical intimacy returned, but it's never been quite the same'.

'How has it been different?' Maria asks gently.

They exchange a glance that carries complex layers of communication.

'There's a guardedness that never fully disappears', Barry explains carefully. 'Moments when Edith seems to go somewhere else mentally, to withdraw even in the midst of physical closeness'.

'Because sometimes I'm suddenly ambushed by images, by questions', Edith admits, visible discomfort breaking through her usual composure. 'Did he do this with her? Did he say these things to her? Was she more exciting, more responsive? Even thirty years later, these thoughts come uninvited'.

This candid exchange reveals how thoroughly the affair has continued to contaminate even their most private connections; physical intimacy becoming yet another arena where the past intrudes into the present, where attempts at connection can unexpectedly transform into painful reminders of betrayal.

After gathering this history, I move to the next stage of our session. 'I'd like to try something different now', I explain, lifting the lids on two wicker baskets filled with pebbles of various sizes, shapes, and colours. 'These stones will help us understand your relationship in a way that sometimes words alone cannot'.

Barry regards the baskets with quiet interest, while Edith's expression suggests cautious curiosity.

'There's no right or wrong way to do this', I assure them. 'I'd like each of you, starting with Barry, to choose one pebble to represent yourself, and place it where it needs to be'.

Barry considers the stones thoughtfully before selecting a substantial, weathered-looking grey pebble with smooth edges worn by time. He places it carefully on the floor, his movements deliberate and measured.

Edith explores the basket more methodically, her fingers moving through the stones before selecting a smaller, white stone flecked with darker minerals. She places it on the floor at a moderate distance from Barry's; not vastly separated but with a clear space between them.

'Now', I continue, 'please select other pebbles to represent important people or elements in your lives and place them where they need to be in relation to you'.

What emerges over the next few minutes is revealing. Barry creates a balanced arrangement, with stones representing their children and five grandchildren forming a loose semicircle that curves between his position and Edith's, as if creating a bridge between them. His friends and remaining family members are positioned in a scattered pattern to his left. Most tellingly, he places a dark, jagged stone at some distance behind his own pebble, not naming it explicitly but positioning it in a way that suggests something he wishes to leave behind but that still casts a shadow.

Edith's constellation tells its complementary story. The children and grandchildren are similarly positioned between herself and Barry, suggesting this is perhaps their primary connection now. Her sister and close friends form a tight cluster near her stone, suggesting important sources of support. Most significantly, she places a small red stone directly between her position and Barry's; when asked, she identifies it simply as 'the affair'. Its central placement in their shared space speaks volumes about its continued significance in their relationship.

'I notice that you've both positioned family members between yourselves', Maria observes gently. 'And Edith, you've placed the red stone representing the affair directly in the space between you'.

Edith nods, her gaze fixed on the small red stone. 'Because that's where it lives', she says simply. 'Always between us, no matter what else is happening'.

'It wasn't my intention to place it there', Barry adds, a note of resignation in his voice as he looks at the constellation. 'But I can't deny that's where it's ended up'.

The room grows quiet as these insights settle around us. Both Barry and Edith stare at the arrangement they've created, perhaps seeing the physical representation of their decades-long impasse from a new perspective.

'I'd like to try something else', I say after allowing this moment to breathe. 'Could each of you now create a constellation that represents your ideal future?'

This second exercise brings meaningful adjustments that suggest hope hasn't been entirely extinguished by their long struggle. In his ideal arrangement, Barry brings his stone somewhat closer to Edith's, though still respecting her separate space. The family stones remain important but are positioned slightly differently, no longer serving as the primary connection between them. Most significantly, the dark, unnamed stone behind his position disappears completely from his ideal constellation.

'I would like to be fully present with Edith', he explains quietly. 'Not constantly looking over my shoulder at a mistake I can't undo, no matter how much I wish I could'.

Edith's ideal arrangement shows more dramatic changes. She moves her stone noticeably closer to Barry's, creating a proximity that hasn't been visible in their actual interactions. The family stones remain important but, like in Barry's arrangement, no longer form the primary bridge between them. Most strikingly, the red stone representing the affair is moved; not removed entirely but repositioned to the periphery of their shared space rather than at its centre.

'What does this repositioning mean to you, Edith?' I ask.

She studies the arrangement thoughtfully. 'I don't think it will ever completely disappear', she says after a moment, her honesty both painful and refreshing. 'But perhaps it could stop being the first thing I see when I look at our relationship. Perhaps it could become part of our history without defining our present'.

This insight, that healing might involve repositioning rather than erasing the painful past, represents a potential shift in perspective that might offer a way forward after decades of stalemate.

As our first session moves into its final hour, we explore the significance of these arrangements. Barry speaks with careful honesty about his growing fear that no amount of remorse or changed behaviour will ever be sufficient, while Edith acknowledges the exhausting toll of carrying active anger for so many years. They begin to identify patterns that have calcified over time: her tendency to interpret any defensiveness on his part as minimising the significance of his betrayal; his habit of withdrawing emotionally when facing another cycle of her distress; their mutual reliance on children and grandchildren as buffers and bridges between them.

'For our next session', I explain as our three and a half hours together draw to a close, 'we'd like you to complete a few exercises that will help us go deeper'. I hand them each a folder containing materials on understanding trauma responses, rebuilding trust, and exercises about handling intrusive thoughts and memories.

'We'd also like you to pay attention to the moments when you feel connected rather than divided by the past', Maria adds. 'However brief or seemingly insignificant these moments might be, simply notice them'.

As they prepare to leave, I observe subtle shifts in their physical bearing. Barry seems simultaneously wearier and somehow lighter, as if the simple act of laying out their struggle has both taxed and relieved him. Edith's vigilant tension has softened almost imperceptibly, her movements carrying a touch less rigidity. They gather their belongings with the coordinated efficiency of long-married couples, yet there's a new quality to their silence; less charged with unspoken resentments, more thoughtful.

'Remember', I say as they reach the door, 'we're available by phone or email between sessions if anything comes up that feels important to discuss'.

They thank us with the courtesy that clearly characterises their interactions with the world, then walk out together, their steps naturally falling into the same rhythm despite the emotional distance between them. As the door closes behind them, Maria and I exchange a glance that acknowledges both the entrenched nature of their struggle and the small signs of potential movement we've observed.

'Fifty years is a long time to be together', Maria observes quietly.

'Yes', I agree. 'And thirty years is a long time to be stuck in the same painful cycle. But they're still here, still trying. That means something'.

I take a walk for thirty minutes to breathe and reset my rhythm between worlds. *We will see the progress of Barry and Edith in Chapter 31.*

Chapter 14

Connection

Watching Barry and Edith sit in my therapy room – physically present but emotionally oceans apart after fifty years together – brought home the critical importance of the second element of the Relationship Paradigm: Connection. They had communication of a sort: they talked about logistics, about their children, about the weather. But the deeper connection – those moments of true intimacy that sustain a relationship through storms – had been severed by betrayal decades ago and never restored. Their story illustrates what happens when couples lose the ability to truly connect, when the moments of intimacy that once bound them together become painful reminders of what's been lost.

If there's one word I hear more than any other when couples first come to therapy, it's 'disconnected'. They might express it in different ways – 'We're like ships passing in the night', 'I feel alone even when we're together', 'We've drifted apart' – but the core experience is the same. Somewhere along the journey, the sense of being meaningfully connected to each other has diminished or disappeared entirely.

DOI: 10.4324/9781003752776-14

Connection is perhaps the most elusive yet essential element of the Relationship Paradigm. Unlike communication, which can be observed and even measured, connection exists in the ineffable space between two people – that sense of being emotionally, intellectually, physically, and sometimes spiritually joined with another human being. It's what transforms a partnership based on practical considerations into a relationship that nourishes the soul.

The Dimensions of Connection

In the Relationship Paradigm, connection operates across multiple dimensions:

Emotional connection: The sense that one's partner understands, values, and responds to one's emotional experience; the feeling of being emotionally 'held' even during difficult times.

Physical connection: Beyond sexuality, this includes all forms of touch, physical proximity, and bodily attunement – from holding hands to synchronised breathing during intimate moments.

Intellectual connection: The sharing of ideas, perspectives, and observations; the stimulation that comes from engaging with another's mind.

Experiential connection: The bond formed through shared experiences, whether extraordinary adventures or ordinary daily rituals.

Spiritual connection: The sense of being aligned in one's deepest values, purpose, and understanding of meaning in life, regardless of formal religious beliefs.

These dimensions don't exist in isolation but interact and reinforce each other. A strong emotional connection often enhances physical intimacy. Shared experiences create opportunities for intellectual exchange. Alignment in values deepens emotional bonds.

When couples report feeling disconnected, it's rarely across all dimensions simultaneously. More commonly, one or two dimensions have weakened, creating a sense of distance that eventually affects the others. The art of rekindling connection lies in identifying which dimensions need attention and finding authentic ways to strengthen them.

Emma and Jonathan: The Space Between

Emma and Jonathan arrived at their first Duo Coaching session with a peculiar combination of politeness and despair. Married for twelve years with two children, they had what many would consider an enviable life – successful careers, a beautiful home, healthy children, and financial stability. Yet sitting before Maria and me, they radiated a quiet desolation that filled the room.

'We don't fight', Emma explained, her voice measured. 'We don't have any real problems to complain about. We just don't ... feel anything for each other anymore'.

Jonathan nodded. 'We're excellent co-parents and business partners. We run our household with military precision. But at night, when the children are asleep and the house is quiet, it's like we're strangers with nothing to say to each other'.

As we explored their history, a familiar pattern emerged. Their early relationship had been filled with passionate conversation, physical affection, and shared dreams. Gradually, as careers advanced and children arrived, these connections had been relegated to the category of 'nice but non-essential' – luxuries they could postpone until some future date when life became less demanding.

'When was the last time you had a conversation that wasn't about the children, the house, or work?' Maria asked.

They exchanged glances, genuinely struggling to remember.

'And physical affection that isn't directly related to sex?' I added.

Emma looked down. 'I can't recall the last time we just held hands or hugged for no reason'.

In our second session, we introduced them to an exercise we call Connection Mapping. Each partner identifies moments in their history when they felt deeply connected across the different dimensions, as well as daily practices that once nurtured their bond but had been abandoned.

The results were revealing. Both independently recalled a holiday in Morocco years earlier as a time of profound connection – intellectually stimulated by exploring a new culture, physically close through both adventure and intimacy, emotionally aligned in their sense of discovery and joy.

'What struck me about your recollections', I observed, 'is how multi-dimensional they are. The experiences you've described involve all your senses, your minds, your emotions, and even a sense of shared purpose or meaning'.

This insight led to a crucial understanding: Emma and Jonathan hadn't simply 'drifted apart' through neglect. Rather, they had unconsciously narrowed their relationship to its most practical dimensions, focusing exclusively on effective co-parenting and household management while starving the emotional, physical, intellectual, and spiritual connections that had once formed the core of their bond.

With this awareness, they began the deliberate work of reconnection. They reinstated date nights but with a twist – each taking turns to plan experiences that would engage multiple dimensions of connection. Jonathan arranged an evening stargazing on a hilltop, combining intellectual discovery with physical closeness and the spiritual awe of contemplating the universe. Emma organised a dance class, activating their physical coordination while creating new shared memories.

Perhaps most importantly, they created 'micro connection rituals' in their daily life – small but meaningful practices that acknowledged each other beyond their functional roles. Each morning, they spent five minutes over coffee sharing something they were thinking about or feeling before discussing any practical matters. They instituted a six-second kiss (timed!) when greeting each other after work, a practice that neurologically shifts the body from stress response to connection. They started a two-person book club, reading the same novel and discussing it for fifteen minutes before bed one night a week.

By our final session, the shift in their physical presence was remarkable. Where they had once sat stiffly separate on our sofa, they now naturally gravitated toward each other. Their eyes met more frequently. They nodded in recognition of each other's experiences. The polite strangers had been replaced by two people visibly tuned in to each other's wavelength.

'I feel like I've rediscovered someone I used to know intimately', Emma reflected. 'Not because Jonathan has changed, but because I'm actually seeing him again'.

Jonathan squeezed her hand. 'We still have the same busy lives, but now I feel like we're in it together rather than just running parallel tracks'.

Priya and Aiden: The Digital Disconnect

While Emma and Jonathan's disconnection had developed gradually over years, Priya and Aiden faced a more acute situation. Dating for three years and recently engaged, they had navigated the COVID lockdowns together, spending nearly every hour in the same small flat. Yet despite this physical proximity – or perhaps because of it – they felt increasingly disconnected.

'We're always together but never really present with each other', Priya explained in our first session. 'Aiden is constantly on his phone, even when we're supposedly spending quality time together'.

Aiden looked defensive. 'That's not fair. You're glued to your laptop all evening, working or scrolling through social media'.

This couple presented a modern paradox Maria and I increasingly encounter: physical togetherness combined with attention that is digitally fragmented, creating a new form of loneliness – the experience of being alone together.

Through careful exploration, we discovered that both had valid perspectives. Aiden checked his phone frequently because he felt Priya was emotionally unavailable, often responding to his attempts at conversation with distracted monosyllables. Priya retreated to her laptop because she felt Aiden wasn't really interested in meaningful interaction, as evidenced by his constant phone checking. They had created a self-reinforcing cycle of disconnection, each responding to the other's withdrawal by further withdrawing themselves.

In our third session, Maria suggested an experiment: 'For one week, I'd like you to create two thirty-minute periods each day that are completely device-free. No phones, laptops, tablets, or television. Just the two of you, fully present with each other'.

They looked simultaneously intrigued and terrified.

'What are we supposed to do during that time?' Aiden asked, genuinely perplexed.

'Whatever you want', I replied. 'Talk, play a game, cook together, be intimate, sit in comfortable silence. The only rule is that you're fully present with each other'.

Their report in the following session was illuminating. The first few device-free periods had been awkward, even anxiety-provoking. Both realised how dependent they'd become on digital distraction to avoid the vulnerability of direct connection.

But by day three, something had shifted. They found themselves actually looking forward to these technology-free islands in their day.

'We had a debate about our favourite films that turned into a really deep conversation about what we value in storytelling', Priya shared. 'It reminded me of the kinds of talks we used to have when we were first dating'.

Aiden nodded. 'And last night, we just sat on the balcony watching the sunset without saying much at all, but it didn't feel awkward. It felt ... connected'.

As we continued working together, Priya and Aiden developed a more nuanced understanding of connection in the digital age. Rather than demonising technology, they learned to be more intentional about how, when, and why they used it. They established clear agreements about device-free zones and times in their relationship. Perhaps most importantly, they recognised that digital connection could complement but never replace the richness of full-presence human connection.

'I realised I was using my phone as a shield', Aiden admitted in our fifth session. 'Whenever I felt emotionally uncertain or vulnerable, I'd check my messages or scroll through news as a way to regulate my anxiety. Now I'm learning to sit with those uncomfortable feelings and actually share them with Priya'.

Priya reached for his hand. 'And I'm learning that connection isn't always about deep conversation. Sometimes it's just about being fully present in the same space, whether we're talking or not'.

The Power of Physical Touch: The Science of Hugging

What fascinates me about connection is how deeply it's rooted in our biology. Humans are neurologically wired for physical touch from birth, and this wiring continues to influence our relationships throughout life. The same neurochemicals that bond an infant to its mother – oxytocin, dopamine, serotonin – are activated in adult relationships during moments of meaningful connection.

One of the simplest yet most powerful forms of physical connection is the humble hug. Virginia Satir, often called the 'Mother of Family Therapy', famously proposed that we need four hugs a day for survival, eight for maintenance, and twelve for growth. While these specific numbers might seem prescriptive, they highlight an essential truth: physical touch isn't a luxury but a biological necessity. Her emphasis on hugging as a healing practice stemmed from understanding that touch directly affects our neurochemistry and emotional well-being.

The science supports her intuition. Research by neuroeconomist Dr Paul Zak has shown that a twenty-second hug releases significant amounts of oxytocin – often called the 'bonding hormone' or 'love hormone' – in both participants. This extended embrace, what I sometimes call the 'twenty-second oxytocin hug', reduces cortisol levels, lowers blood pressure, and creates feelings of trust and connection. It's remarkable how something so simple can have such profound physiological effects.

Maria and I often share this science with couples because understanding the biological basis of connection helps normalise both the longing for it and the distress when it's absent. Disconnection isn't just emotionally painful; it registers in our bodies as a form of threat. This explains why chronic disconnection in relationships often manifests in physical symptoms – tension headaches, digestive issues, compromised immunity, sleep disturbances.

Conversely, moments of genuine physical connection trigger our body's relaxation response. I recall working with Eleanor and Thomas, whose physical connection had diminished over decades of emotional distance. When they began practising daily twenty-second hugs – initially with awkward self-consciousness but gradually with genuine presence – the effects extended far beyond those brief moments. Eleanor reported sleeping better than she had in years. Thomas noticed a decreased desire for his evening glass of whisky, a habit he'd developed to manage stress. Their nervous systems were literally co-regulating through this simple practice of connection.

For couples experiencing physical distance, I often recommend starting with these intentional hugs rather than jumping immediately to more intimate forms of physical connection. There's less performance pressure, yet the neurochemical benefits create a foundation for deeper intimacy. As one client beautifully expressed, 'Through those long hugs, we remembered how to be in the same body space without agenda or expectation. Everything else followed naturally from there'.

This biological perspective offers valuable insight into why certain connection practices are particularly effective. The six-second kiss I recommended to Emma and Jonathan, for instance, isn't arbitrary. Research indicates that prolonged physical contact of this duration triggers oxytocin release, promoting feelings of bonding and trust. Similarly, the synchronised breathing that occurs naturally during close conversation or eye contact has been shown to align partners' cardiac rhythms, creating a physiological state of co-regulation.

The Connection Toolkit

Through years of working with couples, I have developed The Connection Toolkit – practical approaches that help rekindle and maintain this essential element of relationship:

The Daily Connection Ritual: A brief but focused daily practice that acknowledges your partner's presence and importance, such as a proper greeting and farewell, a morning check-in, or a nightly gratitude exchange.

Technology Boundaries: Clear agreements about device-free times and spaces that create opportunities for undivided attention.

Physical Touch Inventory: An exploration of non-sexual physical connection that feels nourishing to each partner, from hand-holding to massage to simply sitting with bodies touching.

Novelty Injection: Regular introduction of new experiences, as novel activities have been shown to recreate some of the neurochemical excitement of early relationship stages.

The Connection Journal: A shared document where partners record moments of felt connection, creating awareness of what specifically nurtures their unique bond.

Bids for Connection Practice: This involves learning to recognise and respond to a partner's attempts to connect, whether through conversation, touch, or shared attention.

These tools aren't complicated, but they require something many couples struggle to give – intentional attention. In a world that constantly pulls our focus in multiple directions, the choice to fully attend to one's partner represents a radical act of love and commitment.

The Bridge to Other Elements

Like Communication, which we explored in the previous chapter, Connection interweaves with all other elements of the Relationship Paradigm. Trust deepens connection by creating emotional safety. Commitment provides the security that allows vulnerability and thus deeper connection. Growth challenges partners to develop new aspects of connection as they and their relationship evolve. Fun creates light-hearted connection that balances the more serious dimensions of partnership.

When couples like Emma and Jonathan or Priya and Aiden rekindle their sense of connection, they often report improvements across all areas of their relationship. Problems that once seemed insurmountable become manageable when approached from a foundation of felt connection. Communication flows more easily when partners feel tuned in to each other. Differences in desire or preference become less threatening when the underlying bond is secure.

Connection may be the most difficult element to define or measure, but its presence or absence is unmistakable in the felt experience of a relationship. When present, it creates a sense of being truly seen, known, and valued by another human being – perhaps our deepest longing as social creatures. When absent, even the most practically successful relationship feels hollow, more arrangement than true partnership.

As I witness couples rediscover their connection in our therapy room, I'm reminded of why this work matters so deeply. Beyond problem-solving or conflict resolution, beyond communication skills or negotiation techniques, we're helping people recover their capacity for that most fundamental human experience: the joy of being fully present with and to another.

Chapter 15

Jon and Sophia – Blindsided by Fate

Learning to See Differently

They arrive with careful coordination that speaks of recently adjusted patterns; Jon guiding Sophia with a light touch at her elbow, Sophia maintaining a precise distance that allows for guidance without dependence. There is something tentative in their movements, a choreography still being learned, its steps not yet committed to muscle memory.

Jon is tall and athletic, his movements carrying the deliberate precision of someone accustomed to solving problems through action. At forty-six, he maintains the physical confidence of a man who has always relied on his body's capabilities. By contrast, Sophia's movements contain a new cautiousness, her eyes: one significantly clouded, the other surrounded by the fading marks of recent surgery, scanning the room with careful attention. At forty-three, she carries herself with dignity clearly being maintained through conscious effort rather than ease.

They settle onto the couch with subtle adjustments; Jon ensuring Sophia knows exactly where the seat begins, Sophia arranging herself with the practised care of someone navigating a world that has become increasingly unpredictable. Once seated, they maintain a small but noticeable distance between them, neither the comfortable proximity of secure connection nor the vast emptiness of active estrangement, but something more complicated; a space filled with unspoken concerns.

'Thank you for coming today', I begin, noting how they both turn toward my voice with slightly different timing, Sophia's movement a fraction delayed. 'Before we explore your situation together, I'd like to start with a simple but important question for each of you. What would you like to have happen in our sessions together?'

Sophia's hands rest in her lap, fingers lightly intertwined. 'I need to understand if we can find a way forward together through this', she says, her voice steady despite the weight of her words. 'My sight is going to continue deteriorating. That's the reality. What I don't know is whether our marriage can survive it'.

Jon shifts slightly, his posture betraying tension he might not be fully aware of. 'I want to be the husband Sophia needs', he says, his voice carrying a controlled frustration. 'I've always been able to fix things, solve problems. But I can't fix this, and I don't know how to ...' he pauses, searching for words, 'how to be with it. With what's happening to us'.

DOI: 10.4324/9781003752776-15

The word 'us' hangs in the air, immediately highlighting a crucial aspect of their struggle: how Sophia's changing physical reality has become a relationship challenge neither knows how to navigate.

Maria says gently, 'Would it be alright if we learn more about your relationship and what you're currently facing?'

What unfolds over the next hour is the story of a marriage built on mutual strength and capability now confronting unexpected vulnerability. Jon and Sophia met in their late twenties through mutual friends at a charity running event. Their connection was immediate and based on shared values; both ambitious professionals with active lifestyles, both valuing independence while seeking genuine partnership. Their courtship was filled with outdoor adventures and travel, each appreciating the other's self-sufficiency and drive.

They married after two years together and built a life that balanced successful careers – Jon in software engineering, Sophia in architectural design – with their shared love of physical activity and exploration. They chose not to have children, preferring to focus on their relationship and professional achievements. For over a decade, their marriage thrived on mutual respect, common interests, and a fundamental assumption of continuing health and capability.

The first signs of trouble appeared three years ago when Sophia began experiencing vision problems. Initially diagnosed as standard age-related changes requiring only reading glasses, her symptoms gradually worsened. After multiple consultations and tests, she was diagnosed with a progressive eye condition that would eventually lead to significant vision loss.

'The first surgery was supposed to halt the progression', Sophia explains, her voice carrying the weariness of someone who has repeated this narrative too many times. 'Then the second was to repair complications from the first. The third was experimental, hoping to preserve what vision remained in my left eye'.

'Each procedure has changed her appearance', Jon adds, his voice carefully neutral in a way that suggests suppressed emotion. 'Scarring around the eyes, asymmetry in how they look, reactions to medications that caused swelling ...'

'And each has failed to stop what's happening', Sophia continues. 'The specialists now say it's not a question of if I'll lose my sight, but when and how much. I might retain some limited vision in my right eye, but I need to prepare for the likelihood of legal blindness'.

As they speak, the architecture of their struggle emerges with increasing clarity. For Sophia, the physical and emotional process of losing her sight has been accompanied by the additional pain of feeling her husband withdraw as her appearance changes and her independence diminishes.

'I can feel Jon pulling away', she admits, sorrow evident beneath her composed exterior. 'Not just physically, though that's part of it. He barely touches me anymore. But also, emotionally. Like he's already mourning the person I used to be, even though I'm still here'.

'I don't know how to help', Jon responds, frustration breaking through his controlled demeanour. 'I've researched every treatment option, connected her with the best specialists, modified our home for better accessibility. But none of it stops what's happening. And I don't know how to look at her without my fear showing, without her seeing how scared I am of what's coming'.

This candid exchange reveals the complex interplay of their individual responses to this crisis: Sophia grieving the loss of her vision while also fearing abandonment, Jon confronting his helplessness to solve an unsolvable problem while struggling with his visceral response to the physical changes in the woman he loves.

After a thoughtful pause, I decide to address directly what seems to be a particularly difficult aspect of their situation. 'I'd like to ask about something couples often find difficult to discuss in circumstances like yours', I say. 'Can you tell me about how intimacy between you has been affected, both physical and emotional?'

The question creates a palpable shift in the atmosphere. Sophia's hands tighten slightly in her lap, while Jon looks briefly toward the window before returning his gaze to the space between us.

'It's almost disappeared', Sophia says finally, her directness clearly costing her effort. 'Jon hasn't initiated any physical intimacy since my last surgery six months ago. When I try to initiate, he finds reasons to avoid it'.

'It's not that I don't want to', Jon says, discomfort evident in his voice. 'It's just ... complicated'.

'In what way?' Maria asks gently.

Jon struggles visibly with how to express himself. 'I worry about hurting her. The area around her eyes is still sensitive sometimes. And I don't want her to think I'm repulsed by the changes, but I also don't want to pretend they're not there, and I get caught in this loop of not knowing what to do, what to say ...'

'So, you do nothing, say nothing', Sophia completes his thought, a hint of barely contained hurt breaking through.

'But it's not just the physical changes', Jon continues, words now coming more rapidly as if a dam has broken. 'It's what they represent. Every surgery, every new limitation is a reminder that I can't stop this from happening. That our life is changing in ways I don't know how to handle. That the future we planned together, all those places we were going to see, things we were going to do, is disappearing'.

'While I'm disappearing for you', Sophia adds quietly.

Jon turns to her then, genuine pain evident in his expression. 'That's not what I meant'.

'But it's what's happening', Sophia responds, her voice steady despite the weight of her words. 'I'm becoming someone, something, different from the woman you married. Someone who needs help instead of being your equal. Someone whose face bears the marks of everything we're losing. And you can't bear to look at me'.

The raw honesty of this exchange reveals how thoroughly their shared crisis has affected not just their physical intimacy but their emotional connection; how Jon's inability to 'fix' Sophia's condition has translated into a sense of broader failure, how Sophia's experience of physical change has become entangled with fears of losing not just her vision but her husband's love and desire.

After gathering this history, I move to the next stage of our session. 'I'd like to try something different now', I explain, opening the lids on two wicker baskets filled with pebbles of various sizes, shapes, and colours. 'These stones will help us understand your relationship in a way that sometimes words alone cannot'.

Jon regards the baskets with cautious interest, while Sophia leans forward, her functioning eye focusing intently on the collected stones.

'There's no right or wrong way to do this', I assure them. 'I'd like each of you, starting with Sophia, to choose one pebble to represent yourself, and place it where it needs to be'.

Sophia explores the basket methodically, her fingers moving over the stones with deliberate attention to their textures and contours. She eventually selects a smooth, medium-sized stone with layers of blue and green minerals running through it. With careful precision, she places it on the floor.

Jon considers the stones more briefly before selecting a larger, rougher grey stone with flecks of quartz catching the light. He places it on the floor at a noticeable distance from Sophia's; not vastly separated but with a clear space between them.

'Now', I continue, 'please select other pebbles to represent important people or elements in your lives and place them where they need to be'.

What emerges over the next few minutes is revealing. Sophia creates a balanced arrangement with stones representing her closest friends positioned in a loose semicircle near her stone. Her parents and brother form another small grouping nearby. Her work, once central to her identity but now increasingly challenging as her vision deteriorates, is represented by a collection of stones arranged in what appears to be a receding line, moving from closest to her position to gradually further away. Most tellingly, she places a clouded white stone directly in front of her own and identifies it simply as 'my changing vision'.

Jon's constellation tells its complementary story. His friends and family are positioned in a similar pattern to Sophia's, suggesting shared social connections. His work is represented by a substantial stone placed prominently to his right. Most significantly, he places a dark, jagged stone between his position and Sophia's; when asked, he identifies it with a single word: 'helplessness'.

'I notice that you've both positioned important elements between yourselves', Maria observes gently. 'Sophia, you've placed the stone representing your vision directly before you, while Jon, you've placed helplessness in the space between you'.

Sophia nods, her gaze fixed on the arrangement. 'Because that's what stands between us now', she says quietly. 'Not just my physical condition, but how differently we're experiencing it'.

'I didn't consciously intend to create distance', Jon adds, looking troubled by the visual representation. 'But seeing it laid out like this ... yes, that's exactly what's happening'.

The room grows quiet as these insights settle around us. Both Jon and Sophia study the constellation they've created, perhaps seeing the physical representation of their emotional reality from a new perspective.

'I'd like to try something else', I say after allowing this moment to breathe. 'Could each of you now create a constellation that represents your ideal future?'

This second exercise brings meaningful adjustments that suggest hope hasn't been extinguished by their current struggle. In her ideal arrangement, Sophia keeps the white stone representing her vision condition; a recognition of unchangeable reality, but repositions it slightly to the side rather than directly before her. The stones representing her work remain present but are arranged differently, suggesting adaptation rather than loss. Most notably, she moves her stone closer to Jon's, with no objects positioned between them.

'My condition isn't going away', she explains with characteristic directness. 'But in my ideal future, it wouldn't stand between us. It would be something we face together, from the same side'.

Jon's ideal arrangement shows significant changes. The stone representing helplessness disappears entirely from between them. His stone moves substantially closer to Sophia's, creating a proximity absent in their current reality. He adds a new element: a smooth river stone that he places beside their now-adjacent stones.

'What does this stone represent for you, Jon?' I ask.

He considers it for a moment. 'Acceptance', he says finally. 'Not resignation, but true acceptance. Of what we can't change, and what we can'.

This simple insight, the distinction between defeating resignation and empowering acceptance, points toward a potentially transformative shift in perspective that might offer a way forward through their current impasse.

As our first session moves into its final hour, we explore the significance of these arrangements. Sophia speaks with careful honesty about her fear that Jon sees her primarily through the lens of her condition rather than as the whole person she remains despite her changing abilities. Jon acknowledges his struggle to reconcile his self-image as a problem-solver with the reality of a situation he cannot fix. They begin to identify patterns that have developed in response to their crisis: his tendency to retreat into practical solutions when emotional connection feels too painful, her habit of pre-emptively withdrawing to protect herself from perceived rejection, their mutual avoidance of the genuine grief that accompanies their changing reality.

'For our next session', I explain as our three and a half hours together draw to a close, 'we'd like you to complete a few exercises that will help us go deeper'. I hand them each a folder containing materials on navigating significant health changes as a couple, rebuilding physical intimacy amid medical challenges, and exercises focused on emotional connection when practical circumstances are shifting.

'We'd also like you to pay attention to the moments when you feel genuinely connected despite the challenges you're facing', Maria adds. 'However brief or seemingly insignificant these moments might be, simply notice them'.

As they prepare to leave, I observe subtle shifts in their physical bearing. Jon seems more present, his movements around Sophia more attentive without being controlling. Sophia's posture carries a touch less tension, her expressions more open than when they arrived. They gather their belongings with increased coordination, small verbal cues between them suggesting renewed awareness of how to navigate together.

'Remember', I say as they reach the door, 'we're available by phone or email between sessions if anything comes up that feels important to discuss'.

Jon helps Sophia navigate the doorway with a guidance that seems more collaborative than directive. As they walk away, their steps gradually synchronising, I notice that while he maintains his supportive position slightly behind her elbow, there's a new quality to their physical coordination: less like someone leading and more like two people finding a shared rhythm.

'They still care deeply for each other', Maria observes as the door closes behind them.

'Yes', I agree. 'The connection remains strong beneath the fear. That gives us a lot to work with'.

Between sessions, I am the shore between tides – receiving, releasing, renewing.

Jon and Sophia will continue exploring in Chapter 33.

Chapter 16

Commitment

Jon and Sophia's journey illuminates Commitment – the third element of the Relationship Paradigm – in its most profound form. When Sophia faced the devastating reality of her progressive vision loss, Jon could have chosen an easier path. Instead, he demonstrated what true commitment means: not just staying together when life is pleasant, but actively choosing your partner when everything changes. Their story shows that commitment isn't a one-time wedding vow – it's a daily decision to nurture and protect the relationship, especially when life delivers blows that test every foundation you've built together.

In our increasingly disposable culture, where dating apps promote an illusion of endless options and 'upgrade mentality' extends from smartphones to spouses, commitment might seem like an outdated concept. Yet in my years of working with

DOI: 10.4324/9781003752776-16

couples, I've observed that commitment remains a cornerstone of truly thriving relationships – though its nature and expression continue to evolve.

Within the Relationship Paradigm, Commitment represents more than the initial decision to form a partnership or the legal structures that may formalise it. It's an ongoing, active choice to remain invested in the relationship through challenges, growth, and change. It's the daily decision to turn toward rather than away from one's partner, to work through difficulties rather than avoiding or abandoning them, to continuously choose the relationship even when momentarily dissatisfied or tempted by alternatives.

The Dimensions of Commitment

Commitment operates across several dimensions in healthy relationships:

Structural commitment: The formal and practical aspects that bind a relationship, from marriage contracts to shared mortgages, from children to intertwined social networks.

Personal commitment: The internal desire to maintain the relationship because it's valued, fulfilling, and aligned with one's identity and goals.

Moral commitment: The sense of obligation to honour one's word and promises, the belief that commitments, once made, should be kept.

Daily commitment: The moment-by-moment choices to prioritise the relationship through attention, energy, and action.

These dimensions don't always align perfectly. A couple might have high structural commitment (children, property, social expectations) but diminished personal commitment (no longer finding joy or meaning in the relationship). Another might have strong personal commitment (deep love and satisfaction) but hesitate to formalise structural commitments. Understanding these nuances helps couples address commitment concerns with greater precision and compassion.

Adrian and Rhiannon: When Commitment Means Different Things

Adrian and Rhiannon came to their first Duo Coaching session with what appeared to be a straightforward issue: after seven years together, Rhiannon wanted marriage, while Adrian was hesitant. On the surface, this seemed like a classic commitment disparity – one partner eager to deepen formal ties, the other reluctant.

As Maria and I explored this dynamic with them, however, a more complex picture emerged.

'It's not that I don't want to be with Rhiannon', Adrian explained, tension visible in his shoulders. 'I just don't see why we need to change anything. We already live together; we've talked about having children someday. Why complicate things with legal entanglements?'

Rhiannon's response revealed the emotional undercurrent: 'When Adrian resists marriage, what I hear is "I'm not sure about you" or "I want to keep my options open". It makes me feel like he's got one foot out the door'.

Through careful conversation, it became clear that Adrian and Rhiannon had different understandings of what commitment meant. For Rhiannon, raised in a traditional family where marriage was highly valued, formal commitment through wedding vows represented emotional security and certainty about the future. For Adrian, whose parents had divorced acrimoniously after twenty years of marriage, daily demonstrations of care and presence felt more meaningful than a legal contract.

'What if we look at this not as a disagreement about marriage itself', I suggested in our second session, 'but as a difference in how you each experience and express commitment?'

This reframing opened a new conversation. Rather than debating the merits of marriage as an institution, Adrian and Rhiannon began exploring the emotional needs underlying their positions. Rhiannon articulated her desire for explicit, verbal commitments that could be witnessed and celebrated. Adrian expressed his value for consistent, daily actions that demonstrated prioritisation of the relationship.

'I realise now that when I ask for marriage, I'm really asking for certainty', Rhiannon acknowledged in our third session. 'I want to know that Adrian sees me in his future without question'.

Adrian nodded slowly. 'And I think I've been resisting because to me, a wedding feels like a performance for others rather than something meaningful between us. But I'm hearing that it would be meaningful to you in ways I hadn't understood'.

Maria guided them through an exercise exploring their commitment histories – how commitment had been modelled in their families of origin, their own experiences with keeping or breaking commitments, and the specific actions that made each feel secure in the relationship.

By our fifth session, they had developed what they called their 'commitment translation dictionary' – a shared understanding of how each experienced and expressed commitment. Adrian had come to appreciate that, for Rhiannon, verbal and ceremonial affirmations weren't empty gestures but meaningful reassurances. Rhiannon recognised that Adrian's daily prioritisation of their relationship – from small household considerations to major life decisions – constituted significant commitment in his framework.

The marriage question hadn't disappeared, but it had transformed. Rather than a binary choice representing commitment versus hesitation, they now saw it as one of many ways they might express and strengthen their mutual investment in their future together.

'We're planning a small commitment ceremony', Rhiannon shared in our final session. 'Not a traditional wedding, but something that honours what matters to both of us. And we're working with a lawyer to create agreements about property and decision-making that address Adrian's concerns about entanglement'.

Adrian reached for her hand. 'I've realised that my resistance wasn't really about commitment to Rhiannon – it was about fear based on my parents' experience. By talking about what commitment actually means to each of us, I've found a way to move forward that feels authentic and right'.

Marcus and Elena: When Commitment Faces External Tests

While Adrian and Rhiannon's commitment challenges were primarily internal, Marcus and Elena came to us facing external pressures that tested their dedication to each other. Engaged after three years together, they were navigating significant opposition from Elena's family, who disapproved of Marcus's different cultural background and religion.

'My parents have made it clear they won't attend our wedding', Elena explained tearfully in our first session. 'They say I'm turning my back on our culture and traditions. My mother has stopped taking my calls'.

Marcus sat beside her, visibly distressed by her pain yet determined. 'I've tried everything to win them over. I've learned Elena's family language, studied their traditions, even offered to incorporate elements of their faith into our ceremony. Nothing changes their minds'.

The situation was creating significant stress for both of them. Elena felt torn between loyalty to her family of origin and her commitment to her chosen partner. Marcus questioned whether he was being selfish by pursuing the relationship despite the pain it caused Elena.

'How do we navigate this?' Elena asked directly. 'Is love enough when it causes this much collateral damage?'

It was a profound question that went to the heart of what commitment means when tested by external opposition. Maria and I recognised that this couple needed not just practical strategies for managing family dynamics but a deeper exploration of their commitment to each other.

'Commitment isn't tested when everything is easy', Maria observed gently. 'It's in moments like this, when continuing the relationship requires genuine sacrifice or difficulty, that we discover its depth and resilience'.

In our second session, we introduced a visualisation exercise, asking both Marcus and Elena to imagine their lives five, ten, and twenty years in the future – both with and without each other. This wasn't about pressuring them to stay together but about helping them connect with their deeper values and desires.

Elena's reflection was revealing: 'When I imagine my future without Marcus, even if it means regaining my parents' approval, I feel a profound emptiness. When I imagine a future with him, even with the pain of family estrangement, I see possibility, growth, and joy'.

Marcus shared similar sentiments but added an important nuance: 'I want a future with Elena, but not at the cost of her happiness. If family connection is fundamental to her well-being, I need to know that she's choosing this with full awareness of what it means'.

This led to a crucial distinction in our work together: differentiating between commitment tested by legitimate external challenges versus commitment undermined by internal doubts or incompatibilities. For Marcus and Elena, their personal commitment to each other remained strong; the challenges came from navigating competing commitments to family and cultural identity.

Over our remaining sessions, we focused on three aspects of their situation:

First, clarifying their commitment to each other despite external opposition, exploring what it would mean to choose their relationship even with the current family difficulties.

Second, developing strategies for maintaining healthy boundaries with Elena's family while leaving the door open for future reconciliation.

Third, creating new rituals and connections that honoured aspects of Elena's cultural heritage she valued, helping her maintain cultural identity even without family support.

By our final session, they had developed a more resilient understanding of their commitment. 'We're not just committing to each other under ideal circumstances', Marcus explained. 'We're committing to supporting each other through the difficult reality we're facing'.

Elena nodded. 'And I've realised that commitment sometimes means making painful choices. I hope my family will eventually accept us, but I'm choosing to build a life with Marcus either way'.

Their situation reminded me that committed relationships don't exist in isolation but within complex webs of other relationships, cultural expectations and social pressures. The strength of commitment isn't measured during easy times, but in how couples navigate these external challenges together. For Elena and Marcus, choosing their relationship despite family opposition didn't diminish their other loyalties – it simply established a priority that allowed them to move forward with integrity rather than remaining perpetually torn.

What struck me most about their journey was not just the decision they reached, but the process through which they reached it. They had moved from viewing external opposition as an insurmountable obstacle to seeing it as a context within which they could still exercise choice. This shift – from feeling controlled by circumstances to recognising their agency within those circumstances – is often where the true power of commitment reveals itself.

Their story illustrates that commitment isn't about the absence of challenges or sacrifices. Rather, it's about making conscious choices about which challenges we're willing to face and which sacrifices feel meaningful in service of what we truly value. Elena might never experience full family acceptance, and Marcus might always carry some guilt about her estrangement, but together they had found a way to honour their commitment without denying its costs.

Chapter 17

Richard and Kaye – The Beautiful Dormouse

When Love Is a Cage

Some days in therapy, you feel the weight of inequality before a single word is spoken. The day Richard and Kaye arrived for their first session was one of those days.

The initial phone conversations had already set the stage. Kaye had called first – her voice tentative yet determined, explaining that she felt unhappy and unfulfilled in their fifteen-year relationship. She spoke of wanting marriage, commitment, faithfulness – basic desires that shouldn't have felt like unreasonable demands. When I contacted Richard for his preliminary conversation, his tone was entirely different: dismissive, slightly bored, agreeing to attend while simultaneously suggesting it would likely be a waste of his valuable time.

'I'll come', he had said with an audible sigh, 'but I'm not sure there's any point. We want different things. That's not going to change'.

The morning of their appointment, Maria and I prepared the room with our usual care – arranging the seating to create equal space for both voices, setting out the wicker baskets of pebbles for possible constellation work, ensuring water and tissues were within easy reach. We briefly discussed our impressions from the intake forms and phone calls, noting the sharp contrast between Kaye's detailed, emotionally transparent responses and Richard's perfunctory, almost dismissive engagement with the process.

Maria had sensed something in Kaye's careful phrasing that concerned her. 'There's a hesitancy there', she observed. 'As if she's measuring her words, afraid of saying too much'.

I nodded. 'And his responses feel like someone completing a tedious administrative task. No real investment'.

Neither of us could have predicted the scene that would unfold.

Kaye arrived first, asked politely where the bathroom was, and excused herself. Moments later, Richard strode in – tall, impeccably dressed in what was clearly a bespoke suit, his confidence filling the room with an almost palpable pressure. He carried himself with the ease of someone accustomed to immediate deference, shaking my hand with the precise pressure of a man who had been taught that a handshake reveals character.

DOI: 10.4324/9781003752776-17

Before I could begin the usual preliminaries, he glanced at his watch – a timepiece that probably cost more than most people's cars – and offered a statement so unexpected I momentarily wondered if I'd misheard him.

'We were running early', he said, his tone casual yet somehow performative. 'So, I had about half an hour to spare. I stopped at the Ferrari garage up the road and had a look. There's a very nice model 599, limited edition, very rare, for sale for just under a million pounds. I'm thinking about whether to take some of my pension pot out to buy it'.

His expression as he delivered this information was extraordinary – a peculiar mix of casualness, as if discussing the weather, combined with a barely concealed expectation of impressed reaction. The subtext couldn't have been clearer if he'd stated it outright: *I have a bigger wallet than you, a bigger life, a bigger everything.*

I maintained a neutral expression. 'That's interesting', I said simply, neither feeding nor challenging his obvious need to establish dominance before the session had even begun.

The moment was interrupted by Maria and Kaye's return. Her physical presence formed an immediate contrast to Richard's commanding stature – petite, carefully but modestly dressed, her body language suggesting someone accustomed to taking up as little space as possible. She smiled nervously as she settled into her seat, automatically positioning herself slightly farther back than Richard, as if this minor physical deference was habitual.

After the standard introduction to our process, I asked what had brought them to therapy. Kaye glanced at Richard, seemingly waiting for permission to speak first. When he made a small gesture with his hand, a gesture I found disquietingly similar to a monarch granting audience, she began.

'We've been together for fifteen years', she said, her voice soft but clear. 'And I ... I feel like we want different things now. Or maybe we always did, but I thought they might change'. She paused, her fingers twisting the simple silver ring she wore – not an engagement ring, I noted. 'I would like us to get married. To make a real commitment to each other'.

Richard sighed, the sound carrying more annoyance than contemplation. 'Kaye knows my views on marriage. It's an outdated institution, and I don't see what it would add to what we already have'.

'And there have been ... other women', Kaye continued, her voice dropping slightly. 'Throughout our relationship. I've asked for faithfulness, but –'

'Nothing serious', Richard interrupted, his tone dismissive. 'Casual arrangements. They don't affect what we have'.

My practised therapeutic neutrality was already being tested. The dynamic unfolding before us wasn't simply a matter of different relationship expectations – it was a profound imbalance of power, respect, and basic consideration.

As the session progressed, this imbalance became increasingly evident. Richard spoke at length about his professional success – the high-powered positions he'd held, the substantial income he commanded, the organisations now courting him after his departure from his previous role. He described his 'beautiful house in Sussex' and their property in the Isles of Scilly as if these possessions somehow validated their relationship itself.

Kaye spoke much less, but when she did, the picture she painted was disturbing in its implications. She worked part-time in a local gallery – 'pin money', as Richard characterised it, a phrase that made Maria and I exchange a brief glance. More tellingly, she revealed that she paid 'rent' to Richard for living in 'his' house, despite their fifteen-year relationship.

'It's a fair arrangement', Richard explained, as if discussing a business contract. 'I own the property; I cover the major expenses. Kaye contributes what she can'.

'Do you pool your resources for other expenses?' Maria asked.

'Not really', Kaye answered quietly. 'I buy the groceries, handle the cleaning, take care of Richard's mother when she visits ...'

'Kaye's wonderful with my mother', Richard interjected, his first truly positive comment about her. 'She has a way of making people comfortable, taking care of details. It's one of her special talents'.

The word 'talents' hung in the air between us, carrying uncomfortable connotations of servitude rather than partnership.

As the session continued, I employed several techniques to try breaking through the rigid patterns between them. When I suggested the pebble constellation exercise, Richard participated with bemused tolerance, selecting a large, polished stone for himself and placing it prominently in the centre. Kaye chose a small, pale pebble for herself and positioned it close to Richard's stone, slightly behind it. The arrangement spoke volumes.

'If you could create an ideal arrangement', I asked Kaye, 'how would it look different?'

She studied the stones for a long moment. 'I suppose ... my stone would be closer to his. Not behind, but beside. And perhaps they would be more similar in size'.

'That's not very realistic, is it?' Richard commented with a smile that didn't reach his eyes. 'I mean, I'm six foot two, you're five foot three. Some differences are just natural'.

His deliberate misinterpretation of the symbolic exercise wasn't lost on any of us.

The most revealing moment came near the end of our session. Richard, perhaps growing bored with the process, reached over and briefly took Kaye's hand; the first physical contact I'd observed between them.

'You know I adore you', he said, his tone softening slightly. 'You're my beautiful dormouse'.

The term of endearment landed like a stone in still water. Kaye smiled reflexively, but the expression didn't reach her eyes. I felt a chill at the inadvertent truth of his metaphor – the dormouse, small and vulnerable, kept for someone else's amusement, existing in captivity while the owner came and went freely.

In that moment, I saw with perfect clarity what our therapy could and could not accomplish. This wasn't a relationship that could be repaired, because it had never been equitable to begin with. Richard wasn't seeking change – he was perfectly satisfied with the arrangement as it stood. Kaye was the only one hoping for transformation, and the changes she sought would require Richard to relinquish power he had no intention of sharing.

'Richard', I said carefully, 'what would happen if the dormouse roared?'

His expression shifted from mild amusement to something harder, more assessing. 'Dormice don't roar', he replied after a moment. 'It's not in their nature'.

I turned to Kaye. 'What would you need to have happen for you to escape the dormouse cage and find your voice; perhaps even your roar?'

The question seemed to startle her. For perhaps the first time in the session, she didn't immediately look to Richard for his reaction. Instead, she gazed downward, her brow furrowed in genuine contemplation.

'I don't know', she said finally. 'I'm not sure I remember what my voice sounds like'.

As our time drew to a close, I offered some reflections on what I'd observed and some possible approaches for future sessions. Richard checked his watch several times during this summary, his disengagement palpable. Kaye listened with intense concentration, occasionally nodding.

'For our next session', I suggested, knowing even as I spoke that there likely wouldn't be one, 'I'd like each of you to complete an exercise about your individual values and priorities. It might help clarify where your visions for the future align and where they diverge'.

Richard stood immediately when I indicated we had reached the end of our time. 'Thank you for your time', he said, with the polite insincerity of someone concluding an unsuccessful business meeting. Kaye gathered her things more slowly, her movements deliberate, as if trying to extend her time in this neutral space.

As they left, I noticed that Richard walked slightly ahead, not looking back to see if Kaye was following. She trailed behind, her gaze fixed on his back with an expression I couldn't quite decipher – resignation mixed with something else, something that might have been the first flicker of resolve.

'Well', Maria said after the door closed behind them. 'That was ...'

'Indeed', I agreed, the single word carrying the weight of our shared concern.

A brief walk outside reconnects me to the wider world and allows me to reacquaint myself with an ice cream, a reminder that each session is but one piece of a greater whole.

We will find out more about Kaye's roar in Chapter 34.

Chapter 18

Fun

One of the saddest revelations in my first session with Richard and Kaye was their answer to my standard question: 'When did you last have fun together?' They looked at each other blankly, unable to remember. Somewhere in the years of building careers and raising children, of meeting obligations and managing responsibilities, they had lost the ability to simply enjoy each other's company. This brought home the importance of Fun – the fourth element of the Relationship Paradigm. It might seem trivial compared to Communication or Commitment, but I've learned that couples who stop playing together often stop staying together. Fun isn't frivolous; it's the lightness that keeps love from becoming a burden.

In the serious business of relationship therapy, fun might seem like a frivolous focus – a luxury rather than a necessity. Couples arrive in my therapy room struggling with communication breakdowns, betrayals, intimacy issues, and parenting conflicts. Rarely does anyone list 'not enough fun' as their presenting problem. Yet as Maria and I work with couples over time, we often discover that the gradual disappearance of playfulness, joy, and shared delight has been a silent contributor to their relationship distress. The question 'and when did the two of you last have fun together?' is often responded to with blank looks, a shuffling of feet, and an embarrassed 'I can't remember'.

DOI: 10.4324/9781003752776-18

Within the Relationship Paradigm, Fun represents more than mere entertainment or distraction. It encompasses the capacity for lightness amidst life's inevitable heaviness, the ability to play together as well as work together, the shared experiences of joy and pleasure that create a reservoir of positive feeling. Fun is the antidote to the grinding seriousness that can gradually erode even the most committed relationships.

The Dimensions of Fun

Fun in relationships manifests across several dimensions:

Playful interaction: The teasing, joking, and banter that create moments of lightness and laughter in everyday exchanges.
Novel experiences: Shared adventures, both grand and small, that interrupt routine and create new memories together.
Physical play: From dancing in the kitchen to weekend hikes, activities that engage the body and release endorphins.
Releasing the child within: Taking down the adult barriers and allowing the freedom of childlike behaviour out.
Intellectual play: The stimulation of games, debates, or exploring ideas together without the pressure of practical application.
Sensual pleasure: The enjoyment of physical sensations, from the taste of a meal to the relaxation of massage to the intimacy of sexual connection.

What constitutes fun varies enormously between couples and often between partners within the same relationship. For some, fun means active adventure; for others, it's quiet companionship around a board game. The essential quality isn't the specific activity but the shared experience of joy, the temporary stepping away from responsibilities and problems to connect through pleasure.

Lisa and Omar: When Fun Disappears

When Lisa and Omar first came to Duo Coaching, their relationship had reached a state of functional misery. Married for eleven years with three children under ten, they operated their household with impressive efficiency but minimal joy. Their schedules were meticulously coordinated, their parenting responsibilities clearly divided, their finances carefully managed. Yet beneath this operational success lay a growing emptiness.

'We're like business partners running a family enterprise', Lisa explained in their first session, her voice flat. 'Everything gets done, but there's no ... sparkle anymore'.

Omar nodded, adding, 'I can't remember the last time we did anything just because it was enjoyable. Every moment feels scheduled and purposeful'.

As Maria and I explored their history, a familiar pattern emerged. Their early relationship had been filled with spontaneous adventures, inside jokes, and playful physical affection. They'd been known among friends for their lively dinner parties and impulsive weekend trips. Gradually, as career pressures mounted and children arrived, these elements had been squeezed out of their relationship, viewed as dispensable compared to the serious business of building careers and raising a family.

'When did you start believing that fun was optional?' I asked in our second session.

The question stopped them both short. After a thoughtful pause, Omar responded, 'I think it happened so gradually we didn't notice. First, we were both working long hours to establish our careers. Then the children came, and any free time went to them. Somewhere along the way, we started seeing enjoyment as something we'd get back to "someday" when life was less demanding'.

Lisa's eyes filled with tears. 'The thing is life never gets less demanding. There's always another work deadline, another child's activity, another household project. If we're waiting for the perfect time to reintroduce fun, it will never come'.

In our third session, Maria introduced an exercise we call the Fun Archaeology Dig. She asked Lisa and Omar to excavate their relationship history for activities, experiences, and interactions that had once brought them genuine joy together, without regard to whether these seemed practical in their current circumstances.

Their list was revealing. Many items were remarkably simple: impromptu dance parties in their kitchen, weekend morning coffee on the balcony without phones or newspapers, making up ridiculous stories about fellow diners at restaurants. Others reflected their pre-children lifestyle: rock climbing, spontaneous road trips, hosting themed dinner parties.

'What strikes me', Maria observed, 'is how many of these involve either spontaneity or physical movement or both – qualities that can be challenging to maintain with young children and demanding careers'.

This insight led to a crucial realisation: Lisa and Omar hadn't stopped valuing fun; they'd simply stopped believing it was possible within the constraints of their current life. The challenge wasn't to convince them that fun mattered but to help them rediscover how it could fit into their reality.

'What if', I suggested, 'instead of trying to reclaim the specific activities of your pre-children life, you focused on identifying the qualities that made those experiences enjoyable? Then you could look for new ways to incorporate those qualities that are compatible with your current circumstances'.

This reframing energised them. They identified several core qualities: physical movement, unpredictability, shared creativity, and temporary escape from responsibility. With these in mind, they began experimenting with new forms of fun that could work within their family life.

By our fourth session, they reported their first successes. They'd instituted 'Dance Party Thursdays' with their children, twenty minutes of music and movement in the living room before bedtime routines began. They'd created a 'Spontaneity Jar' filled with small adventures written on slips of paper – from 'breakfast for dinner' to 'family pillow fight in the living room' – that they would draw from when the weekend felt too scheduled and predictable.

'Last Saturday', Omar shared with evident delight, 'we pulled "garden camping" from the jar. We didn't actually sleep outside because the weather turned, but we set up the tent, made toasted marshmallows on the firepit, and told ghost stories with torches under our chins. The children were thrilled, and Lisa and I remembered what it feels like to be playful together'.

Lisa added, 'The amazing thing is how these small injections of fun seem to change the whole tone of our relationship. Even during the normal routine of making lunches or supervising homework, we're exchanging more smiles, more brief touches. It's like we've given ourselves permission to be light-hearted again'.

By our final session, the change in their physical presence was remarkable. Where they had once sat rigidly apart, they now naturally gravitated toward each other. Their faces were more animated, their voices more expressive. They reported feeling more attracted to each other, with physical intimacy becoming more frequent and satisfying.

'Fun isn't just the icing on the cake', Omar reflected. 'It's more like the yeast in the bread – it might seem like a small ingredient, but without it, everything falls flat'.

Naomi and Patrick: When Fun Means Different Things

While Lisa and Omar's challenge was reclaiming fun within the constraints of family life, Naomi and Patrick presented a different scenario. In their case, fun hadn't disappeared from their relationship – it had become a source of conflict due to fundamentally different definitions of what constituted enjoyment.

'Patrick's idea of a good time is sitting at home with a book', Naomi explained in their first session, frustration evident in her voice. 'I feel like I'm dragging him out of the house for any social activity'.

Patrick sighed. 'And Naomi needs constant stimulation and people around. Her perfect weekend would exhaust me completely'.

Both in their early thirties and childless by choice, Naomi and Patrick had substantial freedom to pursue enjoyable activities. The problem wasn't opportunity but alignment. As an extrovert, Naomi craved social gatherings, active adventures, and novel experiences. Patrick, a classic introvert, found these draining rather than energising, preferring quiet conversations, intellectual pursuits, and familiar routines.

'I feel rejected when Patrick doesn't want to join me for parties or trips with friends', Naomi admitted. 'Like he's choosing books over me'.

Patrick countered, 'And I feel inadequate, like I'm never exciting enough for her. Then I get resentful that my natural preferences are somehow wrong'.

Maria and I recognised a pattern we often see in couples with different temperaments. Rather than viewing their diverse preferences as an opportunity for mutual growth and balanced living, Naomi and Patrick had fallen into seeing them as a fundamental incompatibility. Each interpreted the other's natural inclinations as a personal rejection or criticism.

'What if', Maria suggested in our second session, 'instead of framing this as a problem to solve, we explore how your different approaches to fun might actually complement each other over time?'

This perspective shift opened a productive conversation. We introduced the concept of The Fun Venn Diagram, asking Naomi and Patrick to identify three categories of activities: those only Naomi enjoyed, those only Patrick enjoyed, and a third category of activities they both found genuinely pleasurable.

The exercise revealed more overlap than either had expected. Both enjoyed hiking in nature, though Patrick preferred familiar trails while Naomi sought new destinations. Both valued travel, though Patrick was drawn to the cultural and historical aspects while Naomi focused on adventure and social connections. Both appreciated music, though Patrick preferred listening at home while Naomi enjoyed live concerts.

'The question isn't whether you can find shared enjoyment', I observed, 'but how to structure your leisure time to honour both your overlapping and distinct preferences'.

Over the next few sessions, we helped Naomi and Patrick develop what they called their 'Fun Constitution' – a set of principles and practices for balancing their diverse approaches to enjoyment:

1. Each would have regular time for solo enjoyment without guilt or pressure (Patrick's reading afternoons, Naomi's girls' nights out).
2. They would prioritise the activities in their 'overlap zone', recognising these as the foundation of their shared fun.
3. Each would stretch occasionally into the other's preferred territory, approaching these stretches with curiosity rather than reluctance.
4. They would develop clear communication signals for when social situations became overwhelming for Patrick, allowing them to attend events together but leave at different times if needed.
5. They would practise genuine celebration of each other's enjoyment, even when not participating directly.

By our fifth session, they reported a newfound appreciation for their differences. 'I've started seeing Patrick's introversion as a quality that helps us slow down and savour experiences', Naomi shared. 'He notices details I would miss if I were rushing on to the next thing'.

Patrick nodded. 'And Naomi's extroversion has enriched my life with connections and experiences I would never have sought out myself. I've actually enjoyed some of the new activities she's introduced – just in smaller doses than she might prefer'.

Their case illustrates an important aspect of fun in relationships: it doesn't require identical preferences, just mutual respect and a willingness to create space for both shared and individual enjoyment.

The Neurochemistry of Joy

The importance of fun in relationships isn't just psychological but physiological. Research in affective neuroscience has demonstrated that positive shared experiences trigger the release of several crucial neurochemicals that strengthen bonding:

Dopamine: Released during novel and pleasurable experiences, creating feelings of reward and motivation to seek similar experiences in the future.
Oxytocin: Often called the 'bonding hormone', increases during positive physical touch and shared positive emotions.
Endorphins: Natural mood elevators released during physical activity and laughter.
Serotonin: Linked to feelings of well-being and satisfaction, often elevated during enjoyable social interactions.

When couples regularly engage in activities that activate these neurochemical systems, they create what researchers call 'positive sentiment override' – a general positive feeling about the relationship that helps buffer against inevitable conflicts and stresses. Put simply, couples who play together develop greater resilience for when they must work through problems together.

Maria and I often share this science with couples because it helps them understand that fun isn't frivolous – it's fundamental to relationship health. Creating opportunities for shared joy and pleasure isn't selfish indulgence but an investment in the biochemical foundations of connection.

The Fun Toolkit

Over years of working with couples, we've developed what we call The Fun Toolkit – practical approaches to revitalise this essential element of relationship:

The Pleasure Inventory: A structured exploration of what creates genuine enjoyment for each partner, distinguishing between what they think should be fun and what actually brings them joy.
Novelty Scheduling: Intentionally planning new experiences to activate the brain's novelty response, which heightens attention and creates more vivid shared memories.
The 2-2-2 Principle: Planning dates or experiences at different intervals – every two weeks something small (like a walk in a new park), every two months something medium (like a day trip), and every two years something significant (like a special holiday).

Fun First: Restructuring priorities to ensure enjoyment isn't always deferred until after responsibilities are completed (which often means it never happens).

Play Personalities: Identifying each partner's natural play style (the competitor, the explorer, the collector, the joker, etc.) to better understand their approach to fun.

Joy Journaling: Recording moments of shared delight, however small, to increase awareness of when they occur and create a resource to revisit during more challenging times.

These tools aren't about manufacturing artificial fun or pressuring couples to be more playful than feels natural. Rather, they're about removing the barriers – practical, psychological, and cultural – that often prevent adults from accessing the natural capacity for joy and play that remains within us throughout life.

The Bridge to Other Elements

Like all elements of the Relationship Paradigm, Fun interconnects with the others in dynamic ways. Fun experiences build Trust by creating positive shared history. They strengthen Connection through shared emotional states. They demonstrate Commitment through the prioritisation of the relationship. They facilitate Communication in low-pressure contexts. They create opportunities for Growth through new experiences and challenges.

When couples like Lisa and Omar or Naomi and Patrick rediscover or renegotiate the role of fun in their relationships, the benefits often cascade into these other areas. Problems that once seemed intractable become more manageable when approached from a foundation of shared positive experiences. Difficult conversations flow more easily when embedded in a relationship that includes lightness as well as seriousness.

Perhaps most importantly, fun reminds couples why they chose each other in the first place – not just as practical partners in navigating life's responsibilities but as companions in experiencing life's joys. It reconnects them with the feelings that drew them together initially and creates new iterations of those feelings as they grow and change together.

As I witness couples rediscover playfulness and shared enjoyment in our therapy room, I'm reminded that relationships aren't solely about solving problems or fulfilling obligations. They're also about creating spaces of joy, delight, and pleasure amidst life's inevitable challenges – not as an escape from reality but as an essential part of a full and balanced human experience. In the end, a relationship that cannot play together will likely struggle to stay together through life's more serious passages.

Chapter 19

Be More Penguin – Relationship Wisdom from the Ice

Speaking of fun in relationships, I want to share something that fundamentally changed how I think about partnership – though the lesson came from the most unexpected teachers. It was November when I found myself standing on a beach in South Georgia, following in the footsteps of Ernest Shackleton, and what I witnessed there would offer insights into connection that even decades of therapy work had not fully revealed. Sometimes wisdom arrives not from academic theory or clinical experience, but from simply paying attention to how other beings navigate the very things we humans struggle with most.

The cold air filled my lungs as I gazed out at a sight that would fundamentally shift my perception of relationships forever: penguins, hundreds of thousands of them, stretching as far as the eye could see.

Humans tend to believe we have cornered the market on meaningful connection. We write poetry about love, develop elaborate theories of attachment, and spend millions on self-help books. We fancy ourselves the sophisticated species, looking down – quite literally in this case – on the 'simple' bonds formed by other creatures.

And then you meet a colony of king penguins, and everything you thought you knew is suddenly up for reconsideration.

Tears on the Shoreline

I remember the moment vividly. We had spotted specks from our Discovery yacht – some stationary, some mobile – and through binoculars, they resolved into penguin forms. Some were marching determinedly down the beach into the water, others were leaping back onto the shore, and still others stood quietly, seemingly contemplating the horizon.

My curiosity drew me to the shore. I wanted to see these creatures up close, in their natural habitat. As our dinghy approached and I climbed onto the beach, I was struck by their nonchalance. They noticed us, I'm certain of that, but they didn't scatter in fear or approach with aggression. They simply carried on with their penguin lives, allowing us to exist in their space without particular concern.

DOI: 10.4324/9781003752776-19

I walked further up the sloping beach and stopped, stunned into immobility. Ahead of me, to my sides, everywhere I looked, were penguins. Not dozens or hundreds, but hundreds of thousands. The scale was incomprehensible. I felt tears streaming down my cheeks before I even registered the emotion welling up inside me.

'What's wrong?' asked my wife, concerned by my unexpected reaction.

'Nothing's wrong', I managed to say. 'Everything's right. That's what's so overwhelming'.

And it was true. Looking out at this vast colony, I was witnessing something remarkable: a community functioning in perfect harmony. No arguments over territory. No visible hierarchy disputes. No individuals hoarding resources or neglecting responsibilities. Just a vast, collaborative network of beings, each playing their part in the whole.

As a relationship therapist, I couldn't help but wonder – what might my human clients learn if they could stand where I was standing?

My penguin observations weren't limited to the king penguins of South Georgia. Later in our expedition, I found myself standing on the Antarctic peninsula itself, witnessing one of nature's most charming courtship rituals within a bustling colony of Gentoo penguins. I watched, captivated, as male Gentoos diligently searched the rocky landscape for the perfect pebble; not just any stone would do.

When a male found what he deemed worthy, he would waddle back to his chosen female, presenting this small token with what could only be described as penguin hopefulness. The ritual held all the tension of human courtship; the female would either accept this offering, adding it to her nest and strengthening their bond, or reject it outright, sending the disappointed suitor back to search for a better pebble or perhaps a more receptive partner.

There was something profoundly moving about the simplicity of this exchange; a small stone representing much larger intentions. No elaborate promises or complicated negotiations, just a straightforward offering that said, 'I choose you, and I'll help build our home'.

It struck me that in human relationships, we often overlook these small, meaningful gestures, the everyday 'pebbles' that, when accumulated over time, construct the foundation of lasting connection. The Gentoos reminded me that sometimes the most profound expressions of commitment come not in grand declarations but in these consistent, intentional offerings of care.

The Myth of Human Superiority

We humans pride ourselves on our intelligence, our complexity, our supposedly superior capacity for love and connection. We measure our superiority in academic achievements, technological advancements, and elaborate social structures. We create IQ tests that – surprise, surprise – confirm our own brilliance while failing to capture forms of intelligence that don't align with our specific capabilities.

Yet here, on this frozen landscape, was a display of relationship intelligence that made our human efforts appear clumsy and underdeveloped by comparison.

Consider this: king penguins can identify their mate's call among tens of thousands of nearly identical vocalisations. Can you pick out your partner's voice in a noisy restaurant? Many of my clients would answer with an emphatic 'no', followed by complaints about their spouse mumbling.

These penguins take turns incubating their precious egg, sometimes standing in place for weeks while their partner journeys up to thirty miles away to hunt for food. The returning partner relieves them without argument or resentment. No 'but I did it last time' or 'can't you see how tired I am?' Just seamless cooperation based on mutual understanding of shared purpose.

I once worked with a couple who had a three-day standoff over whose turn it was to empty the dishwasher.

'What would your relationship look like', I now wonder, 'if you approached it with penguin-like clarity of purpose?'

Serial Monogamy: The Penguin Way

It's worth noting that king penguins are serially monogamous. They typically find a new mate each breeding season, though they may reunite with previous partners. This is neither better nor worse than the human ideal of lifelong monogamy – it's simply a different way of structuring relationships that works perfectly for their species and environment.

What's remarkable isn't the structure but the execution. When penguins commit to a partner for the breeding season, that commitment is absolute. There's no penguin equivalent of 'I need space' or 'I'm not sure this is working'. No penguin marriage counsellors needed to help them navigate conflicting expectations or communication breakdowns.

This observation isn't meant to suggest we should emulate their relationship structure – humans are different creatures with different needs. But there's something to be learned from their clarity of purpose and commitment.

I recall working with Harriet and Ed. Ed's affair had shattered the trust between them, and rebuilding required months of painful conversations and intentional reconnection. As they struggled through this process, I sometimes wondered what would have been different if they'd had the penguin-like clarity of commitment from the start.

Would Ed have strayed if he'd understood his relationship with the unwavering certainty that a penguin appears to possess? Would Harriet have built walls of silent resentment if she'd approached their relationship with the direct, purposeful communication that penguins seem to manage so effortlessly?

Community without Competition

One of the most striking aspects of the penguin colony was the sense of community without competition. In human relationships, we often find ourselves comparing our partnerships to others, measuring our success against external standards, competing for resources or recognition.

'John and Sarah went to Bali for their anniversary. Why do we always just go to the same local restaurant?'

'Look how attentive Michael is with their baby. Why can't you be more like that?'

The penguins showed no such comparisons. Each pair was focused on their own relationship, their own egg or chick, their own responsibilities. Yet this individual focus didn't translate to isolation or selfishness. The colony functioned as a cohesive whole, with individuals benefiting from the collective warmth, protection, and wisdom of the group.

Standing there on that beach, I had a moment of clarity about the relationship issues that so many of my clients struggle with. Perhaps our human problems stem not from our complexity but from our loss of simplicity. We've added layers of comparison, expectation, and ego that obscure the fundamental purpose of partnership: to support each other, to care for our young, to find joy in connection.

The Penguin Relationship Paradigm

As I watched the colony go about their daily business, I couldn't help but map their behaviours onto my own Relationship Paradigm – the six elements I've identified as essential for healthy human partnerships: Communication, Connection, Commitment, Fun, Growth, and Trust.

The penguins excelled at all six, though in their own distinctly penguin way:

Communication: Clear, consistent, and effective. No passive-aggressive sighs or cryptic 'I'm fine' responses when they're clearly not fine. When a penguin has something to communicate, they do so directly and unmistakably.

I once watched a returning parent call to their chick among thousands of nearly identical youngsters in a crèche. The specific pattern of their call, like an acoustic fingerprint, allowed the chick to identify its parent instantly. The precision of this communication would put many human couples to shame.

Connection: Physical and emotional bonds maintained through ritualistic behaviours – mutual preening, synchronised movements, physical proximity. No penguin seems to wonder, 'Does my partner still desire me?' or 'Are we growing apart?'

I observed pairs standing together, flippers touching, in what appeared to be moments of quiet companionship. There was something deeply moving about the simplicity of this connection.

Commitment: Absolute dedication to shared goals. Once paired, penguins don't seem to experience commitment doubts or wonder if another penguin might make them happier.

I watched as pairs took turns incubating their egg, each enduring harsh conditions while their partner fed, neither shirking responsibility nor questioning their role.

Fun: Yes, penguins have fun! I witnessed groups swimming and 'porpoising' (leaping out of the water), engaging in what appeared to be play behaviour that had no immediate survival value but seemed to bring joy.

This reminded me of how often human couples forget to play together, becoming so consumed by responsibilities that they lose the lightness that initially drew them together.

Growth: Adaptation to changing conditions and challenges. Penguins don't become static or complacent; they continuously develop skills and strategies to thrive in their harsh environment.

I wondered how many human relationships stagnate because partners stop growing together, falling into comfortable but limiting patterns.

Trust: Perhaps most impressively, penguins demonstrate unwavering trust in their partners. When one leaves to hunt, sometimes for weeks, the other doesn't appear to worry about abandonment or betrayal.

How many human relationships are undermined by trust issues, by the nagging worry that we can't fully rely on our partner?

The Penguin in the Therapy Room

Since that profound experience in South Georgia and Antarctica, I've found myself bringing penguins into my therapy room – not literally, of course (though I imagine that would certainly liven up sessions), but as a powerful metaphor for relationship potential.

When couples become entangled in complex power dynamics, I sometimes ask, 'What would the penguins do?' The question often breaks tension with laughter, but it also invites a shift in perspective. It encourages couples to step back from their elaborate human narratives and consider the essential purpose of their partnership.

Take Stuart and Clare, whose story I shared earlier. Their relationship had become bogged down in control issues and cultural differences. When I introduced the penguin perspective, Stuart initially scoffed.

'Penguins don't have mortgages or career demands or difficult ex-spouses', he pointed out.

'True', I acknowledged. 'But they navigate life-threatening conditions, care for vulnerable offspring in harsh environments, and manage to do it without the resentment that's building between you two'.

This reframing helped them see their challenges differently. Instead of viewing their relationship as uniquely difficult, they began to recognise that partnership always involves challenges – the question is how we approach them.

The Human Challenge

Of course, I'm not suggesting we can or should literally 'be penguins'. Human relationships are indeed more cognitively complex, embedded in cultural contexts that penguins don't navigate. We have abstract concepts like justice, fairness, personal growth, and self-actualisation that shape our expectations of partnerships.

Yet I wonder if this cognitive complexity – supposedly our evolutionary advantage – sometimes becomes our relationship downfall. We overthink, we ruminate, we create elaborate narratives about what is happening instead of simply experiencing and responding to what is.

A penguin doesn't appear to spend time wondering if they're with the 'right' mate or if they could be happier with a different partner. They don't seem to construct stories about their partner's intentions or ruminate on past disappointments. They respond to the present reality, adapting as needed, without the burden of what we might call 'relationship anxiety'.

I've worked with countless couples caught in cycles of what I call 'paralysis by analysis' – so caught up in thinking about their relationship that they've lost the ability to simply be in it. They interpret each interaction through lenses of past hurt, future worry, or comparative dissatisfaction. They're so busy evaluating their relationship that they're no longer experiencing it.

Standing on that beach in South Georgia, surrounded by hundreds of thousands of penguins getting on with the business of connection without apparent angst or uncertainty, I had a profound realisation: perhaps the pinnacle of relationship evolution isn't more complexity, but a return to essentials.

From Provider to Partner

Modern human relationships have evolved beyond the purely functional. We no longer partner primarily for survival or resource sharing (though these elements remain). We seek emotional fulfilment, intellectual stimulation, personal growth, and a sense of shared purpose and meaning.

Yet in this evolution toward more sophisticated connection, we've perhaps lost touch with the foundational elements that the penguins demonstrate so beautifully: clarity of purpose, direct communication, present-moment attention, and collaborative spirit.

I'm not advocating we abandon the depth and richness of human connection for penguin-like simplicity. Rather, I'm suggesting that perhaps these seemingly simpler creatures have mastered fundamentals that we, in our complexity, have forgotten or obscured.

The penguins reminded me that beneath all our elaborate relationship theories and therapeutic models lies a simple truth: we are beings designed for connection, for partnership, for collaboration. When we strip away the layers of expectation, comparison, ego, and fear, we find our natural capacity for the kind of straightforward, purposeful togetherness that the penguins display so effortlessly.

Be More Penguin

As I left that beach, reluctantly returning to the dinghy that would take me back to the ship, to explore more penguin colonies on South Georgia and Antarctica, I took one last look at the vast colony. The tableau before me – thousands of beings, each distinct yet part of a harmonious whole – seemed to offer a vision of relationship potential that I've carried with me ever since.

Now, when couples ask me for the secret to a thriving relationship, I sometimes smile and say, 'Be more penguin'. The suggestion usually earns me a puzzled look, giving me the opportunity to explain:

Be clear in your communication, like a penguin who calls to their mate across a noisy colony.

Be collaborative in your goals, like penguins who take turns nurturing their shared future.

Be present in your connection, like penguins who attend fully to each interaction rather than dwelling on past disappointments or future anxieties.

Be playful in your partnership, finding joy in simply being together.

Be committed to your shared purpose, approaching challenges as a team rather than adversaries.

Be trusting in your bond, believing in your partner's essential goodwill even when circumstances are difficult.

Of course, this advice is a simplification – human relationships will never be as straightforward as they appear to be in a penguin colony. But the metaphor serves as a powerful reminder of what's possible when we approach connection with clarity, purpose, and presence.

I often wonder what those penguins would make of our relationship struggles if they could observe us as we observed them. Would they be puzzled by our tendency to complicate what they manage so naturally? Would they be amused by our elaborate relationship theories and therapeutic interventions? Or would they simply continue doing what they do, unwittingly modelling a way of being together that we, with all our sophistication, still strive to achieve?

Whatever the case, my time with the penguins offered me a different perspective on relationships – one that continues to inform my work and my own approach to connection. In our quest for deeper, more fulfilling partnerships, perhaps we would all do well to occasionally ask ourselves: What would a penguin do?

And in moments of relationship confusion or conflict, I now offer this simple but profound advice: Be more penguin.

Chapter 20

The View from the Second Chair

What You Don't See

Eight years in this chair, and today I'm going to reveal what you never see.

Throughout this book, you've witnessed Neil's perspective on the couples who have walked through our door – Rebecca and James, Sam and Suzy, Barry and Edith, John and Sarah.

You've read about their transformations, heard their stories, followed their journeys. But there's another story woven through these sessions, one that happens in the spaces between words, in the silent exchanges between two therapists, in the moments when I see what the couple cannot yet see, or when I notice something Neil has missed.

This is the view from the second chair – not the origin story I've shared elsewhere, but the living reality of what happens behind the scenes when we work with couples whose stories you already know.

The Silent Language: Rebecca and James

I still remember the phone call from Neil the night before Rebecca and James's session following her discovery at the cottage. 'She's found more', he said, his voice carrying that particular tension I'd come to recognise. 'Hidden journals. Three years' worth. She's devastated'.

What he couldn't have known from that phone conversation was what I would notice the moment Rebecca and James walked through our door the next morning. Neil saw what he expected: tension, potential crisis, a couple on the brink. But I saw something else entirely – something in the way Rebecca's hand briefly touched James's arm as he held the door, a gesture so fleeting it might have been accidental, yet carried such tenderness it made my breath catch.

While Neil began gently exploring what Rebecca had discovered, I watched James. Not his words or even his overall demeanour, but the micro-expressions that flickered across his face when Rebecca spoke. When she said, 'I want to leave him', his jaw tightened – but not defensively. It was the clench of someone bracing for deserved punishment while simultaneously heartbroken at the thought of losing her. His eyes never left her face, even when she couldn't look at him.

DOI: 10.4324/9781003752776-20

And Rebecca – throughout Neil's careful questioning about whether Sarah might have deliberately planted the evidence, I noticed Rebecca's fingers. They kept moving toward her wedding ring, twisting it slightly, but never attempting to remove it. A telling distinction. Couples who are truly done often unconsciously remove their rings during sessions, or at minimum, stop engaging with them. Rebecca was still holding on.

About forty minutes into the session, Neil paused to review some notes. In that brief silence, I saw it – the moment James shifted almost imperceptibly toward Rebecca on the couch, and she didn't move away. Such a tiny adjustment, perhaps just an inch, but in the vocabulary of bodies under stress, it spoke volumes.

'Rebecca', I said softly, and both she and Neil looked at me. 'I've been watching you both as you talk about this devastating discovery. And I'm noticing something. Would you be open to hearing what I'm seeing?'

She nodded, though her expression suggested scepticism.

'You're using the word "want" – "I want to leave him". But your body is telling me something different. The way you oriented toward him when you sat down. How you've unconsciously turned your wedding ring three times in the last five minutes, but never moved to remove it. How, when Neil asked whether this changes your future, you said it might, but you looked at James as you said it, checking his response. These aren't the movements of someone who has decided. They're the movements of someone who is still hoping'.

The room went quiet. Rebecca's eyes filled with tears, and she finally looked directly at James. 'I don't want to want you', she whispered. 'It would be so much easier if I could just hate you'.

'But you can't', James said, and for the first time that morning, his voice broke.

That's when I knew they would make it. Not because the discovery didn't matter – it did, devastatingly – but because underneath the justified anger was something more foundational that trauma hadn't quite destroyed.

Neil caught my eye, and in that glance was the whole conversation we'd have later: *You saw it before I did. Thank you.*

When We Disagree: The Sam and Suzy Dilemma

Not every session flows smoothly between us. Sometimes Neil and I have fundamentally different reads on what's happening, and Sam and Suzy's first session was one of those times.

They arrived showing all the classic signs of a relationship under siege from external forces – Sam's ex-wife Glenda was waging what could only be described as a systematic campaign to destabilise their blended family. As Neil laid out the situation, I found myself increasingly uneasy. His instinct was to focus immediately on boundary-setting strategies with Glenda, practical tools for managing the custody conflicts, communication protocols for dealing with the constant crises.

All of which made perfect sense from a solution-focused perspective. Except I couldn't shake the feeling we were missing something crucial.

During one of Neil's more detailed explanations about parallel parenting strategies, I noticed something: every time he mentioned Glenda by name, Suzy's entire body tensed, but Sam barely reacted. And when Sam described the latest custody manipulation, Suzy's face showed not just frustration but something much deeper – a kind of haunted vigilance that went beyond the specific situations being described.

I waited for a natural pause. 'Neil, might I suggest something?' He nodded, immediately giving me space. 'I'm wondering if we might explore something before we get to the strategies. Sam, Suzy, I'm noticing different physical responses when Rebecca is discussed. Would you be open to helping me understand what's actually happening inside each of you when these situations arise?'

Neil shifted slightly in his chair. I knew that micro-movement – it was his 'I'm not sure where you're going with this but I trust your instinct' posture. To an outside observer, nothing had changed, but between us, an entire conversation had just occurred.

What emerged in the next forty minutes was crucial: Suzy's mother had been manipulative and controlling in ways that closely mirrored Glenda's tactics. When Sam's ex-wife deployed similar strategies, Suzy wasn't just responding to the present situation – she was re-experiencing childhood trauma. No amount of boundary-setting would work until we addressed why these particular behaviours were hitting Suzy with such disproportionate force.

'I need to push back gently on where we were heading', I said, directing this primarily to Neil. 'The strategies you were outlining are excellent for a couple who are fundamentally aligned. But I don't think Sam and Suzy are there yet. I think Sam is experiencing this as an external problem to be managed, while Suzy is experiencing it as an existential threat that's triggering her core abandonment wounds'.

Neil paused, his expression thoughtful. 'Say more about what you're seeing'.

'Watch Suzy when you describe Glenda as "difficult but manageable". She physically withdraws. Sam nods in agreement, but Suzy's going somewhere else entirely. I think she needs Sam to understand that for her, this isn't just difficult – it's reactivating her deepest fears about being displaced, about not being chosen, about powerful people using children as weapons'.

Sam's face underwent a visible transformation as this landed. 'Oh God', he said quietly. 'I've been trying to reassure you by minimising the threat. But that's made you feel more alone, hasn't it?'

Suzy's tears confirmed it before her words did.

After the session, Neil and I debriefed in our usual way. 'I was too quick to problem-solve', he admitted. 'I missed the attachment piece'.

'And I might have been too focused on the past trauma and missed that they also need practical tools', I countered. 'But I think we need to address her trauma responses first, or the strategies won't hold'.

'Agreed. We'll split the next session – you work with Suzy on her maternal history and attachment wounds, I'll work with Sam on understanding trauma responses, then we bring them back together to co-create strategies from that foundation'.

This is the dance we do – not always in perfect step, but always willing to let the other lead when they see something more clearly. And importantly, we do it visibly enough that couples see that disagreement and course-correction are part of healthy partnership, not threats to it.

What I Saw before the Miracle: Barry and Edith

Of all the couples in this book, Barry and Edith's transformation was the most dramatic. Thirty years of unresolved trauma from betrayal, decades of Edith being ambushed by triggering memories, Barry's patient but increasingly hopeless endurance of her pain. By the time they reached us, they seemed destined to live out their remaining years in the prison they'd built together.

But in our second session, I saw something Neil didn't – couldn't, perhaps, because he was actively engaged with Edith while she described another triggering episode. I was in observation mode, which meant I could watch Barry.

Neil has written about this case, focusing quite rightly on the Timeline Therapy breakthrough with Edith. What he couldn't see from where he was sitting was the moment I knew Edith could heal.

It happened about ninety minutes into that second session. Edith was describing, with characteristic precision, how she'd been 'ambushed' by memories in a department store – the same store where Barry had bought gifts for his affair partner thirty years earlier. As she spoke, her breath became shallow, her pupils dilated slightly, her voice took on that particular flatness that signals dissociation beginning to occur. She was being re-traumatised in real time, just by talking about the experience.

And Barry – I watched Barry watch her go somewhere else. His hands were perfectly still in his lap, but his face... his face showed something I hadn't seen before. Not guilt, not defensiveness, not even his usual weary patience. It was grief. Pure, uncomplicated grief at watching the woman he loved suffer from a wound he'd inflicted three decades earlier.

I caught his eye for just a moment. In that glance, I saw something that made me lean forward slightly. He wasn't defending anymore. He wasn't minimising. He wasn't even hoping she'd get past it. He was simply, utterly present with her pain in a way I hadn't seen before.

'Barry', I said softly, interrupting Neil's gentle questioning. Both he and Edith looked at me. 'I'm going to ask you something that might seem strange. When you watch Edith describe these experiences, what happens inside you?'

He was quiet for a long moment. 'I feel ... responsible', he said finally. 'Not in the defensive way I usually mean that. But truly responsible. Like I created this suffering and watching her endure it is the least I can do. The very least'.

'And if you could take it from her, would you?'

'Without hesitation. In an instant. Even if it meant carrying it myself for the rest of my life'.

Edith had gone very still, watching him with an expression I couldn't quite read.

'That's different from what you usually hear from me, isn't it?' Barry said to her directly.

She nodded slowly. 'You've apologised a thousand times. But this is the first time I've actually felt that you see it. Really see what you did'.

That was the moment. Right there. Not when we did the Timeline Therapy – though that was crucial. Not during the hypnotherapy – though that created space for healing. The real turning point was Barry dropping his defences so completely that Edith could finally feel seen in her pain. Only then could her nervous system begin to trust that it might be safe to let go of the hypervigilance that had protected her for three decades.

After that session, I pulled Neil aside. 'I think we need to offer Edith individual trauma work, but I don't think that's actually the key anymore'.

'What is?'

'Barry just showed up differently. Did you see it?'

'I saw something shift in him, but I was focused on Edith's trauma response'.

'She needs the trauma work, absolutely. But I think she was only staying stuck because she didn't trust that Barry truly understood what he'd done. The moment she felt genuinely seen by him – not just apologised to, but seen – her whole body changed. I think the Timeline work will be effective now in a way it might not have been before'.

Neil nodded slowly. 'You're right. I was so focused on the trauma symptoms that I was missing the relational piece. She needed his witness before she could let go'.

'We both see different things', I reminded him. 'That's why we're better together'.

The Preparation You Don't See

Before every session begins, Neil and I meet in the therapy room for what we simply call 'preparation'. For couples you've read about in this book, this wasn't just reviewing notes. It was entering into relationship with their story before they walked through the door.

Before Rebecca and James's first session, I read through the intake forms Neil had already reviewed and something caught my eye: Rebecca had survived a serious health crisis five years earlier. James had mentioned his learning disability and the shame he carried. Both had described themselves as high-achievers who'd built their identities around competence and control.

'I think we're going to see two people who are terrified of being "found out" as inadequate', I told Neil as we reviewed the case. 'The affair might be less about desire and more about James finding someone who didn't need him to be perfect'.

'And Rebecca's question isn't really about trust', Neil added, following the thread. 'It's about whether she's enough'.

'Exactly. So when we work with them, we need to address the shame driving the affair, not just the betrayal of it'.

This kind of preparation means that when the couple arrives, we're not starting cold. We've already identified patterns, anticipated themes, considered which techniques might be most effective. We've discussed which of us should take the lead on different aspects, where our skills complement each other, what we each need to watch for.

Before Sam and Suzy's first session, we spent significant time discussing blended family dynamics and, specifically, the particular challenges when one co-parent is deliberately destructive. We reviewed the research on parental alienation, discussed our own experiences with similar cases, and made a crucial decision: we would not let Glenda's campaign dominate the narrative, even though that was clearly the presenting crisis.

'If we make it all about managing Glenda', I argued, 'we risk reinforcing the dynamic where she's the centre of their relationship. We need to help them reclaim their own story'.

'Agreed', Neil said. 'But they're so worn down by the constant siege that they might not even remember what their story is beyond crisis management'.

'Then we help them remember. But carefully. They're not ready to hear that they have agency until they feel less alone with the threat'.

This kind of strategic thinking happens before every session, shaping how we show up, what we listen for, when we intervene, and when we wait.

The Debrief: What We Learn from Each Couple

After every session – sometimes immediately after, sometimes later – Neil and I debrief. Not just 'how did that go?' but deep analysis of what we learned, what worked, what we missed, what we need to adjust for next time.

After John and Sarah's first session (where they arrived as polite strangers after years of parallel lives), Neil and I had a fascinating disagreement.

'I think Sarah's efficiency and organisation are defensive', Neil said. 'She's created structure to manage her anxiety about chaos'.

'I think Sarah's efficiency is actually her love language', I countered. 'I watched her face when she talked about planning their holiday. She was showing John love through taking care of logistics, and he's experienced it as controlling rather than caring'.

We debated this for probably thirty minutes, pulling apart our observations, testing our assumptions. Eventually we landed on: both are true. Sarah does use organisation to manage anxiety, and she also genuinely expresses care through service and planning. The problem isn't the behaviour itself but John's interpretation of it through his lens of feeling smothered.

This kind of post-session analysis makes us better. We challenge each other, we notice each other's blind spots, we refine our hypotheses, we plan our approach to the next session based on a fuller understanding than either of us could have achieved alone.

After Barry and Edith's final session, where the transformation was so dramatic, Neil and I sat in that therapy room for almost two hours, trying to understand what had actually created the change.

'Was it the Timeline Therapy?' Neil wondered. 'That session with Edith alone was clearly pivotal'.

'Yes, but not just the technique', I said. 'Remember that moment in session two when Barry showed up differently? When he stopped defending and just witnessed her pain? I think that created the psychological safety she needed for the trauma work to be effective. The technique was crucial, but the relational shift made it possible'.

'So it was both', Neil concluded. 'The right technique at the right time, but only because the relationship had shifted enough for her nervous system to feel safe releasing the hypervigilance'.

'Exactly. Which means with other couples carrying long-term betrayal trauma, we need to watch for that relational shift before we do the deeper trauma work, or it might not hold'.

This is how we grow as practitioners – by deeply analysing not just what happened, but why it happened, how it happened, what made this particular intervention work with this particular couple at this particular time. Every couple teaches us something we bring to the next session with someone else.

What I'm Still Learning: The Growing Edge

Eight years in, and there are still moments when I feel the old imposter syndrome creep in. Just last month, working with a couple struggling with intimacy after the birth of their first child, Neil mentioned a concept from sexology that I wasn't familiar with. For just a moment, I felt that familiar flutter: *Am I qualified enough? Do I know enough? Should I be here?*

But here's what eight years has taught me: the point isn't to know everything Neil knows. The point is to bring what I know that he doesn't.

When that same couple returned for their second session, the wife mentioned feeling 'trapped' between her identities as mother and sexual being. I recognised something Neil might not have, given the differences in our training. 'This sounds like what we call "role collision" in attachment theory', I said. 'The same person – your baby – evokes your caregiving system and your sexual system is inhibited by that. For many women, the solution isn't just about desire; it's about creating enough psychological separation between "mother mode" and "partner mode" that your brain can shift gears'.

Neil gave me that look – the one that says *I didn't see that angle, and I'm glad you did.*

That's the dance we do. Not competing for who knows more, but filling in each other's gaps, creating a fuller picture together than either could create alone.

My growing edge now isn't about learning more modalities, though I continue to train in new approaches. It's about trusting my instincts more quickly. There are still moments when I notice something – a micro-expression, a shift in energy, a pattern emerging – but hesitate to interrupt Neil's flow to name it. I'm learning that those intuitions are often correct, and that Neil wants me to interrupt, wants me to share what I'm seeing, even if it means temporarily shifting direction.

I'm also learning about what happens in longer-term relationships where one partner has betrayed the other, because I see it from an angle Neil sometimes doesn't. With Rebecca and James, with Barry and Edith, even with Sam's ex-wife Glenda's manipulation of Sam – I notice the women's experience of betrayal in particular ways. The vigilance, the hyper-awareness, the way trust isn't just broken but shattered into sharp pieces that keep cutting long after the initial wound. Neil can understand this intellectually, but I feel it viscerally. That felt sense informs how I sit with the pain, what I notice, when I intervene.

The Privilege of This Perspective

Sometimes, during particularly powerful moments in sessions – when Rebecca read her 'I Am' poem, when Sam and Suzy finally addressed their intimacy issues, when Edith described feeling 'freedom from the past's power', when John and Sarah hugged each other after years of distance – I look across at Neil, and we share a glance that holds everything.

We've just witnessed something sacred. We've held space for transformation. We've seen two people choose each other again, sometimes against overwhelming odds.

The view from the second chair isn't always easy. It requires constant vigilance, comfort with uncertainty, willingness to disagree, and the humility to be wrong. It demands that I show up fully in every session, bringing all my training, all my intuition, all my humanity.

But it offers something irreplaceable: the privilege of witnessing love in its full complexity – its wounds and its healing, its breakdowns and its breakthroughs, its ordinary struggles and its extraordinary courage.

The couples in this book trusted us with their most vulnerable truths. They showed up week after week, doing the hard work of looking at themselves and each other with honest eyes. They let us into their pain and, eventually, their healing.

From this second chair, I've watched them transform. Not because we had magic answers – we didn't. Not because therapy is easy – it isn't. But because they were willing to do something remarkable: they were willing to change.

And I remain profoundly grateful for every single one of them.

As I prepare for our next couple to arrive, I take a moment to centre myself, to remember what a gift this work is. Alone we can do so little; together – Neil and I, each couple we serve, the web of connection we're all part of – together we can do so much.

That's the view from the second chair. That's what you don't see when you read the stories in this book. But it's there in every session, every transformation, every moment of healing.

And it's the honour of my professional life.

Chapter 21

The Agony and the Ecstasy

There is a wand on the bookshelf in my therapy room. I purchased it years ago after hearing one too many clients say, ‘If only you had a magic wand’. When appropriate, I reach for it, press the button on its side that makes it sparkle and light up, and show them that, indeed, I do have one. It usually breaks the tension, brings a smile, perhaps even laughter.

But we all know it isn’t real. In my darkest moments, I sometimes wish it were. I wish I could wave it and instantly heal the pain I see before me, reconnect the disconnected, rebuild the trust that has been shattered like glass on concrete. But even if it were a genuine magic wand, bestowed upon me by some benevolent wizard or fairy godmother, I’m not convinced I would use it.

Because what I’ve learned in my years of sitting alongside Maria, bearing witness to the intimate struggles of couples, is that there is no shortcut to relationship healing. The agony must be felt before the ecstasy can be experienced. The lessons must be learned, not circumvented by magic.

DOI: 10.4324/9781003752776-21

This chapter is about those twin experiences, the agony and the ecstasy, that form the emotional landscape of relationship therapy. It's about what it feels like to sit in my chair, day after day, witnessing both the remarkable resilience of human connection and its devastating fragility.

The Moments of Ecstasy

I can always tell when a breakthrough has happened, even before a couple says a word. It's in how they enter the room for their follow-up session. Where previously they might have kept a careful distance, now they walk closer together. Where once they avoided eye contact, now they exchange small glances, private smiles. Their bodies often incline toward each other rather than away. Sometimes they're holding hands, a gesture that would have felt impossible just weeks before.

These physical signs are the visible manifestation of an invisible shift, a reconnection that has begun to heal the wounds that brought them to therapy. When I see these changes, I feel a surge of quiet joy. This, after all, is why I do this work.

I remember Alicia and Andrew, who came to therapy after fifteen years of marriage. They entered our first session like two foreign diplomats at a tense negotiation, maintaining formal politeness while radiating suspicion and hurt. By our third session, just one month into our work together, they arrived laughing together about something that had happened on the drive over. As they settled into their seats, Andrew automatically reached for Alicia's hand, and she squeezed his in return, a gesture so natural neither of them seemed conscious of it.

'Something's different', Maria observed with a smile.

Alicia nodded. 'We talked all night on Tuesday. Really talked, for the first time in years. It was like finding my best friend again'.

Andrew looked at her with wonder. 'I'd forgotten who we were before the kids, the mortgage, the promotions. I'd forgotten how much I just like being with her'.

These moments of reconnection aren't just heartwarming; they're profound in their implications. When a couple finds their way back to each other, the effects ripple outward, touching everyone in their orbit. Their children witness what loving repair looks like. Their friends see that relationships can be renewed. Their parents experience the relief of knowing their adult children are cared for.

The healing extends beyond the couple, creating what I think of as spirals of positivity that can influence generations. I often liken this to the Fibonacci sequence, that remarkable mathematical pattern found throughout nature – in the arrangement of leaves on a stem, the bracts of a pinecone, the curve of a shell. Each number in the sequence is the sum of the two preceding ones: 0, 1, 1, 2, 3, 5, 8, 13, 21, and so on, creating an exponential spiral of growth.

Relationship healing follows a similar pattern. What begins as a small shift between two people grows exponentially as it affects their immediate family, then friends, then community, then potentially future generations. The child who witnesses parents resolving conflict with respect and vulnerability carries that model into their own relationships, teaching it to their children in turn. The spiral expands, each generation building upon the healing of the last.

Sometimes the breakthroughs are quieter but no less significant. I recall Angie and Tim, both in their seventies, married for forty-eight years. They came to therapy not because of any dramatic crisis but because, as Angie put it, 'We've become excellent roommates and poor partners'. Their sessions involved a gentle rekindling of curiosity about each other, a slow rebuilding of intimacy that had been eroded by routine and assumption.

In our final session, Tim said something I've never forgotten: 'I thought I knew everything about her. We've shared a bed for nearly fifty years. But I'm discovering her all over again, and it's lovely'.

The look they exchanged then, full of tenderness and renewed interest, was the essence of what I consider ecstasy in this work, not the fireworks of passion but the warm glow of genuine connection.

These moments sustain me. They are the fuel that keeps me going through the more difficult aspects of this profession. They remind me that human beings have a remarkable capacity for growth, change, and deepening love, even after decades of disappointment or disconnection.

When I witness a couple move from defensive posturing to vulnerable honesty, from blame to understanding, from disconnection to renewed intimacy, I feel privileged to have played some small part in their journey. In these moments, I know with absolute certainty that this work matters, that relationships matter, that the quality of human connection is perhaps the single greatest determinant of happiness and well-being.

The ecstasy isn't just in the successful outcomes; it's in the courage I witness every day. It's watching someone risk sharing a painful truth they've hidden for years. It's seeing a partner truly listen, perhaps for the first time, to the emotions beneath their loved one's words. It's the moment when understanding dawns and someone says, 'I never saw it that way before'. These instances of bravery and growth are sacred, and I never take for granted my role as witness to them.

The Reality of Agony

Yet for all these moments of breakthrough and connection, there are also times of profound difficulty, what I can only describe as agony. Not every couple finds their way back to each other. Not every story has a happy ending. And sometimes, the therapy room becomes the space where this painful truth must be acknowledged.

There are sessions where I feel almost physically ill with the awareness that one partner is being dishonest, not just with their spouse but with themselves and with us. I recall a man who insisted throughout three sessions that his affair was over, that he was committed to rebuilding his marriage, while Maria and I both sensed his continued deception. We couldn't prove it, and direct confrontation would likely have only reinforced his defensive stance. The agony was in watching his wife cautiously opening herself to trust again, knowing that she was likely to be hurt once more.

As it happened, the truth emerged in our fourth session when his phone, which he'd forgotten to silence, pinged with a message from his affair partner that appeared on his screen. The devastation on his wife's face is something I will never forget.

There are couples who use therapy as a way to say they 'tried everything' before ending the relationship. They come not with any genuine hope or intention to repair what's broken, but to tick a box, to deflect future guilt or criticism. I can usually detect this agenda quite early, but helping the couple acknowledge it is another matter entirely. The agony here is in being used as an unwitting accomplice in what amounts to a performance of concern rather than its reality.

Perhaps most painful are the couples who genuinely want to reconnect but have waited too long to seek help. Their patterns of interaction have become so deeply entrenched, their wounds so profound, that the mountain between them seems insurmountable. They've lived parallel lives for so many years that the bridge back to each other feels impossible to build.

I remember Gloria and Daniel, who came to therapy after twenty-three years of marriage. They were unfailingly polite to each other, almost like strangers meeting at a dinner party. When I asked about their relationship history, it became clear that they had begun drifting apart after the birth of their first child and had never found their way back. Years of unspoken resentments, unexpressed needs, and unshared joys had created a chasm between them that seemed unbridgeable.

'I don't hate him', Gloria told me privately. 'I just don't feel anything anymore'.

Over the course of our six sessions spread across three months, it became clear that while Daniel desperately wanted to revitalise their marriage, Gloria had emotionally checked out years ago. She was going through the motions of therapy to ease her guilt about wanting to leave.

The agony in such cases is multilayered. There's the pain of watching someone realise that their hope for reconciliation isn't shared. There's the sadness of seeing a family about to undergo the seismic shift of separation. And there's my own sense of limitation, the knowledge that no amount of skill or experience on my part can manufacture desire or commitment where it no longer exists.

In these moments, the weight of what's at stake feels almost unbearable. I know that the outcomes of these sessions will affect not just the couple before me, but their children, their extended families, their friends, and potentially generations to come. The ripple effects of relationship breakdown can be just as profound as those of relationship healing, though in the opposite direction.

When Ending Is the Answer

Not all relationship endings represent failure, however. There are times when the most compassionate, healthy outcome is for a couple to part ways. In such cases, therapy becomes not about saving the relationship but about helping it end with minimal damage, maximal learning, and preserved dignity.

The agony and the ecstasy can sometimes coexist in these scenarios. There is real pain in witnessing the death of a relationship, especially a long-term one with shared history, children, and interconnected lives. Yet there can also be a kind of liberation, a sense of authenticity finally achieved, when a couple honestly acknowledges that their relationship has run its course.

Fiona and Michael came to us after seventeen years of marriage, presenting with what they called 'communication problems'. As we worked together, it became apparent that they had fundamentally different values, desires, and visions for the future. They had married young and grown in divergent directions. Their 'communication problems' weren't about how they talked to each other but about the fact that they were essentially speaking different languages altogether.

After several months of therapy, they made the brave decision to separate. Our final sessions focused not on reconnection but on how to disentangle their lives with mutual respect and minimal harm to their teenage children. They drafted new boundaries, discussed co-parenting strategies, and planned how to tell friends and family.

Crucially, we also devoted significant time to understanding what had gone wrong in their relationship and the roles they each had played in its dissolution. This wasn't about assigning blame but about learning. Fiona recognised how her tendency to avoid conflict had prevented necessary conversations from happening years earlier. Michael acknowledged how his workaholic tendencies had created emotional distance that became impossible to bridge.

This self-reflection is essential. Without it, people tend to carry their unexamined patterns into future relationships, often recreating the same problems with different partners. They cling to comfortable narratives that place all blame on the other person, preventing their own growth and healing. By understanding their part in what went wrong, Fiona and Michael were giving themselves the gift of future relationships unencumbered by old, destructive patterns.

At our last session, Fiona said something that has stayed with me: 'I was so afraid that ending our marriage meant we had failed. Now I see that the real failure would have been continuing to live a half-life together when we could each be whole apart'.

This perspective represents a kind of wisdom that isn't often celebrated in our culture, which tends to view any relationship ending as a failure. But I've come to see that sometimes, the most loving choice two people can make is to release each other.

In these cases, the work becomes about helping couples have what I call a 'good ending'. This means an ending where both people feel heard and validated, where they can acknowledge what was valuable in their time together, where they can take responsibility for their contributions to the relationship's breakdown without shame or blame, and where they can create a vision for their separate futures that honours their shared past.

A good ending is not painless, but it minimises unnecessary suffering. It allows couples to move forward without the toxic residue of bitterness and recrimination.

And if children are involved, it gives them a model of how adults can disagree, even on fundamental matters, while still treating each other with dignity and respect.

Facilitating these good endings involves its own kind of agony and ecstasy, the pain of witnessing the death of a dream alongside the relief of seeing people liberated from patterns that have kept them small or suffering.

The Complexity of Being the Therapist

Sitting in the therapist's chair through these extremes of human experience is both a privilege and a burden. The privilege lies in being trusted with people's most intimate struggles, in being allowed to witness their courage, vulnerability, and growth. The burden is in carrying the weight of what's at stake, in knowing that my interventions, my insights, my very presence in the room can influence the trajectory of people's lives in profound ways.

There are nights when I lie awake replaying moments from sessions, wondering if I said the right thing, pushed too hard or not hard enough, missed a crucial cue. There are cases that haunt me, where despite my best efforts, I couldn't help a couple find their way through to healing. There are faces I remember years later, voices that echo in my mind during quiet moments.

In the realm of relationship therapy, particularly within our Duo Coaching approach, there are few phrases that carry as much weight as 'you are our last chance'. When couples utter these words, they're not merely scheduling an appointment – they're placing their most intimate hopes and deepest vulnerabilities in your hands. This declaration creates a complex emotional landscape for Maria and me: a profound responsibility that can feel simultaneously flattering and terrifying. Each couple arrives with their unique history, their accumulated hurts, and their dwindling reserves of hope, all carefully packaged in this simple phrase. The burden lies in knowing that failure might mean the end of something that once brought two people immeasurable joy, whilst success could rescue decades of shared history from dissolution. Yet within this pressure lives an exhilarating challenge – the opportunity to guide people back to each other when they've lost their way, to help them rediscover connection when all familiar paths seem overgrown. The privilege of standing at this critical juncture in people's lives demands not just technical skill but profound humility, recognising that we are neither saviours nor miracle workers, but simply guides offering tools, perspective, and a safe harbour for the difficult work of relationship repair.

The emotional labour of this work is substantial. To be effective, I must be fully present, fully engaged, bringing my whole self to each session. I must allow myself to feel enough of my clients' pain to understand it without becoming overwhelmed by it. I must maintain hope even when the situation seems hopeless, yet I must also be honest about the realities I see.

Maria's presence beside me is invaluable in this complex emotional terrain. We support each other, offer different perspectives, and share the weight of responsibility. Having a co-therapist means never being alone with the difficult feelings this work can evoke, never being the sole witness to either the agony or the ecstasy of the couples we serve.

Together, we've learned to celebrate the victories, however small, and to accept the limitations of what we can accomplish. We've learned that our job isn't to save relationships but to create a space where healing and growth become possible, where honest conversations can happen, where new understandings can emerge. What couples do with that space is ultimately up to them.

The Magic of Doing the Work

I keep that pretend magic wand on my shelf as a reminder that real change doesn't come from shortcuts or external solutions. It comes from the difficult, messy, often painful work of honest self-examination, vulnerable communication, and committed practice of new ways of being together.

If I could wave a wand and instantly fix a couple's problems, I would be robbing them of the growth that comes from working through those problems themselves. I would be depriving them of the profound intimacy that can develop when two people struggle together toward a shared goal. I would be taking away the very experiences that can transform a troubled relationship into a resilient one.

The real magic happens not when problems disappear but when couples discover their capacity to face those problems together. It happens when they learn to listen beneath the words to the emotions driving them. It happens when they develop compassion for each other's weaknesses and appreciation for each other's strengths. It happens when they build new patterns of interaction that allow both partners to feel seen, heard, and valued.

This kind of magic can't be conjured instantly. It unfolds gradually, often painfully, over our six sessions spread across a few months of committed effort. It requires courage, patience, and the willingness to sit with discomfort rather than running from it. It demands that couples confront the gap between the relationship they have and the one they want, and then do the daily work of bridging that gap.

As a therapist, my role is not to perform magic but to guide couples through this challenging terrain. I can offer tools, insights, and a safe space for vulnerable conversations. I can help them see patterns they're too close to notice. I can teach them new ways of listening and communicating. But I cannot do the work for them. I cannot want healing for them more than they want it for themselves.

The agony and the ecstasy of my profession lies in this fundamental truth: I can guide, but I cannot control. I can witness, but I cannot decide. I can hope, but I cannot guarantee. Each couple must find their own way, make their own choices, create their own future together or apart.

A Privilege beyond Measure

Despite the emotional complexity of this work, despite the nights I lie awake wondering about a particular couple, despite the weight of responsibility I feel, I consider my role a privilege beyond measure.

To be invited into the most intimate struggles of people's lives, to be trusted with their hopes, fears, and deepest vulnerabilities, to be allowed to witness both their pain and their healing, is an honour I never take for granted. It is sacred work, handling the fragile, precious material of human hearts and human bonds.

In the therapy room, I am witness to the full spectrum of human experience, from the deepest betrayals to the most profound reconciliations, from bitter endings to beautiful new beginnings. I see people at their worst and at their best, in their moments of greatest weakness and their displays of remarkable strength.

The agony and the ecstasy of relationship therapy are, I've come to believe, simply the agony and ecstasy of human connection itself, magnified and concentrated in the crucible of the therapeutic process. In witnessing these extremes, in helping couples navigate between them, I touch something essential about what it means to be human, to love, to hurt, to heal, to grow.

And so, I continue this work, day after day, couple after couple, holding space for both the pain and the possibility, the despair and the hope, the endings and the beginnings. I keep my pretend magic wand on the shelf, a reminder that real healing comes not from external magic but from the courageous inner work that couples do when they commit to their own growth and connection.

Chapter 22

Rebecca and James – The Power of Second Chances

When I first met Rebecca and James, they sat on opposite ends of my sofa, the invisible gulf between them carved by his affair. Rebecca carried her pain like armour, while James bore the weight of her choices with quiet desperation. Through five sessions of therapy, they had begun the painstaking work of rebuilding what betrayal had shattered – or so I thought.

The phone call came just a day before our scheduled final session with Rebecca and James. Rebecca's distressed voice immediately told me our recent progress was in jeopardy.

What should have been a routine visit to their country cottage had turned into an archaeological dig of betrayal. In every drawer, every cupboard, tucked away in the most unexpected places, she had found evidence of Sarah's presence; personal items, love notes, and intimate photographs that spoke of a deeper connection than she had been led to believe.

'We'd just returned from four wonderful days in Portugal', Rebecca explained, her voice cracking. 'I was going to tell you how wonderfully we were connecting, and then ...'

She paused, fighting for composure. 'I found a journal hidden behind the bookshelf. It contained entries dating back three years. Three years! James told me their affair only began last summer'.

During our hour-long phone conversation, I worked to help Rebecca process this discovery. Through years of experience, I've observed what we call the 'betrayal response spectrum'. Betrayed partners typically fall somewhere between two extremes: those who seek to punish ('I hate you; I will make you suffer as I am suffering') and those who take a more pragmatic approach ('I acknowledge I may have co-created this situation, I love you and want to recover'). Despite her immediate pain, Rebecca's response showed remarkable potential for the latter, more healing approach.

The discovery had shaken her to her core. 'I want to leave him', she declared. 'Everything he told me was a lie'.

As we talked, I gently explored different possibilities. Could these items have been deliberately arranged by Sarah as an act of revenge? Was this a calculated attempt to prove her former importance in James's life? Or perhaps it was simply

DOI: 10.4324/9781003752776-22

vindictiveness – if she couldn't have James, she would ensure no one else could either. I focused on helping Rebecca look beyond the immediate pain. Yes, James had lied, but did this new information necessarily change their potential future? Given James's natural aversion to causing pain, could this have been his misguided attempt to deliver difficult truths in smaller, more manageable doses?

This crisis highlighted why we maintain our 24/7 availability policy for clients. The journey from crisis to healing rarely follows a straight line, and being available during these crucial moments can make the difference between breakdown and breakthrough.

The next day, as the couple entered our therapy room, I was grateful for Maria's presence beside me. Her calm energy helped balance the space, and I've learned to value how her perspective often catches nuances I might miss in these delicate situations. Instead of the tension we had expected, there was a palpable positive energy between Rebecca and James. Their body language, the way they sat together, their shared glances – all spoke of connection rather than division.

'We had a wonderful time in Portugal', Rebecca shared, her eyes bright despite the recent discovery. 'We connected in ways we haven't for years – really connected. The intimacy issues we'd discussed. Resolved. But it wasn't just the physical connection; it was the emotional openness, the lack of pressure, the feeling of being close again'.

Throughout the session, Maria's gentle presence seemed to create a safe container for both Rebecca and James to express themselves fully. James, though clearly ashamed about the recent revelations, showed significant growth in his understanding of the situation. 'I always thought Sarah was straightforward', he said quietly. 'But I'm beginning to see the manipulation in her actions. There needs to be a clear ending – for all our sakes'.

When James mentioned feeling he should spend years making amends for his actions, I intervened. 'Given the progress you've made in just a few weeks, years of penance sounds excessive. Your energy would be better spent creating your new future together'.

Their shared vision for the future revealed a beautiful alignment of dreams – traveling to places they'd always wanted to see, creating new memories together, and rediscovering shared passions they'd neglected. The practical matters still needed attention: what to do with the cottage, how to clear it of painful associations, and how to balance work and personal time to make their dreams possible.

As part of their homework, I assigned them the task of studying my Toxic Triangle – a framework I developed for ending affairs and refocusing energy on the primary relationship. I also asked them to work together on finally clearing Sarah's presence from their lives, both physically and emotionally.

What impressed me most was Rebecca's remarkable resilience. She had transformed what could have been a relationship-ending crisis into an opportunity for deeper honesty and connection. James had finally shared the complete truth, and as Rebecca noted, 'Now that he's done that, we can move forward. I believe him now'.

As they left our office that day, Maria and I exchanged knowing looks. We had witnessed something rare: a couple who had turned a potential breaking point into a breakthrough. 'They're choosing love over fear', Maria observed softly, 'and that makes all the difference'. Sometimes, I reflected, it's not just the therapeutic process but the energy in the room that helps facilitate healing. Maria's intuitive understanding had once again helped create the safe space needed for true honesty to emerge.

When Rebecca and James returned for their final session two weeks later, the transformation was remarkable. They arrived together, their movements synchronised in a way that spoke of renewed connection. They settled onto the three-seater couch with an ease that contrasted sharply with the rigid distance of their first meeting.

'We've been working through the exercises you suggested', James began, his voice carrying a confidence I hadn't heard before. 'The "I Am" poems were particularly powerful'.

Rebecca nodded, her eyes bright with emotion. 'May I read mine?' she asked, unfolding a carefully prepared page.

I am the girl who climbed mountains to prove her worth
I am the child who learned that vulnerability was weakness
I am the woman who built walls around her heart for protection
I am the wife who mistook independence for strength
I am the survivor who fought illness alone, afraid to burden others
I am the executive whose success couldn't fill the emptiness inside
I am now learning that courage isn't always about endurance
I am discovering that trust can be rebuilt, stone by careful stone
I am finding my voice after years of silence
I am seeing my partner with new eyes, beyond his mistake
I am beginning to forgive him, and perhaps more importantly, myself
I am creating space for imperfection and growth
I am still healing, still hoping, still here.

The room fell silent as her words resonated. James reached for her hand, a gesture both protective and reverent.

'Your turn', she said softly to him.

James cleared his throat and began:

I am the boy who feared being discovered as inadequate
I am the student who worked twice as hard to hide his struggles
I am the man who built his identity on perceived competence
I am the husband who couldn't admit his fears or failures
I am the academic whose papers couldn't express his inner turmoil
I am the betrayer who sought validation in the wrong places
I am now understanding the damage caused by my silence

I am learning that vulnerability creates connection, not rejection
I am finding courage to be seen fully, flaws and all
I am grateful for the chance to rebuild what almost was lost
I am beginning to trust my own voice, to speak my truth
I am discovering that perfection matters less than presence
I am still apologetic, still growing, still yours if you'll have me.

The raw honesty of their words filled the room. In just six sessions, they had traversed territory that many couples never manage to explore in decades together.

'What will you carry forward from our time together?' I asked as our final session drew to a close.

Rebecca considered the question thoughtfully. 'The understanding that silence doesn't protect – it isolates', she said. 'For years, we both kept our fears and needs locked away, thinking we were sparing each other. But all we did was create distance'.

'And I've learned that true intimacy requires truthfulness', James added. 'Not just about the big things, but about our daily struggles, our uncertainties, our dreams. I've spent a lifetime hiding parts of myself, and it nearly cost me everything that matters'.

As they prepared to leave for the last time, I observed how differently they moved together – a natural synchronicity that had replaced their former careful distance. They paused at the door, turning back toward us.

'Thank you', Rebecca said simply, the words carrying the weight of genuine gratitude.

'For helping us find each other again', James completed her thought.

Maria and I watched through the window as they walked to their car, her head briefly resting against his shoulder, his arm protectively around her waist. Their future wasn't guaranteed – no relationship ever is – but they had developed tools and awareness that made continued growth possible.

In the quiet of our practice room, with the energy of their presence still lingering, I reflected on the privilege of witnessing such transformations. The affair that had brought them to the brink of separation had become, paradoxically, the catalyst for deeper connection. The silence that had slowly eroded their bond had finally been broken, allowing new growth to emerge from what once seemed irreparably damaged.

Chapter 23

Growth

Watching Rebecca and James in that session, I saw two people caught in the painful space between who they had been and who they needed to become. James's affair hadn't happened in a vacuum – it emerged from years of him growing and changing while Rebecca remained fixed in patterns that no longer served them.

DOI: 10.4324/9781003752776-23

Their crisis illuminated Growth – the fifth element of the Relationship Paradigm. Relationships cannot survive on autopilot. Both partners must continue evolving as individuals, and the relationship itself must adapt to accommodate that evolution. Without growth, relationships calcify; with it, they can transform even the deepest wounds into wisdom.

'We've grown apart'. This phrase echoes through our therapy room with remarkable frequency, offered as both diagnosis and resignation by couples contemplating the end of their relationships. It's presented as an unfortunate but inevitable outcome, as if relationships naturally diverge without constant correction, like ships on slightly different headings eventually finding themselves in entirely separate oceans.

Yet my experience suggests a different truth: relationships don't simply grow apart passively. Rather, they fail to intentionally grow together. Within the Relationship Paradigm, Growth represents the understanding that both individuals and their relationship must evolve over time – not away from each other, but in coordination with each other. This evolution isn't accidental but deliberate, requiring awareness, communication, and mutual support.

The Dimensions of Growth

Growth in relationships manifests across several dimensions:

Individual development: Each partner's personal evolution – intellectually, emotionally, professionally, and spiritually – supported by the relationship rather than constrained by it.

Relationship development: The partnership itself maturing over time, developing more sophisticated ways of communicating, resolving conflict, and creating intimacy.

Mutual expansion: Partners introducing each other to new perspectives, experiences, and possibilities, expanding each other's worlds rather than contracting them.

Shared purpose: The couple's evolving vision of what they're building together, their 'third entity' beyond individual goals.

Adaptive capacity: The relationship's ability to transform in response to changing circumstances, from external challenges like career changes or health crises to internal shifts in individual needs and desires.

When couples maintain growth across these dimensions, their relationship remains vibrant and relevant as life changes around and within them. When growth stagnates, the relationship risks becoming a constraining force rather than a catalysing one, leading to resentment, restlessness, and eventually, that sense of having 'grown apart'.

Charlotte and Ben: When One Partner Outgrows the Other

Charlotte and Ben arrived at their first Duo Coaching session with a tension that filled the room before they'd spoken a word. Married for seventeen years with two teenagers, they sat at opposite ends of our sofa, Charlotte perched forward with nervous energy, Ben slumped back with apparent resignation.

'I feel like I'm suffocating', Charlotte began bluntly. 'The life we've built together made sense for years, but now it feels like a cage rather than a home'.

Ben stared at the floor. 'Charlotte's changed. She used to be happy with our life. Now suddenly nothing's good enough'.

As we explored their history, a clearer picture emerged. For most of their marriage, they'd followed a traditional arrangement: Ben focused on his accounting career while Charlotte managed their home and raised their children. This arrangement had worked well while the children were young and Charlotte found fulfilment in her maternal role.

But three years earlier, with both children in secondary school, Charlotte had returned to university to complete the degree she'd abandoned when she became pregnant with their first child. This step back into education had catalysed profound changes in her. She'd discovered passions for environmental science and community activism. She'd developed new friendships with politically engaged classmates. She'd begun questioning aspects of their suburban lifestyle that had previously gone unexamined.

'I feel like I've woken up from a long sleep', Charlotte explained. 'I can see possibilities and problems I was blind to before. But when I try to talk to Ben about any of it, he acts like I've been infected with some strange virus that needs to be cured'.

Ben's perspective revealed his sense of betrayal and abandonment. 'We had an agreement about our life. I've kept my end of the bargain – providing for the family, being faithful, coaching the kids' football teams. Now Charlotte's suddenly decided that's not enough. She's becoming someone I don't recognise, someone who seems embarrassed by the life we've built'.

This pattern – one partner experiencing significant personal growth while the other remains static – is one Maria and I encounter frequently. It often coincides with major life transitions: children leaving home, career changes, health crises, or educational opportunities. One partner evolves rapidly in response to new circumstances while the other clings to established patterns, creating an expanding gap in worldviews, interests, and aspirations.

'Growth in a relationship isn't necessarily synchronised', Maria observed in our second session. 'The challenge is how to accommodate individual evolution without sacrificing the connection between you'.

This framing helped shift both partners' perspective. Rather than seeing Charlotte's development as a rejection of their shared life or Ben's resistance as simple stubbornness, they began to recognise the natural tension between stability and change that exists in all relationships.

In our third session, we introduced an exercise we call Growth Mapping. We asked Charlotte and Ben to each create three lists: areas where they'd experienced significant personal change in recent years, aspects of themselves that had remained consistent, and directions they anticipated evolving in the future. They then shared these maps with each other, looking for points of convergence, divergence, and potential complementarity.

The exercise revealed important insights. While Charlotte had indeed changed dramatically in her intellectual interests and social awareness, her core values around family loyalty and personal integrity remained steadfast. And while Ben presented himself as unchanging, he'd actually evolved considerably in his approach to fathering teenagers versus young children, developing greater flexibility and emotional openness than he recognised in himself.

'What I'm hearing', I reflected, 'is that you're both evolving, just in different domains and at different rates. The question isn't whether change should happen but how you navigate it together'.

This recognition led to a crucial conversation about support versus constraint in their relationship. Ben acknowledged that his resistance stemmed partly from fear – fear of being left behind as Charlotte developed new interests and relationships, fear of being judged for his more traditional perspectives, fear that her growth would inevitably lead her away from him.

'I feel like I'm losing you', he admitted quietly. 'Like you're becoming too good for what we've built together'.

Charlotte's eyes softened as she heard the vulnerability beneath his resistance. 'I'm not becoming better than our life – I'm becoming more myself. I don't want to leave what we've built; I want to build more. But I need you to make space for these new parts of me instead of trying to stuff them back into the box I used to fit in'.

Over our remaining sessions, Charlotte and Ben developed a new framework for supporting each other's growth while maintaining their connection. Ben began joining Charlotte at occasional campus events, not pretending interest he didn't feel but approaching her new world with curiosity rather than defensiveness. Charlotte became more sensitive to acknowledging the value of the stable foundation Ben had helped create, which had made her educational reinvention possible.

Most importantly, they established regular 'growth conversations' – scheduled times to share their evolving thoughts, interests, and questions without judgement or immediate problem-solving. These conversations created space for Charlotte's development while including Ben in the journey rather than leaving him behind.

By our final session, the physical distance between them on our sofa had noticeably decreased. They still faced significant challenges in reconciling their different paces and directions of growth, but they had replaced antagonism with collaboration, viewing Charlotte's evolution as a potential enrichment of their shared life rather than a threat to it.

'I've realised I don't need Ben to change in all the same ways I am', Charlotte reflected. 'I just need him to be interested in my changes and to consider new possibilities alongside me sometimes'.

Ben nodded. 'And I've recognised that Charlotte's growth doesn't diminish what we've built together. It actually has the potential to make our next chapter even more interesting than the last one – if I can be brave enough to turn the page with her'.

Jules and David: When the Relationship Outgrows Its Original Form

While Charlotte and Ben were navigating one partner's significant personal growth, Jules and David presented a different growth challenge. Their individual development remained relatively synchronised, but the relationship itself had reached a developmental impasse.

Together for eleven years since university, Jules and David had built their relationship around shared passions for travel, outdoor adventure, and their careers in tech. They'd intentionally chosen not to have children, valuing their freedom and flexibility. Their partnership had thrived in this context, with frequent relocations for career opportunities and extended backpacking trips during career breaks.

But at thirty-six, they found themselves unexpectedly questioning the foundations of their relationship. A serious rock-climbing accident had left David temporarily disabled and facing a lengthy rehabilitation. This enforced period of stillness had triggered soul-searching for both of them.

'We've built our relationship around constant motion and achievement', Jules explained in their first session. 'Now that we've had to slow down, I'm wondering what's actually at the core of our connection. Who are we to each other when we're not summiting mountains or launching products?'

David nodded. 'The accident made me realise how fleeting all this could be. I keep asking myself: is this enough? Are we building something meaningful together, or just collecting experiences?'

As Maria and I explored their history, we recognised a pattern common among high-achieving couples. Jules and David had created a relationship perfectly designed for a particular life phase – one centred on exploration, career establishment, and personal freedom. That design had served them well for a decade. But as they entered their mid-thirties and faced questions of mortality and meaning, the relationship structure itself needed to evolve to accommodate new developmental needs.

'Relationships, like people, go through developmental stages', Maria explained in our second session. 'A structure that works beautifully in one stage may become constraining in the next. The question isn't whether your original relationship design was wrong, but whether it can evolve to meet your emerging needs'.

This framing resonated with both men, who were accustomed to thinking in terms of product development in their professional lives. They began to approach their relationship challenges not as failures but as design problems: how could they evolve their partnership to incorporate emerging values around rootedness, contribution, and legacy without abandoning the adventure and freedom they still cherished?

In our third session, we introduced an exercise called Values Evolution Mapping. Jules and David each identified values that had guided their relationship in its first decade, values that were emerging as important now, and values they anticipated becoming more central in the future. They then explored how their relationship structure might need to change to honour both enduring and emerging values.

The exercise revealed significant alignment in their evolving priorities. Both were feeling drawn toward greater community involvement, more sustained creative projects, and a sense of contributing to something larger than themselves. Neither wanted children, but both were feeling called to mentorship roles with younger colleagues and extended family members.

'We've been so focused on experiencing the world', David reflected, 'that we haven't given much thought to what we might contribute to it'.

This insight led to a profound shift in how they conceptualised their relationship's next phase. Rather than seeing David's accident as a temporary interruption to their established pattern, they began viewing it as a catalyst for necessary evolution. They started exploring ways to maintain the adventure and mobility they valued while incorporating new dimensions of meaning and contribution.

By our fifth session, they had drafted what they called their 'Relationship 2.0 Blueprint' – a vision for this next developmental stage. It included establishing a more permanent home base while preserving extended periods for travel. It involved each committing to long-term creative or community projects that would create legacy beyond experiences. It incorporated regular 'contribution sabbaticals' where they would offer their professional skills to organisations aligned with their values.

'What's powerful about this blueprint', I observed, 'is that it doesn't reject what made your first decade together special. It builds upon that foundation to create something more expansive – like renovating and adding to a beloved home rather than abandoning it for a completely different one'.

Jules smiled at the metaphor. 'That's exactly it. We're not becoming entirely different people or creating an unrecognisable relationship. We're growing into a more mature version of us'.

Their case illustrates how relationships themselves have developmental trajectories. Just as individuals must navigate various life stages, partnerships must evolve through their own developmental phases, from the initial merging and establishment phase through various transitions as both partners and external circumstances change. Relationships that cannot adapt their structure and focus to accommodate these natural developmental shifts often stagnate or fracture.

The Neuroscience of Growth

The importance of growth in relationships isn't just psychological but neurological. Research in neuroscience has demonstrated that novelty, learning, and moderate challenge are essential for maintaining neuroplasticity – the brain's ability to form new neural connections and pathways. When we stop learning and growing, our neural networks become more rigid and less adaptable. This neurological reality has profound implications for relationships. Partnerships that prioritise growth and new experiences literally help keep partners' brains younger and more adaptive. Conversely, relationships that fall into rigid routines and avoid challenges may contribute to neural stagnation, making both partners less able to adapt to changing circumstances and potentially accelerating cognitive ageing.

Maria and I often share this science with couples because it helps them understand that growth isn't just a psychological preference but a biological necessity. Our brains are designed to learn, adapt, and evolve throughout our lives. When relationships support this natural process, they align with our neurological needs. When they constrain it, they work against our brain's inherent drive for development.

The Growth Toolkit

Through years of working with couples, we've developed The Growth Toolkit – practical approaches that help nurture this essential element of relationship:

The Growth Interview: A structured conversation where partners periodically interview each other about their evolving thoughts, interests, dreams, and questions, approaching each other with the curiosity they might bring to a fascinating new acquaintance.

Developmental Stocktaking: Regular reflection on how both individuals and the relationship itself have evolved over specific time periods, celebrating growth already experienced while identifying areas where development may have stalled.

The Learning Lab: Intentionally trying new activities, reading materials outside their usual interests, or exploring unfamiliar perspectives together, creating shared growth experiences.

Growth Visioning: Periodically creating explicit pictures of desired future development – individually and as a couple – then identifying steps toward those visions.

Growth Storytelling: Crafting and sharing narratives about how each partner has helped the other develop and how the relationship itself has matured over time.

The 70/30 Principle: Maintaining roughly 70% shared activities and interests while devoting 30% to individual pursuits that broaden each partner's horizons and bring new energy into the relationship.

These tools help couples intentionally nurture growth rather than allowing development to happen haphazardly or not at all. They create structures that support evolution while maintaining connection, preventing the 'growing apart' phenomenon that so many couples experience as inevitable.

The Bridge to Other Elements

Like all elements of the Relationship Paradigm, Growth interconnects with the others in dynamic ways. Growth requires Trust that exploration won't threaten the relationship's foundation. It demands Communication about evolving needs and desires. It demonstrates Commitment to the relationship's continued development. It creates opportunities for new forms of Connection as partners evolve. It introduces novelty that contributes to Fun and play.

When couples like Charlotte and Ben or Jules and David intentionally nurture growth in their relationships, the benefits often cascade into these other areas. Problems that once seemed intractable become more manageable when approached from a development perspective. Static patterns that created recurring conflicts can be transformed through intentional evolution.

Perhaps most importantly, growth keeps relationships relevant through life's inevitable changes. Rather than becoming relics of an earlier life phase – preserved but increasingly disconnected from current reality – relationships that prioritise development remain vital resources for navigating life's journey.

As I witness couples rediscover their capacity for mutual evolution in our therapy room, I'm reminded that relationships aren't static achievements to be attained once and preserved unchanged. They are living systems that must grow and adapt to remain viable. Just as a tree must continuously extend new branches and deepen its roots to thrive, relationships must continuously evolve to remain sources of nourishment rather than constraint.

In the end, the opposite of growing apart isn't remaining the same – it's growing together. Not in identical directions or at identical rates, but in awareness of each other's evolution, in support of each other's development, and in continuous adaptation of the relationship itself to accommodate who you both are becoming.

Chapter 24

Stuart and Clare – Finding Grace in Goodbye

Stuart and Clare had arrived months earlier carrying the accumulated weight of cultural differences, a blended family resistant to their union, and years of drifting apart while maintaining the appearance of connection. As a high-powered businessman and a devoted mother protecting her children, they had built separate kingdoms that happened to share a border. Now, as their therapy journey continued, the question remained: could those kingdoms ever truly merge, or was it time to acknowledge the border as a permanent boundary?

In their third session, the complexities of their blended family came into sharper focus. Clare arrived visibly distressed, explaining that her oldest daughter had confronted her after learning about the therapy sessions.

'She told me I was wasting my time', Clare shared, her voice tight with emotion. 'That Stuart would never change, and I was a fool for trying again after all these years'.

Stuart's reaction was telling – a flash of anger quickly subdued, his large hands gripping his knees as he worked to contain his response. 'They've never given me a chance', he said finally. 'From day one, I was cast as the villain in their story'.

Maria gently guided the conversation toward the roots of this family dynamic. 'Tell us about the early days of blending your families', she suggested.

What emerged was a portrait of good intentions derailed by cultural differences, competing expectations, and the ghost of Clare's ex-husband, who had remained actively involved with his children while consistently undermining Stuart's position. Stuart had entered the marriage believing his financial provision would naturally translate into respect and authority. Clare's children, however, already had a father figure and viewed Stuart as an unwelcome intruder.

'I tried to be firm but fair', Stuart explained, his South African directness coming through. 'In my family, you said what you meant, you set boundaries, you expected respect'.

'But to my children, it felt like harshness', Clare countered. 'In our French culture, especially among my family, there was more softness, more discussion, less dictating'.

These fundamental differences in communication style had created a chasm not just between Stuart and his stepchildren but between the couple themselves. Each

DOI: 10.4324/9781003752776-24

interaction became laden with misunderstandings, each misunderstanding reinforcing negative perceptions until they calcified into seemingly immutable truths.

The reality of their situation remained stubbornly present. When we discussed how to navigate the resistance from Clare's children, the fundamental differences in their perspectives became apparent once again.

'They're adults now', Stuart argued. 'They need to respect our marriage, our relationship'.

'They're still my children', Clare countered, her loyalty evident. 'Their feelings matter to me. I can't simply dismiss their concerns'.

The session ended with a tentative agreement to try some communication exercises at home, but as Maria and I debriefed afterward, we shared concerns about whether real change was possible within the existing family dynamics.

'The children have become a proxy for all their unresolved issues', Maria observed. 'And Clare's identity as a mother seems to outweigh her identity as a wife'.

I nodded, thinking of the pebble constellation they had created. 'And Stuart's desire to "reset" may not acknowledge how much repair needs to happen before real connection is possible'.

Sometimes, I've learned, the greatest service we can offer couples isn't helping them stay together at all costs but creating a space where honest truths can finally be spoken. For Stuart and Clare, that truth was beginning to take shape, though neither seemed quite ready to name it yet.

Their fifth session began differently. They arrived separately – Clare first, then Stuart fifteen minutes later. The physical distance between them on the couch seemed greater, yet paradoxically, there was less tension in the air. Something had shifted.

'We've had a long conversation', Clare began, her voice steadier than I'd heard before. 'After our last session, when we tried those communication exercises ...'

'We kept hitting the same wall', Stuart completed her thought, a new gentleness in his tone. 'Every time we seemed to make progress, something would happen with one of the kids'.

Clare nodded. 'My daughter Pam found the workbook you gave us. She was ... upset. Said I was betraying them by trying to make things work with Stuart'.

'And your response?' Maria asked carefully.

'I defended our right to try', Clare said, then paused. 'But later that night, I found myself wondering why I always feel torn in two. Why, after all these years, am I still caught between being a mother and being a wife?'

Stuart's expression was surprisingly tender. 'And I realised I've been asking her to choose. Not explicitly, but in the way I respond to her children, in my expectations'.

What unfolded over the next two hours was one of the most profound conversations I've witnessed in my practice: a couple gradually, respectfully, coming to terms with the reality that their paths might need to diverge. Not in anger or betrayal, but with a growing understanding that some divisions cannot be bridged without requiring sacrifices that would ultimately hollow out their individual lives.

'The truth is', Stuart said, turning to face Clare directly, 'I will never be accepted by your older children. After thirty years, that's not likely to change. And your relationship with them is too important to damage further'.

Clare's eyes filled with tears. 'And the truth is, I don't know if I can ever feel truly safe with you, Stuart. Not because you're a bad person, but because our fundamental needs and communication styles are so different. I need gentleness and emotional openness; you need directness and practical solutions'.

We moved to the pebble constellation exercise again, asking them to represent their current reality. The arrangement they created was striking – Stuart placed his stone and Clare's at a respectful distance from each other, with a small, smooth stone between them.

'What does this middle stone represent?' I asked.

'Mutual care', Stuart answered quietly. 'I still care deeply about Clare's well-being. That hasn't changed, even if our marriage needs to'.

Clare nodded, adding, 'And respect. I respect Stuart's journey, his willingness to look at himself, to try to change. I just don't think either of us should have to change our essence to make this work'.

This is a moment I've witnessed before – when a couple comes to therapy ostensibly to save their relationship but discovers instead a path toward mindful separation. It's not a failure of the therapeutic process but often its deepest success; creating space for truths that have been suppressed for years, sometimes decades.

'What would a respectful separation look like for you?' Maria asked, opening the door to this possibility.

Their responses revealed how much healing had already begun. Stuart spoke of wanting Clare to have financial security, to keep the family home where her children and grandchildren gathered. Clare expressed concern for Stuart's well-being, his need for connection and community as he aged.

We spent the remainder of the session outlining a framework for separation that honoured their shared history while acknowledging the reality of their situation. This wasn't an impulsive decision but the culmination of years of struggle, the recognition that some differences cannot be reconciled without causing deeper damage.

When they returned for our sixth session three weeks later, the transformation in both of them was remarkable. Stuart arrived wearing a crisp button-down shirt rather than his usual work clothes, his dusty boots replaced by polished loafers. Clare wore colours I hadn't seen her in before: vibrant blues rather than the muted tones that had seemed to help her fade into the background.

'We've told the children', Stuart began, a new steadiness in his voice. 'All of them, together. It was ... difficult but necessary'.

'How did they respond?' I asked.

'My older ones were relieved', Clare admitted. 'They said they'd been worried about me for years. Our younger two were upset at first, but when they saw that there wasn't going to be anger and fighting, they seemed to accept it'.

'We've found a place for me', Stuart added. 'Not far, but separate. Enough distance for both of us to establish our independent lives, but close enough to cooperate on practical matters'.

What struck me most was the genuine care they showed toward each other: handing tissues when emotions welled up, acknowledging each other's concerns, even sharing a moment of unexpected laughter over a memory from their early days together.

Stuart looked directly at Clare. 'I want you to know that even though our marriage is ending, I'm committed to being a better co-parent, a better person'.

'That means a lot to me', Clare responded, genuine warmth in her voice. 'I've started painting again; something I gave up years ago because it took time away from family responsibilities. It feels like ... rediscovering a part of myself'.

For their final exercise, I asked them to create their 'I Am' poems once more, reflecting their current journey. Stuart's revealed the profound transformation beginning within him:

I am the man learning that vulnerability is not weakness
I am the father seeking to repair relationships with patience
I am the former husband carrying gratitude alongside grief
I am the human being discovering that control is an illusion
I am learning to listen more and pronounce judgement less
I am finding my voice without needing to raise it
I am discovering that being right matters less than being kind
I am embracing solitude without fear of loneliness
I am becoming the person I always wanted to be
I am still growing, still hoping, still worthy of connection.

Clare's poem showed her own evolution:

I am the woman reclaiming spaces long surrendered
I am the mother who can love her children without losing herself
I am the artist remembering how creation heals
I am the friend learning to set boundaries with compassion
I am discovering courage I didn't know I possessed
I am making peace with choices both right and difficult
I am allowing joy to return without guilt
I am breathing freely for the first time in decades
I am grateful for endings that contain new beginnings
I am still nurturing, still dreaming, still becoming.

As our final session drew to a close, I shared my observations of their remarkable journey: how they had moved from entrenched opposition to mutual respect, how they had found a way to honour their shared history while acknowledging the necessity of separate futures.

'You've demonstrated extraordinary courage', I told them. 'Not in staying together at all costs, but in recognising what would truly allow both of you to thrive'.

'It's strange', Stuart reflected. 'I came here hoping to save our marriage, but what I'm saving instead is my relationship with myself, with my kids, and yes, even with Clare; just in a different form'.

Clare nodded. 'For years, I thought my choices were either miserable togetherness or bitter separation. I never imagined there could be grace in goodbye'.

As they prepared to leave for the last time, I observed how differently they moved in relation to each other; no longer the careful distance of strangers nor the tense proximity of adversaries, but the mindful space of two people who had found a way to honour both their connection and their necessary separation.

At the door, they paused. 'Thank you', Stuart said, genuine emotion in his voice. 'For helping us find a better ending than we could have written ourselves'.

'And perhaps better beginnings, too', Clare added softly.

As they walked to their separate cars, I watched from the window. There was sadness in their parting, certainly, but also a palpable sense of rightness, of paths diverging not in anger but in mutual recognition of a deeper truth.

Maria joined me at the window. 'Not every love story has a traditional happy ending', she observed.

'No', I agreed. 'But some endings are happier than the continuation would have been'.

In the quiet of our therapy room, with the energy of their presence still lingering, I reflected on the privilege of witnessing such transformations. Sometimes our work is about helping couples find their way back to each other, but sometimes it's about helping them find their way forward: separately, respectfully, with their dignity and essential selves intact.

Chapter 25

Trust

Stuart and Clare's story revealed how Trust – the sixth element of the Relationship Paradigm – can erode not through dramatic betrayal but through countless small disappointments. Clare stopped trusting that Stuart would prioritise their relationship over his work demands. Stuart stopped trusting that Clare would accept him as he was rather than who she wanted him to become. Their protective children didn't trust that their parents' new relationship would last. When trust fractures in multiple directions like this, even tremendous effort cannot always restore it. Yet understanding trust's centrality helps us recognise what we're fighting for – and sometimes, what we must grieve when it proves irretrievable.

When I ask couples in their first session to identify the foundations of a healthy relationship, trust invariably makes the list. Yet when I probe deeper – 'What exactly do you mean by trust?' – the answers become surprisingly diverse and often vague. 'Knowing they won't cheat', one might say. 'Being reliable', offers another. 'Feeling safe', a third suggests.

DOI: 10.4324/9781003752776-25

This ambiguity around such a fundamental concept reflects its complexity. Trust isn't a single quality but a multifaceted element that permeates every aspect of relationship functioning. Within the Relationship Paradigm, Trust represents the confidence that allows vulnerability, the reliability that enables interdependence, and the safety that permits growth. It's both the foundation upon which other elements rest and the outcome they collectively produce.

The Dimensions of Trust

Trust in relationships manifests across several dimensions:

Fidelity trust: Confidence in a partner's commitment to agreed boundaries around physical and emotional intimacy with others.

Reliability trust: The belief that a partner will follow through on commitments, whether daily promises or long-term responsibilities.

Emotional trust: The security to be vulnerable, knowing one's feelings will be handled with care rather than dismissed or weaponised.

Competence trust: Faith in a partner's abilities and judgement in areas where they hold responsibility.

Integrity trust: Belief that a partner's words align with their actions and that they operate from consistent values.

Financial trust: Confidence in responsible management of shared resources and transparency around financial decisions.

Disclosure trust: The expectation of honesty and appropriate sharing of significant information.

These dimensions don't always develop in tandem. A couple might have strong reliability trust while struggling with emotional trust. Another might have complete confidence in each other's fidelity while harbouring suspicions about financial management. Understanding these distinctions helps couples address trust issues with precision rather than treating trust as a monolithic quality that's either present or absent.

Andrea and Marcus: When Trust Is Shattered

When Andrea and Marcus arrived for their first Duo Coaching session, the atmosphere crackled with tension. They sat at opposite ends of our sofa, Andrea's arms tightly crossed, Marcus leaning forward with the desperate energy of someone trying to prevent something precious from slipping away.

'I don't know if we can come back from this', Andrea stated flatly. 'How can I ever trust him again?'

The 'this' was Marcus's six-month affair with a colleague, discovered when Andrea found intimate messages on his unlocked phone. The affair had ended two months before our session, immediately upon discovery, but the damage to their fourteen-year marriage felt catastrophic to both of them.

'I know what I did was unforgivable', Marcus said, his voice thick with emotion. 'I've ended all contact with her. I've changed jobs. I've given Andrea complete access to my phone, email, everything. I'll do whatever it takes, but nothing seems to make any difference'.

Andrea shook her head. 'I check his location twenty times a day. I read every text, scrutinise every late meeting. This isn't a marriage anymore; it's a surveillance operation. I hate who I've become, but I don't know how else to feel safe'.

Their situation illustrates a fundamental truth about trust: it's far easier to destroy than to rebuild. Trust typically develops gradually through consistent, positive experiences over time. But it can be shattered in an instant by a single significant betrayal. The path to rebuilding requires not just the absence of further betrayals but the active, consistent demonstration of trustworthiness across multiple dimensions.

'Trust is both emotional and rational', Maria explained in our second session. 'Right now, Andrea, your rational mind might acknowledge Marcus's efforts, but your emotional brain remains in high alert. That's not a failure of willpower; it's your brain doing exactly what it evolved to do – protect you from further harm'.

This normalisation of Andrea's experience was crucial. Many betrayed partners feel shame about their hypervigilance, interpreting it as weakness or vindictiveness rather than a natural protective response. Meanwhile, partners who have broken trust often grow frustrated with the slow pace of rebuilding, expecting their immediate remorse and changed behaviour to produce immediate forgiveness.

'Rebuilding trust isn't just about providing evidence of change', I added. 'It's about creating enough new experiences of trustworthiness that the brain gradually rewires its threat response. This doesn't happen quickly, and it can't be forced through rational argument'.

Over our next few sessions, we helped Andrea and Marcus understand the stages of trust rebuilding after betrayal:

1. **Crisis stabilisation**: Establishing basic safety through transparency, consistent availability, and respect for the betrayed partner's emotional reactions.
2. **Understanding the breach**: Exploring the context and meaning of the betrayal without excusing it – what vulnerabilities in the relationship and in Marcus himself had created fertile ground for the affair?
3. **Vision clarification**: Determining whether both genuinely want to rebuild the relationship and what kind of partnership they hope to create.
4. **Creating a new relationship**: This is not about putting a sticking plaster over the old; this is about taking the opportunity to reset and create a new and better relationship with each other.
5. **Repair work**: Active efforts to rebuild trust through consistent behaviours that directly address the specific dimensions of trust that were violated.
6. **Integration**: Incorporating the experience into a new understanding of the relationship – neither defined solely by the betrayal nor pretending it never happened.

Marcus initially fixated on providing logistical transparency – sharing passwords, location tracking, detailed accounts of his daily movements. While these steps were necessary, they addressed only the most basic level of safety. The deeper work involved helping him understand what had made him vulnerable to the affair and developing the emotional awareness and communication skills to address future relationship challenges without betrayal.

'I realise now I was completely disconnected from my own feelings', Marcus reflected in our fourth session. 'I couldn't talk to Andrea about feeling inadequate at work or unattractive as I got older because I could barely admit those feelings to myself. The affair was a way to escape those feelings rather than face them'.

This honesty represented a crucial step in rebuilding emotional trust. Marcus wasn't just demonstrating fidelity in the present; he was developing the self-awareness and communication capacity that would make future betrayals less likely.

For Andrea, the journey involved both holding Marcus accountable and gradually relinquishing the hypervigilance that had become exhausting. We introduced the concept of 'trust testing' versus 'trust building', helping her see how constant checking created an illusion of safety while actually reinforcing her trauma response.

'The surveillance gives me momentary relief but never lasting peace', she acknowledged. 'I need to find a way to feel safe without needing to control everything'.

By our final session, significant healing had occurred. Andrea no longer checked Marcus's phone daily, and they had established new patterns of emotional communication that addressed the disconnection that had preceded the affair. The betrayal hadn't been forgotten – it had been integrated into their shared narrative as a painful chapter that had ultimately led to greater authenticity and connection.

'I still have moments of panic', Andrea shared. 'But they're less frequent now. And when they happen, I can talk about them without Marcus getting defensive. That alone helps me feel safer'.

Marcus nodded. 'I understand now that rebuilding trust isn't just about proving I'm not cheating. It's about showing up emotionally in all the ways I didn't before – being reliable with everything from household tasks to difficult conversations'.

Their case illustrates how trust recovery requires attention to multiple dimensions. For Andrea and Marcus, fidelity trust had been most dramatically broken, but fully rebuilding their relationship required strengthening emotional trust, disclosure trust, and integrity trust as well.

Katie and Daniel: When Trust Was Never Established

While Andrea and Marcus were working to rebuild trust after a clear betrayal, Katie and Daniel presented a different challenge. Together for three years but not married, they had never fully established trust in the first place.

'I feel like I'm always waiting for the other shoe to drop', Katie explained in their first session. 'Daniel hasn't done anything wrong exactly, but I never feel completely secure with him'.

Daniel sighed heavily. 'Nothing I do is ever enough. I text when I'm going to be late. I introduce her to all my friends. I've never given her any reason not to trust me, but she's constantly questioning me'.

As Maria and I explored their history, we discovered that both brought significant trust injuries from previous relationships and family experiences. Katie's father had abandoned the family when she was twelve, disappearing without explanation. Her first serious boyfriend had maintained a 'backup' relationship throughout their time together, revealed only when the other woman became pregnant.

Daniel's trust landscape was similarly complicated. Raised by a mother with undiagnosed borderline personality disorder, he had grown up walking on eggshells, never knowing what might trigger her rage or rejection. His previous girlfriend had used emotional manipulation, threatening self-harm when he attempted to establish boundaries.

These histories created a perfect storm for trust issues. Katie, hypervigilant to signs of abandonment or betrayal, interpreted ambiguous situations as threatening. Daniel, hypersensitive to emotional control, withdrew when Katie expressed insecurity, perceiving her need for reassurance as manipulation.

'You're both responding more to your past experiences than to each other', Maria observed in our second session. 'Katie, when Daniel is vague about his plans, your brain doesn't register it as simple oversight but as potential evidence of concealment. Daniel, when Katie asks for more information, you don't experience it as normal curiosity but as the beginning of the control you feared from your mother and ex-girlfriend'.

This reframing helped shift their perspective. Rather than seeing their trust issues as evidence of relationship incompatibility, they began to recognise how their individual histories created specific vulnerabilities that could be addressed directly.

In our third session, we introduced the concept of 'trust building blocks' – specific behaviours that create security for each partner based on their unique history and needs. Katie identified several actions that helped her feel secure: Daniel proactively sharing information about his whereabouts and plans, introducing her to new friends and colleagues, and responding to messages within a reasonable timeframe. Daniel identified behaviours that helped him feel trusted: Katie asking directly about concerns rather than monitoring his behaviour, acknowledging when her fears stemmed from past experiences rather than his actions, and respecting his need for occasional solitude without suspicion.

'The goal isn't perfect trust without any vulnerability', I explained. 'That's neither possible nor desirable. The goal is creating enough security that you can acknowledge uncertainty without being overwhelmed by it'.

Over our remaining sessions, Katie and Daniel developed new patterns of interaction around trust. Katie practised distinguishing between evidence-based concerns and anxiety triggered by past experiences. Daniel worked on proactive transparency rather than defensiveness when Katie expressed insecurity.

'I've realised that trust isn't something Katie should just automatically give me', Daniel reflected in our fifth session. 'It's something we build together through hundreds of small moments of reliability and honesty'.

Katie nodded. 'And I've learned that some of my trust issues aren't about Daniel at all – they're wounds I need to heal regardless of who I'm with. When I separate my past from my present, I can see how trustworthy he actually is'.

By our final session, they had developed what they called their 'trust toolkit' – specific agreements and practices that addressed their particular vulnerabilities while respecting each other's autonomy. These weren't universal trust solutions but customised approaches based on their unique histories and needs.

Their case illustrates an important truth: establishing trust isn't a one-size-fits-all process. What creates security for one person may be irrelevant or even counterproductive for another. The key is identifying each partner's specific trust requirements and working collaboratively to meet them without sacrificing healthy autonomy.

The Neurobiology of Trust

The complexity of trust in relationships becomes clearer when we understand its neurobiological underpinnings. Trust isn't merely a cognitive assessment but a whole-brain experience involving our threat-detection system (primarily the amygdala), our social connection circuits (involving oxytocin and vasopressin), our pleasure pathways (dopamine), and our rational planning centres (prefrontal cortex).

When trust is broken, the amygdala becomes hyperactivated, triggering our threat response. This neurological reaction explains why logical reassurances often fail to restore emotional trust after betrayal – the primitive brain stem and limbic system aren't primarily responsive to language and reason but to consistent experiences of safety over time.

Conversely, when we experience reliable trustworthiness from a partner, our brain releases oxytocin, often called the 'bonding hormone', which promotes feelings of connection and security. This creates a positive feedback loop: trust produces biochemical rewards that encourage further trust.

Maria and I often share this science with couples because it helps normalise both the immediate neurological impacts of betrayal and the biological processes involved in rebuilding trust. Understanding that trust has neurochemical dimensions helps couples approach it with greater patience and precision, recognising that both the breakdown and the rebuilding of trust involve the brain's structure and chemistry, not just conscious choices.

The Trust Toolkit

Through years of working with couples, we've developed The Trust Toolkit – practical approaches that help establish, maintain, or rebuild this essential element of relationship:

Trust Specificity Assessment: Identifying exactly which dimensions of trust are strong or vulnerable in the relationship, allowing for targeted attention rather than generalised anxiety.

Proactive Transparency: Voluntarily sharing information that matters to a partner before being asked, demonstrating consideration for their security needs.

Reliability Practices: Consistent follow-through on commitments, from being on time to completing agreed tasks, which builds evidence of dependability in everyday interactions.

Trust Building Blocks: Customised behaviours that address each partner's specific security needs based on their history and attachment style.

The Apology Process: A structured approach to acknowledging breaches of trust that includes recognition of the specific harm caused, taking responsibility without defensiveness, genuine remorse, concrete plans for change, and patience with the healing process.

Trust Repair Tracking: Documenting efforts to rebuild trust and progress over time, providing evidence of change that might otherwise go unnoticed during emotional fluctuations.

These tools provide practical strategies for addressing trust issues at various stages – from establishing basic trust in new relationships to rebuilding after significant betrayals. They acknowledge that trust is both emotional and practical, requiring consistent attention to both dimensions.

The Bridge to Other Elements

Like all elements of the Relationship Paradigm, Trust interconnects with the others in dynamic ways. Trust creates the safety necessary for vulnerable Communication. It forms the foundation for deep Connection. It represents an essential aspect of Commitment to the relationship. It allows the vulnerability needed for Growth. It enables the spontaneity required for true Fun.

When couples like Andrea and Marcus or Katie and Daniel strengthen trust in their relationships, the benefits cascade into these other areas. Problems that once seemed insurmountable become more manageable when approached from a foundation of basic security and confidence in each other's fundamental goodwill.

Perhaps most importantly, trust creates the conditions for genuine intimacy. Without trust, partners hold parts of themselves back, protecting against potential hurt by limiting vulnerability. With trust, they can bring their full selves into the relationship, creating deeper connection and more authentic partnership.

As I witness couples rebuild trust in our therapy room, I'm reminded of trust's paradoxical nature: it requires vulnerability to establish yet creates the safety that makes vulnerability possible. Breaking through this paradox – finding the courage to trust enough to begin building greater trust – represents one of the most transformative journeys couples can undertake together.

In the end, trust isn't an achievement to be completed but a quality to be continuously nurtured. Like a garden that requires regular attention rather than occasional intensive effort, trust thrives on consistent care – daily choices to be honest even when difficult, reliable even when inconvenient, emotionally responsive even when challenging. It's in these small, cumulative moments of trustworthiness that relationships develop the security that allows them to weather inevitable storms and grow deeper roots over time.

Chapter 26

Thomas and Eleanor – Shared Horizons

Charting a New Course Together

Five months had passed since Thomas and Eleanor first walked into our therapy room on that January afternoon, their careful distance from each other speaking volumes about the years of gradual disconnection. Now, as I watched them approach our building through the window, something fundamental had shifted.

They walked side by side, Eleanor laughing at something Thomas had said, his hand resting lightly at the small of her back. It wasn't the giddy closeness of new lovers but something perhaps more precious: the comfortable intimacy of two people who had rediscovered each other after a long separation.

'They look different', Maria observed, coming to stand beside me at the window.

'They do', I agreed. 'It's in how they move together'.

When they entered the room, the change was even more apparent. Where before they had automatically sat with a careful buffer of space between them, now they sat close enough that their elbows occasionally brushed. Thomas looked more relaxed than I'd ever seen him, his customary formal posture softened. Eleanor's face was animated, her eyes bright with an energy that had been muted during our early sessions.

'Welcome to your fifth session', I said, smiling at them both. 'Before we begin, I'm curious; how does it feel to be here today compared to when we first met in January?'

They exchanged a glance, a silent communication passing between them that hadn't been possible months earlier.

'It feels like we're coming to share good news rather than seek emergency assistance', Thomas replied, the stiff formality that had characterised his earlier speech notably absent.

Eleanor nodded. 'The first time we came, I felt like we were bringing you a relationship that had flatlined, hoping for a miracle revival. Today, I feel like we're coming to celebrate its renewed health'.

'That's a powerful metaphor', Maria noted. 'What's contributed to this revival, from your perspective?'

'Communication', Thomas said promptly. 'Actually, talking about what matters to us instead of making assumptions'.

DOI: 10.4324/9781003752776-26

'And listening', Eleanor added. 'Really hearing each other instead of just waiting for our turn to speak'.

I smiled, recalling how in our early sessions, they had frequently talked past each other, each so entrenched in their own narrative that they couldn't truly absorb the other's perspective.

'Let's reflect on the journey you've taken over these past months', I suggested. 'What stands out to you as particularly significant moments or realisations?'

Thomas considered this thoughtfully. 'For me, a turning point came during our second session when we drew those pictures of our current lives and our ideal futures. I realised I'd been so focused on retirement as the end of something – the end of my career, my professional identity – that I hadn't considered it as the beginning of something new'.

'That exercise was revealing for me too', Eleanor said. 'I saw how my picture of an ideal future was full of connection, with Thomas, our children, grandchildren, friends, while my picture of the present was dominated by solitude and responsibilities. It clarified what I was actually longing for'.

This was precisely why we used creative exercises like drawing; they often bypassed intellectual defences and revealed emotional truths that might otherwise remain hidden.

'The Ikigai exercise was transformative for me', Thomas continued, referring to the Japanese concept we'd explored in our third session, helping him identify the intersection of what he loved, what he was good at, what the world needed, and what he could be rewarded for. 'I've spent my entire career focusing almost exclusively on financial provision. Looking at those other dimensions made me realise there are ways to feel purposeful beyond traditional work'.

I recalled how animated he had become during that session, particularly when discussing his lifelong interest in maritime history; a passion he'd never had time to properly explore. 'You've begun volunteering at the maritime museum, haven't you?' I asked.

He nodded, a boyish enthusiasm lighting his face. 'Two days a week. I'm helping them catalogue some recently acquired navigation instruments. It's fascinating work, and I've met some remarkable people'.

'He comes home brimming with stories', Eleanor said, her affection evident. 'It's wonderful to see him so engaged with something he truly loves'.

'And you've made some changes too, haven't you, Eleanor?' Maria prompted.

'Yes', she replied. 'I've reduced my hours at the gallery to three days a week, which has given me time to take that watercolour class I've been talking about for years. And I've been more intentional about connecting with friends and family. Our daughter Rebecca and her children now come for Sunday lunch every fortnight; something I'd always wanted but never quite managed to establish as a tradition'.

Their individual pursuits might seem peripheral to their relationship issues, but I knew from experience that when people begin nurturing their authentic interests and connections, they bring a fuller, more contented self to their partnership.

'What about your discussions regarding the house?' I asked, recalling the significant tension this had created during our first session.

'We've made a decision', Thomas said, glancing at Eleanor with a smile. 'We're selling it'.

'But not immediately', Eleanor added. 'We're going to take a year to find or create exactly the right next home. Something that reflects who we are now and what we want for this next chapter'.

'In the meantime', Thomas continued, 'we've reconfigured some spaces in our current house. We've converted one of the unused bedrooms into a studio for Eleanor's painting, and the formal dining room we never used is now my study for researching maritime history'.

'The house feels different now', Eleanor reflected. 'More aligned with our current lives rather than preserved as a museum to our past'.

This evolution, from rigid entrenchment in opposing positions to flexible, collaborative problem-solving, was exactly what we hoped to see.

'You mentioned your dream board last time', Maria said. 'How has that been developing?'

Their faces lit up simultaneously, and Thomas reached for a tablet in his bag. 'We'd like to show you', he said, opening it to reveal a digital collage of images, quotes, and notes. 'We decided a digital version would be easier to add to as new ideas emerge'.

He turned the screen toward us, revealing a rich tapestry of possibilities. There were images of coastal cottages, paintings of sailboats, snapshots of their grandchildren, photos of exotic destinations, quotes about learning and growth.

'We've booked our first major trip', Eleanor said, pointing to an image of a rugged coastline. 'Cornwall in September. Thomas has always wanted to explore the maritime museums there, and I'm looking forward to painting the landscapes'.

'And we're considering a longer adventure next year', Thomas added. 'Perhaps New Zealand for several months. Eleanor's sister lives there, and we've never been able to visit properly due to my work constraints'.

The contrast with their first session was striking. Then, they had been focused on what separated them: his attachment to their home versus her desire for change, his imminent retirement creating anxiety rather than anticipation. Now, they were actively co-creating a future rich with shared experiences and mutual support for individual pursuits.

'What's been most challenging about this process?' I asked, knowing that genuine transformation rarely comes without struggle.

They exchanged another glance, this one carrying a different weight.

'Learning to disagree productively', Thomas admitted. 'For so many years, we avoided conflict. Eleanor would acquiesce to keep the peace, or I would retreat into work. Actually, staying present during disagreements, trying to understand rather than win; that's been difficult'.

'We still have moments where we fall back into old patterns', Eleanor acknowledged. 'Times when I feel unheard and withdraw, or when Thomas becomes defensive. The difference is that now we recognise what's happening more quickly'.

'The "State of the Union" meetings have been invaluable for that', Thomas said, referring to another tool we'd introduced: a structured weekly conversation to check in on their relationship. 'Having that dedicated time to discuss what's working and what isn't prevents issues from festering'.

This acknowledgement of ongoing challenges was actually a positive sign. Couples who claim their problems have completely vanished are often in denial; those who can articulate specific difficulties and their strategies for addressing them are usually on a more sustainable path.

'If you were to offer advice to another couple in a similar situation, long married but disconnected, what would you tell them?' I asked.

Eleanor considered this thoughtfully. 'I'd say it's never too late to create something new together. We spent years going through the motions, managing logistics but not really seeing each other. I had resigned myself to that being the remainder of our marriage. Now I realise how much richness was still possible'.

'I would advise them to be honest about what they truly want', Thomas added. 'For so long, I thought I was doing what was expected of me, focusing on providing, maintaining the family home, planning for financial security. I never stopped to question whether those priorities were serving our actual happiness'.

As our session continued, they spoke with growing animation about their plans and discoveries: how they'd established new rituals of connection, from morning coffee in the garden to reading aloud to each other in the evenings; how they'd begun socialising more as a couple, rekindling old friendships and forming new ones; how physical intimacy had gradually returned, tentative at first but increasingly natural.

'The Hunt the Good Stuff exercise transformed our daily interactions', Eleanor noted, referring to another tool we'd introduced in our first session. 'Sharing three positive observations every evening has become a cherished ritual. It trains your attention to notice moments of joy or beauty that might otherwise slip past'.

'It's remarkable how something so simple can shift your perspective', Thomas agreed. 'Yesterday, I found myself mentally noting things throughout the day: the perfect espresso at that new café, the amusing conversation with our grandson about dinosaurs, the way the evening light caught Eleanor's hair as she was painting, specifically because I knew we'd be sharing our observations later'.

This practice, while indeed simple, often creates profound shifts. It counters the brain's natural negativity bias, gradually retraining couples to notice and appreciate what's going well rather than fixating on problems.

As our time together drew to a close, I asked them one final question: 'What do you most hope for in your relationship moving forward?'

'Continued discovery', Eleanor said after a moment's reflection. 'Of each other, of ourselves, of the world we want to explore together. I feel like we've only just begun a new journey'.

Thomas reached for her hand, intertwining his fingers with hers. 'I hope we maintain this attentiveness we've developed: truly seeing each other, making deliberate choices about how we spend our time and energy, creating a life that reflects our shared values rather than just accumulating more years together'.

Their words carried the weight of genuine insight, hard-earned through months of honest reflection and deliberate practice. This wasn't the superficial optimism sometimes seen at the end of therapy, but a deeper understanding of both the work they'd done and the work that lay ahead.

'Before we conclude', Maria said, 'is there anything specific you feel you still need support with?'

They exchanged one more glance, a silent consultation that spoke volumes about their renewed connection.

'I think we've developed the tools we need to continue our journey together', Thomas replied. 'Knowing that you're available if we encounter obstacles we can't navigate is reassuring, but I feel confident in our ability to move forward'.

Eleanor nodded in agreement. 'You've helped us rediscover how to be partners rather than just housemates. That foundation feels solid now'.

As we said our goodbyes, I felt the particular satisfaction that comes from witnessing genuine transformation. Thomas and Eleanor had arrived five months earlier as two people who had gradually drifted into parallel lives despite sharing a home and history. They were leaving as partners actively engaged in creating a meaningful shared future.

Outside the window, the early summer afternoon painted everything in warmth and possibility. Thomas and Eleanor walked to their car: not a large executive sedan as before, but a comfortable mid-sized vehicle they'd purchased together after deciding to sell Thomas's company car. This time, they departed as they had arrived: together, their steps naturally falling into the same rhythm, the space between them now filled with renewed connection rather than careful distance.

'That', Maria said as we watched them drive away, 'is why we do this work'.

'Indeed', I agreed, feeling both the satisfaction of a successful conclusion and a touch of sadness at saying goodbye to a couple who had shared such an important journey with us. 'From parallel lives to shared adventures: not a bad transformation for five months' work'.

As I turned back to my desk to prepare for our next clients, I found myself hoping that Thomas and Eleanor were heading home to continue adding to their dream board, planning their Cornwall trip, or perhaps simply enjoying one of their newfound rituals of connection. Their story would continue long after our formal work together had concluded; and that continuation, with all its inevitable challenges and discoveries, was now theirs to write together.

This is the ultimate goal of our relationship therapy – not creating permanent dependence on the therapist, but equipping couples with the awareness, skills, and connection to navigate their journey independently. Thomas and Eleanor had arrived as virtual strangers despite their decades together, each orbiting in isolation while technically sharing a home. They were departing now as rediscovered partners, not with perfect solutions to every challenge retirement might bring, but with a renewed sense of shared purpose and possibility.

As Maria and I prepared our notes, I reflected on how their transformation embodied the essence of the Relationship Paradigm. Their communication had evolved from logistical exchanges to meaningful dialogue. Their connection, nearly severed by years of physical and emotional distance, had begun to reestablish itself through intentional presence. Their commitment had shifted from obligation based on history to active choice based on desire. They had rediscovered how to have fun together, were embracing continued growth rather than stagnation, and were rebuilding trust in their shared future.

In the quiet of the therapy room, with the afternoon sun casting long shadows across the floor, I felt that particular satisfaction that comes only from witnessing people find their way back to each other across what once seemed an unbridgeable divide. Not all stories in my practice have such promising conclusions, but those that do serve as powerful reminders of why this work matters – and of the extraordinary capacity for renewal that exists within human relationships, even after decades of disconnect.

Chapter 27

Sex

The Unspoken Language of Intimacy

When Thomas and Eleanor first came to see me, they lived like polite strangers sharing a house. Part of reclaiming their relationship involved addressing what neither wanted to discuss: their physical intimacy, or rather, its absence. Over the years, I've learned that while the six elements of the Relationship Paradigm provide the foundation, there's a seventh dimension that weaves through all of them yet deserves its own exploration – Sex and physical intimacy. It's often the unspoken language of connection, the barometer of trust, the place where vulnerability meets desire. Thomas and Eleanor's renewed physical connection didn't just happen after they reconnected emotionally – it became part of how they reconnected.

In the gently lit sanctuary of our therapy room, I've witnessed a remarkable phenomenon hundreds of times. A couple who have been avoiding eye contact, speaking in careful, measured tones about finances, parenting disagreements, or work stress, suddenly falls silent. There's a palpable shift in energy. Sometimes it's preceded by a deep breath, sometimes by a nervous laugh. It feels the right time for me to ask the killer question; 'Tell us about intimacy and sex in your relationship'.

DOI: 10.4324/9781003752776-27

Sex. This three-letter word carries immense weight in relationships. It represents not just a physical act but a complex language of desire, connection, vulnerability, power, pleasure, and identity. Yet for many couples, particularly those who have been together for years, it becomes the proverbial elephant in the room – too large to ignore but too uncomfortable to address directly.

The Fading of Desire

One of the most common patterns I observe in long-term relationships is the gradual diminishing of sexual connection. This transition is so widespread that many couples assume it's inevitable – just another stage in the life cycle of a relationship. Harriet articulated this sentiment when she said, 'I thought that's just what happens. The passion dies down, and you focus on other things'.

But if this change is accepted as inevitable, why does it cause so much distress? Why do partners lie awake at night, wondering if they're still desired, still desirable? Why do they measure the health of their relationship against the frequency of sexual encounters? Why does the absence of physical intimacy often create such profound loneliness, even in relationships that are otherwise supportive and loving?

The answer lies in understanding the deeper purpose of sex in committed relationships. Sex is rarely just about sex.

Beyond Reproduction: The Many Functions of Sex

From a purely biological perspective, sex serves the function of reproduction. But human sexuality has evolved far beyond this basic purpose. In the context of intimate relationships, sex can serve multiple functions:

Connection and bonding: Sexual intimacy triggers the release of oxytocin, often called the 'bonding hormone', which promotes feelings of trust and attachment. This neurochemical response helps explain why sex can create feelings of closeness that transcend the physical act itself.

Communication: Sex is a form of nonverbal communication. Through physical intimacy, we express desires, boundaries, playfulness, trust, and vulnerability in ways that words cannot always capture.

Pleasure and play: Human beings are among the few species that engage in sexual activity for pleasure. This capacity for pleasure and playfulness is not incidental but fundamental to our well-being.

Affirmation: Sexual desire can function as a powerful form of affirmation, a way of saying, 'I see you, I want you, I choose you'. In a world where we often feel invisible or taken for granted, being desired sexually can be profoundly validating.

Transcendence: At its most profound, sexual intimacy can create a sense of transcendence – a temporary dissolution of the boundaries between self and other, a sacred space of connection that feels timeless.

Given these multiple dimensions, it's no wonder that when sex fades from a relationship, the impact extends far beyond physical frustration. Partners often experience this change as a loss of connection, communication, affirmation, and transcendence – in short, a loss of intimacy in its broadest sense.

The Silence around Sex

Despite its importance, sex remains one of the most difficult aspects of relationships for couples to discuss openly. In my therapy room, I've heard countless variations of the same confession: 'We talk about everything else – money, parenting, politics, religion – but never about what's happening, or not happening, in our bedroom'.

This silence stems from multiple sources:

Vulnerability: Sexual desires, fantasies, and needs make us profoundly vulnerable. To express them is to risk rejection, judgement, or misunderstanding.

Shame: Many of us carry sexual shame from childhood messages, religious teachings, cultural norms, or past experiences. This shame creates a barrier to honest communication.

Fear of hurting the other: Partners often avoid sexual discussions for fear of hurting each other. 'What if I tell him I'm unsatisfied and it damages his confidence?' 'What if I admit I don't desire her as I once did?'

Lack of language: Many adults simply lack the vocabulary to discuss sex comfortably and clearly. Without this language, conversations quickly become awkward or confusing.

The myth of sexual telepathy: There's a persistent cultural myth that good sex should 'just happen' naturally, without explicit communication. Partners 'should' intuitively know what the other wants and needs.

These barriers to communication create a cycle of silence, misunderstanding, and disconnection. And in this silence, assumptions flourish. One partner assumes the other has lost interest; the other assumes they're no longer desirable. One believes the problem is physical; the other knows it's emotional. Without conversation, these assumptions become entrenched as 'truths'.

Creating a Liminal Space for Sexual Honesty

In my work with couples, I've found that creating what I call a 'liminal space' – a safe, transitional space outside ordinary life – allows for remarkable honesty about sexual needs and desires. Within the container of therapy, couples often find the courage to speak truths they've kept hidden for years, sometimes decades.

The transformation can be astonishing. Let me share a few vignettes from couples who discovered the power of sexual honesty in our sessions:

Brian and Cathy: The Physical Becomes Emotional

Brian and Cathy had been married for twenty-two years when they came to see me. Their sexual relationship had dwindled to occasional, brief encounters that left both feeling unsatisfied. In our third session, when I gently asked about their intimate life, Cathy stared at the floor while Brian explained their situation in clinical terms, as if discussing someone else's relationship.

'We used to be very active', he said, 'but over the last few years, it's become less frequent. I think it's mostly physical changes – Cathy experienced some pain after menopause, and I sometimes have trouble maintaining an erection'.

When I invited Cathy to share her perspective, she remained silent for a long moment. Then, to both my and Brian's surprise, she began to cry.

'It's not about physical changes', she said finally. 'At least, not for me. It's that I don't feel seen anymore. You come home from work and talk about your day. You ask about the kids. You even remember to ask about my mother's health. But you never really look at me. You haven't really seen me in years'.

Brian's expression shifted from confusion to recognition. 'I thought ... I thought you weren't interested anymore', he said quietly. 'You always seemed so busy, so wrapped up in everything else. I felt like I'd become an afterthought'.

In that moment of mutual vulnerability, something shifted between them. They were no longer discussing 'sex' as a separate category of their relationship but their fundamental need to be seen, recognised, and valued by each other. What had appeared to be a physical issue revealed itself as a deeply emotional one.

Over subsequent sessions, Brian and Cathy developed new rituals of connection – daily check-ins where they made eye contact and truly listened to each other, a weekly date night, even a code word for when one of them felt invisible. Their sexual relationship gradually rekindled, not because they addressed physical symptoms but because they restored the foundation of emotional intimacy that made physical intimacy meaningful.

Garry and Billy: The Fantasy Question

Garry and Billy sought therapy after fifteen years together, concerned that their sexual relationship had become, in Garry's words, 'routine to the point of boredom'. They described a pattern familiar to many long-term couples: the same positions, the same sequence, the same time of day.

In our safe space, I invited them to discuss a topic many couples find particularly challenging: fantasies. What desires did they harbour but had never expressed to each other?

Billy was initially hesitant, but Garry surprised him by going first. 'I've always been curious about role-play', he admitted. 'Not anything extreme, but just ... being different people sometimes. Having different dynamics'. He quickly added, 'But I never suggested it because I thought Billy would think it was silly'.

Billy looked stunned. 'I've had the exact same thought for years', he said. 'I even bought a book about it once, but I hid it because I assumed you'd judge me for it'.

Their shared laughter at this revelation dissolved years of assumptions. They realised they had both been censoring their desires based on what they imagined the other would think, creating a sexual relationship that reflected neither of their true desires.

In subsequent sessions, they developed a simple but effective tool: the Yes/No/Maybe list. They independently marked various activities as 'yes' (enthusiastic interest), 'no' (boundary), or 'maybe' (willing to explore under certain conditions). When they compared lists, they were amazed by how many 'yes' items they shared but had never discussed.

Their story illustrates how easily we project our own fears and assumptions onto our partners, limiting the potential of our sexual connection without ever giving them the chance to surprise us.

Enid and Trevor: The Initiator's Dilemma

Enid and Trevor sought help after seven years of marriage. Their sexual relationship had virtually disappeared, with neither partner initiating intimacy for months at a time. In our therapy space, they described a painfully familiar dynamic: each was waiting for the other to make the first move.

'I stopped initiating because I couldn't bear the rejection', Enid explained. 'Trevor would always have a reason – he was too tired, too stressed, too preoccupied. After a while, it just felt humiliating to keep trying'.

Trevor listened intently before responding. 'I felt the same way', he said. 'Early in our relationship, when I would initiate, Enid would often say she wasn't in the mood. It hurt so much that eventually I just stopped trying'.

As we explored this dynamic further, a more nuanced picture emerged. Enid's rejections had often come during a period of postpartum depression after their first child – a connection she hadn't fully recognised. Trevor's withdrawals had coincided with a stressful career change. Neither had communicated the context of their changing desires, leaving the other to create narratives based on incomplete information.

In the safe container of therapy, they were able to separate their individual experiences from the meanings they had assigned to those experiences. Trevor hadn't been rejecting Enid; he had been responding to his own stress. Enid hadn't been dismissing Trevor; she had been navigating a significant life transition with hormonal and emotional components.

With this new understanding, they developed a communication system that allowed them to express interest without risking outright rejection. They created a 0–10 scale for indicating their level of desire on any given day. This simple tool allowed them to understand each other's state without taking it personally and to find creative ways to connect even when their desire levels differed. Sometimes a

'3' day could become a '7' with the right approach; other times, they would find non-sexual ways to maintain intimacy when one was truly at '0'.

Their story highlights how easily misunderstandings about initiation and rejection can create cycles that become increasingly difficult to break without intervention.

Common Patterns and Pathways Forward

These vignettes illustrate some of the most common patterns I observe in couples whose sexual relationship has faded:

The Assumption Trap: Partners make assumptions about each other's desires, boundaries, or feelings without verification.
The Initiation Imbalance: One partner becomes the primary or sole initiator, creating pressure and potential resentment.
The Meaning Gap: Sex carries different meanings and serves different purposes for each partner, but these differences remain undiscussed.
The Feedback Void: Without specific, constructive feedback about preferences and pleasures, sexual encounters become less satisfying over time.
The Context Conundrum: Sexual desire is highly context-dependent, but couples rarely create the contexts that facilitate desire.
The Prioritisation Problem: In busy lives, sex becomes a 'nice to have' rather than an essential component of relationship maintenance.

In working through these patterns, I've found several approaches particularly helpful:

Decoupling identity from sexuality: Helping partners understand that sexual challenges are not reflections of their worth as individuals or the value of their relationship.
Expanding the definition of intimacy: Moving beyond the narrow focus on intercourse to embrace a broader range of intimate encounters.
Scheduling rather than spontaneity: Challenging the myth that 'scheduling sex' is unromantic by reframing it as prioritisation and anticipation.
Sensate focus exercises: Structured touch experiences that reduce performance pressure and increase awareness of physical sensations.
Desire mapping: Exploring the specific contexts that enhance or inhibit desire for each partner.
Communication tools: Providing concrete frameworks for discussing needs, boundaries, and preferences without shame or judgement.

Beyond the Bedroom: Sex as a Relationship Barometer

Throughout this chapter, I've emphasised that sex is rarely just about sex. It's also true that sexual issues are rarely just about sex. The sexual relationship often functions as a barometer for the relationship as a whole, reflecting underlying dynamics of power, communication, trust, and emotional intimacy.

When Simon and Cat began working with me, their sexual relationship had been dormant for years. As we explored this issue, it became clear that their sexual disconnection mirrored broader patterns in their relationship. Cat's feeling of being 'controlled' in daily life manifested as sexual withdrawal; Simon's sense of being 'disrespected' expressed itself as lack of desire.

As they addressed these fundamental relationship dynamics, their sexual connection began to rekindle naturally. This pattern is common: when couples restore trust, improve communication, balance power, and increase emotional intimacy, sexual desire often follows without direct intervention.

This doesn't mean sexual issues should be ignored until other relationship problems are resolved. Rather, it suggests that addressing sexual concerns in isolation is rarely effective. The most successful approaches consider the whole relationship system, recognising that sexuality is both influenced by and influences every other aspect of the partnership.

Conclusion: From Elephant to Integration

For too many couples, sex becomes the elephant in the room – an imposing presence they carefully manoeuvre around, pretending not to notice even as it takes up more and more space. The goal of therapy isn't to remove the elephant (sexuality is and should remain an important aspect of most intimate relationships) but to integrate it – to transform it from a source of tension or avoidance into a natural, positive dimension of the relationship.

This integration happens when couples develop the courage to speak honestly about their needs and desires, the compassion to listen without judgement, and the creativity to find new pathways to connection. In the safe, liminal space of therapy, I've witnessed this transformation countless times: the nervous glances give way to direct eye contact; euphemisms are replaced by clear, specific language; shame dissolves into acceptance; and what was once unspeakable becomes a source of playfulness, connection, and joy.

As Harriet told me in our final session, after she and Ed had rebuilt their intimate relationship: 'It's not just that we're having sex again. It's that we can talk about having sex – what we want, what feels good, what doesn't work anymore. Being able to talk about it changes everything'.

Sexual intimacy, at its best, isn't separate from the rest of the relationship but an extension and expression of it – another language through which partners communicate their love, trust, and commitment to each other's well-being. When couples learn to speak this language with clarity and compassion, they add a dimension of connection that enriches every aspect of their shared life.

Chapter 28

John and Sarah – The Power of Turning Toward

John and Sarah had been living parallel lives for years, their constant arguments serving as the only real contact points in an otherwise disconnected marriage. He felt unheard and undervalued; she felt unsupported and alone. Their home was less a sanctuary than a battleground where small irritations escalated into warfare. The question that brought them to therapy was stark: after all these years of fighting, could they learn to turn toward each other instead of away?

Six sessions, seventeen weeks, and countless small revelations later, John and Sarah arrive for their final scheduled meeting. Their entrance carries a different energy now; they walk in together rather than one leading the other, their pace aligned rather than discordant. John holds the door for Sarah, not from old-fashioned courtesy but with a genuine attentiveness that speaks of new awareness.

They settle onto the three-seater couch differently too. The vast empty space that once stretched between them has narrowed considerably. John sits with greater confidence, his posture open rather than collapsed. Sarah's rigid precision has softened, her body angled slightly toward him rather than facing straight ahead. Most tellingly, her handbag rests on the floor now, not positioned as a barrier between them.

'Welcome', I say as Maria offers them water. 'How have things been since our last meeting?'

John glances at Sarah, not to seek permission to speak but to invite connection. 'Better', he says with quiet certainty. 'Different in important ways'.

'We had a significant conversation about Jacob's school situation', Sarah adds, her voice carrying the same crisp efficiency but with a new warmth underneath. 'It was the first time in years we've approached a parenting decision as true partners rather than just dividing responsibilities'.

This simple statement encapsulates so much of their progress, the shift from parallel management to genuine collaboration, from organised coexistence to true partnership.

'Tell us more about this conversation', Maria encourages. 'What was different about it?'

John shifts slightly, turning more fully toward the centre of the couch. 'I didn't just defer to Sarah's decision. For years, that's been our pattern, she researches

DOI: 10.4324/9781003752776-28

everything thoroughly, presents the logical conclusion, and I go along with it because, well, she's usually right'.

'And I didn't just present John with a fait accompli', Sarah continues. 'I caught myself preparing a complete analysis with a recommended course of action, but then I remembered what we've been working on about shared decision-making'.

'So, what happened instead?' I ask.

'We sat down after the children were in bed', John explains, 'and I shared my concerns about Jacob feeling lost in such a large school environment. Sarah had data about academic outcomes, which was important, but we both recognised there were emotional factors to consider too'.

'It wasn't efficient', Sarah admits with a small smile that transforms her face. 'It took three separate conversations over a week to reach a decision. But it felt ...' she searches for the right word, '... complete. Like we were considering the whole picture together'.

This example illuminates their journey perfectly, the integration of her analytical strengths and his emotional awareness, the willingness to sacrifice efficiency for depth of connection, the creation of space where both voices carry equal weight.

As our final two-and-a-half-hour session unfolds, more evidence of transformation emerges. They speak of implementing their weekly 'State of the Union' meetings, a structured time to connect beyond logistics. John describes finding his voice again, not just at home but at work as well, setting boundaries around his time that allow him to be more present with the children. Sarah shares her discovery that relinquishing some control actually reduces her anxiety rather than increasing it.

'The Love Languages exercise was surprisingly revealing', Sarah says, referring to one of the tools we provided. 'I've always expressed love through acts of service, managing the household, organising everyone's lives, and I resented that it wasn't appreciated'.

'And I never understood why leaving a note or sending a text meant so much to her', John adds. 'I thought they were just words, not real actions. But they're what make her feel seen'.

'Words of affirmation', Maria nods. 'And what did you discover about yourself, John?'

'Quality time', he replies without hesitation. 'Not just being in the same room but truly engaged with each other. That's what I've been missing for years'.

The way they discuss these insights shows how far they've come, speaking directly to each other rather than through us, truly listening rather than simply waiting to respond, owning their patterns without blame or defensiveness.

'We've started something new', Sarah shares, with uncharacteristic hesitation. 'It might sound silly, but it's been important'.

'Go on', I encourage.

'We're taking a cooking class together every Thursday evening', John explains. 'Neither of us is particularly good at it, which is actually perfect. We're both beginners, both slightly out of our comfort zones'.

'It gives us something to laugh about', Sarah adds, and the mention of laughter feels significant. 'And it's just for us, not about the children, not about our careers, just something new we're learning together'.

This simple shared activity represents a profound shift, creating space for play and discovery in a relationship that had been dominated by productivity and performance. They are allowing themselves to be imperfect together, to explore rather than achieve.

'The exercise Ten Things I Love About You was difficult at first', John admits. 'We've respected each other for so long, but when did we stop really seeing the things we love?'

'I keep mine by my bedside', Sarah says softly. 'When I wake up feeling overwhelmed by everything that needs to be done, I read it first, before checking my emails or making lists'.

As we move toward the conclusion of our work together, I ask them the question that bookends our process: 'What have you gained from these sessions that you want to carry forward?'

John considers this thoughtfully. 'I've learned that withdrawal isn't protection, it's a slow form of disappearing. Every time I chose silence over speaking up, I wasn't just avoiding conflict, I was erasing a little bit of myself from our relationship'.

Sarah nods in recognition. 'And I've realised that efficiency isn't the same as connection. I was so focused on optimising our family life that I forgot relationships aren't meant to be optimised, they're meant to be experienced, with all the messiness that entails'.

'What most surprised you about this process?' Maria asks.

'That it wasn't about learning new communication techniques as much as it was about unlearning old patterns', Sarah replies. 'I came in thinking we needed new skills, but what we really needed was to recognise what we were already doing that wasn't serving us'.

'And that small changes can shift everything', John adds. 'Like the Bids for Connection work, just noticing when Sarah is reaching out, even in small ways, and turning toward her instead of away. That one adjustment has rippled through our entire relationship'.

They speak now with the quiet confidence of people who have glimpsed a new possibility and found it within their reach. Not a perfect relationship; they still have their distinct personalities and challenges, but a vital one, alive with genuine connection rather than merely functioning with transactional efficiency.

As our final minutes approach, I share my observations of their journey, their courage in examining patterns established over years, their willingness to risk vulnerability after long periods of emotional distance, the small brave steps they've taken toward reconnection.

'You came to us as two capable individuals living parallel lives', I tell them. 'What I see now are two people turning toward each other again, creating something more meaningful than mere efficiency'.

'It feels sustainable now', Sarah says, surprising us with this choice of word. 'Before, our good moments felt fragile, like they could disappear at any moment. Now there's something solid underneath'.

'We're remembering why we chose each other in the first place', John says simply. 'Beyond all the practical compatibility, there was something else, a way we made each other feel more alive'.

As they prepare to leave for the last time, I observe how differently they gather their belongings compared to that first session. There is a natural awareness between them now, small glances and subtle adjustments that speak of attentiveness rather than distance. John helps Sarah with her coat, their hands brushing briefly in a moment of casual intimacy that would have been unthinkable weeks ago.

'Remember you can always reach out if you need a refresher session', Maria reminds them. 'Though I have a feeling you have the tools you need now'.

At the door, they pause. 'Thank you', Sarah says, her customary efficiency giving way to genuine emotion. 'For helping us find each other again'.

As they walk toward their car, I watch them from the window. The physical space between them has shifted, not dramatically, but perceptibly. They walk close enough now that their shoulders occasionally brush against each other, and their pace has synchronised in a way that suggests genuine togetherness rather than merely travelling in the same direction.

Most tellingly, just before they reach the car, John says something that makes Sarah laugh, a spontaneous, unguarded sound that carries even through the glass. They then stop and hug each other closely. In that moment of shared humour and connection, I glimpse the future they've begun building, one where efficiency and connection, respect and love, practical partnership and emotional intimacy can coexist rather than compete.

Maria joins me at the window. 'They're going to be all right, aren't they?' she asks quietly.

'Yes', I reply, watching as they drive away. 'They've remembered how to turn toward each other. Everything else will follow from that'.

In the quiet of our practice room, with the energy of their presence still lingering, I reflect on the privilege of witnessing such transformations. Not dramatic reinventions but subtle, profound shifts that allow people to rediscover what drew them together initially. John and Sarah haven't become different people; he is still thoughtful and somewhat reserved, she remains organised and efficiency-minded, but they have expanded their capacity to value each other's natural ways of being, to make space for connection alongside achievement.

As another couple will soon arrive for their own journey, I prepare the room, refreshing water glasses and looking at the wicker baskets of pebbles. Each stone carries its own story, its own potential to reveal what words alone cannot express. Like the couples we work with, these simple objects hold complexities visible only when one takes the time to truly look, to hold them in the light, to see the patterns formed by years of pressure and transformation.

Chapter 29

Sam and Suzy – Reforged Bonds

The Final Threshold

Sam and Suzy's love story had been under siege from the moment they met, attacked by Sam's toxic ex-wife who wielded their shared children as weapons. Suzy, trying to be the supportive partner, felt increasingly like an intruder in the very relationship she was trying to build. Sam, caught between protecting his children and nurturing his new love, felt pulled apart by competing loyalties. Their first sessions revealed a couple not lacking love but drowning in the chaos created by forces beyond their control.

Three months and a few revelations later, Sam and Suzy arrive for their final scheduled meeting. They walk in together with a synchronicity that would have seemed impossible at our first encounter: not the careful navigation of separate orbits but the natural rhythm of two people accustomed to moving through the world as a unit.

They settle onto the three-seater couch differently too. The empty middle cushion that once symbolised their emotional distance has disappeared entirely. They sit close enough for their shoulders to occasionally brush, a casual physical proximity that speaks of rebuilt comfort with each other's presence. Sam's perpetual stoop has lessened, his posture more open and grounded. Suzy's movements have lost the hypervigilant quality they once carried, replaced by a more natural ease.

'Welcome', I say as Maria offers them water. 'How have things been since our last session?'

They exchange a glance that carries communication rather than assessment; a silent acknowledgement of shared understanding before Suzy speaks.

'There's been another incident with Glenda', she begins, and I note that her voice, while serious, doesn't carry the same tension it once did when mentioning Sam's ex-wife. 'She tried to keep Maya from coming for our scheduled weekend because of a suddenly arranged "special outing" that conveniently fell during our time'.

'But we handled it differently', Sam continues, the 'we' significant in itself. 'Instead of me dealing with it alone while Suzy simmered in the background, we approached it together. We called Glenda on speakerphone, both calmly reiterated the custody arrangement, offered to accommodate the special event by swapping days instead of simply losing our time'.

DOI: 10.4324/9781003752776-29

'She didn't like it', Suzy adds with a small smile that suggests understatement. 'Having both of us present, unified, not rising to her provocations. But she didn't have much choice once we didn't engage with the drama'.

'And Maya came as scheduled', Sam concludes. 'We even managed to incorporate part of the "special outing" into our weekend plans, so she didn't miss out on anything'.

This seemingly simple story represents profound progress; a shift from reactive, divided response to proactive, unified strategy. The external challenge hasn't changed, but their approach to it has transformed completely.

'That's significant progress', Maria acknowledges. 'How did it feel to handle things this way?'

'Empowering', Suzy says without hesitation. 'For years it's felt like we're constantly playing defence, always reacting to whatever Glenda throws at us. This felt like reclaiming some control, remembering we have choices in how we respond'.

'And it reminded me we're stronger together', Sam adds, his hand briefly touching Suzy's in a casual gesture of connection that would have been unthinkable in our early sessions. 'I've been handling Glenda alone for so long, first during the marriage, then after the divorce, that I forgot what it's like to have a genuine ally'.

As our final two-and-a-half-hour session unfolds, more evidence of transformation emerges. They speak of implementing regular 'family meetings' that include both children, creating space for concerns to be aired and solutions developed collectively. Sam describes establishing firmer boundaries with Glenda, including communicating exclusively through a co-parenting app that documents all interactions. Suzy shares how she's stopped taking Glenda's attacks personally, recognising them as expressions of the other woman's pain rather than accurate reflections of reality.

'The biggest change', Sam says thoughtfully, 'is that we've stopped letting Glenda set the agenda for our household. We make decisions based on what works for our family, not in reaction to whatever she's doing'.

'We still get it wrong sometimes', Suzy adds with refreshing honesty. 'There are days when it all feels overwhelming again. But now we have tools to recognise when we're slipping back into old patterns, and ways to reset'.

Perhaps most significantly, they've rebuilt their intimate connection, something they discuss with a blend of discretion and genuine joy.

'The intimacy exercises were ... enlightening', Sam admits, a slight flush colouring his cheeks. 'I had fallen into thinking of physical intimacy as yet another demand at the end of exhausting days, rather than a source of connection and renewal'.

'And I'd got so used to compartmentalising everything, being a mother, a professional, a household manager, that I'd forgotten how to transition into being a lover, a partner', Suzy adds. 'Learning to create intentional space for intimacy, treating it as essential rather than optional ... that's been transformative'.

'We've reclaimed our bedroom as our space', Sam continues. 'No more falling asleep to anxious discussions about Glenda's latest manoeuvre or tomorrow's logistical challenges'.

'We're not perfect', Suzy acknowledges with a soft laugh. 'Life with children never allows for perfect. But we're prioritising our connection again, finding each other amid everything else'.

The way they discuss these deeply personal aspects of their relationship shows how far they've come: speaking with mutual respect and without embarrassment, balancing honesty with appropriate boundaries, and most importantly, approaching intimacy as a shared journey rather than a source of tension or obligation.

As we approach the final portion of our session, I said, 'Today, we'd like you both to share something you've been working on between sessions: your "I Am" poems'.

This exercise, which invites each partner to reflect on the journey of their life through a series of 'I am' statements, often reveals deeper values and experiences that shape current patterns. Sam and Suzy have each crafted their poems independently and now will hear the others for the first time.

'Who would like to begin?' Maria asks.

'I will', Sam says, unfolding a sheet of paper. This simple willingness to go first, to lead with vulnerability, represents its own kind of progress for a man who once held his experiences so tightly contained. He takes a deep breath and begins to read:

I am the boy who learned early that conflict meant danger
I am the child of arguments that never resolved, only paused
I am the teenager seeking peace through achievement
I am the young man building life on foundations of compromise
I am the husband who confused silence with harmony
I am the father fiercely determined to protect and shelter
I am the ex-husband caught in endless battles never chosen
I am the man who found unexpected love in shared understanding
I am the stepfather blessed with trust I hadn't earned
I am the husband relearning the courage of standing firm
I am the father still learning to balance protection with empowerment
I am the partner who sometimes retreats when most needed
I am learning that peace isn't the absence of conflict but its resolution
I am discovering strength in vulnerability, power in openness
I am beginning to believe in family beyond biology
I am finding the voice silenced by years of defensive quiet
I am reclaiming joy from the shadow of constant vigilance
I am still growing, still learning, still yours.

His voice remains steady throughout, though emotion coloured the final lines. Suzy watches him with undisguised tenderness, her hand finding his when he finishes.

'Thank you', she says simply, the two words carrying the weight of genuine appreciation.
After a moment, Suzy unfolds her own paper and begins, her voice clear and present:

I am the girl raised to be strong at all costs
I am the child taking care of adults who should have cared for me
I am the teenager hiding vulnerability behind capability
I am the young woman believing love meant constant vigilance
I am the wife who confused control with care
I am the mother fierce in protection, sometimes forgetting self-care
I am the ex-wife freed and broken in equal measure
I am the woman who found unlikely sanctuary in shared scars
I am the stepmother navigating labyrinths of loyalty and love
I am the wife relearning the courage of letting go
I am the mother still learning to balance nurture with release
I am the partner who sometimes controls when feeling powerless
I am learning that strength lives in softness as well as steel
I am discovering peace in shared burdens, not solitary endurance
I am beginning to trust the family we're building day by day
I am finding the rest denied by years of constant readiness
I am reclaiming intimacy from the grip of defensive solitude
I am still hoping, still trying, still here.

The parallels between their independent poems are striking: similar wounds leading to complementary coping mechanisms, shared values expressed through different temperaments, matching journeys toward a more integrated way of being. The final lines, with their echoes of commitment phrased in their distinct voices, seem to perfectly capture their relationship: two people with different approaches but aligned intentions.

As we move toward the conclusion of our work together, I ask them the question that bookends our process: 'What have you gained from these sessions that you want to carry forward?'

Sam considers this thoughtfully. 'I've learned that protecting my family sometimes means engaging with conflict rather than avoiding it', he says finally. 'For so long, I equated peace with absence of confrontation. I'm beginning to see that true peace sometimes requires standing firm, setting boundaries, even when that creates temporary discord'.

Suzy nods in recognition. 'And I've realised that taking care of everyone doesn't have to mean carrying everything alone', she adds. 'I thought strength meant handling whatever came our way without complaint, without help. I'm learning that true resilience comes from connection, not isolation'.

'What surprised you most about this process?' Maria asks.

'That external circumstances haven't changed nearly as much as our response to them', Sam replies. 'Glenda is still Glenda. The challenges of blending our family remain complex. But those realities don't dictate our experience the way they once did'.

'And that intimacy can flourish even amid challenges, maybe especially amid challenges', Suzy adds with a warmth that transforms her face. 'I had this idea that we needed to "fix" everything else before we could reconnect as partners. Now I understand that nurturing our connection is what gives us strength to face everything else'.

They speak now with the quiet confidence of people who have glimpsed a new possibility and found it within their reach. Not a perfect family; they still face extraordinary challenges and pressures; but a resilient one, held together by choice and commitment rather than merely circumstance or obligation.

As our final minutes approach, I share my observations of their journey: their courage in examining patterns established over years, their willingness to reshape responses to situations they cannot control, the small brave steps they've taken toward reclaiming their relationship from external pressures.

'You came to us as two people united in purpose but divided in approach', I tell them. 'What I see now are two people who have learned to function as a genuine team, bringing your individual strengths to shared challenges'.

'It feels sustainable now', Sam says thoughtfully. 'Before, every day felt like barely keeping our heads above water. Now, even when the challenges are just as intense, we have a foundation that doesn't crumble under pressure'.

'And we remember to seek joy, not just manage crises', Suzy adds. 'Creating positive experiences for our family rather than just defending against negative ones'.

As they prepare to leave for the last time, I observe how differently they move together compared to that first session. There is an ease between them now, a natural coordination that speaks of renewed connection. Sam helps Suzy with her coat, their interaction marked by small, unconscious moments of physical awareness that were absent sixteen weeks ago.

'Remember you can always reach out if you need us', Maria reminds them. 'Though I have a feeling you have the tools you need now'.

At the door, they pause. 'Thank you', Suzy says, genuine emotion in her voice. 'For helping us remember we're partners, not just co-managers of chaos'.

As they walk toward their car, I watch them from the window. Sam's arm rests lightly across Suzy's shoulders, a casual intimacy that would have seemed forced in their early sessions. They move in conversation, their faces animated in a way that suggests they're already engaging with each other rather than merely departing together.

Maria joins me at the window. 'They've found their strength as a unit, haven't they?' she asks softly.

'Yes', I reply, watching as they drive away. 'Not by eliminating their challenges, but by facing them together. That's the real victory'.

In the quiet of our practice room, with the energy of their presence still lingering, I reflect on the privilege of witnessing such transformations. Sam and Suzy haven't become different people; he remains the thoughtful protector, she the capable nurturer, but they have expanded their capacity to blend these traits into a cohesive partnership, to create a sanctuary of connection amid external storms.

Chapter 30

The Power of Tears

Embracing Emotional Expression

In a world that often equates strength with stoicism, there exists a profound power in allowing ourselves to cry. Tears, whether born from sorrow, joy, or relief, represent one of humanity's most authentic forms of expression, yet many of us, particularly men, have been conditioned to suppress this natural release.

Breaking the 'Big Boys Don't Cry' Myth

'Big boys don't cry'. These five words have shaped generations of men, creating an emotional prison that has robbed many of the healing power of tears. This cultural directive has left countless men unable to access their full emotional spectrum, creating a disconnect not only within themselves but in their most important relationships.

When a man finds the courage to cry in front of others, something transformative happens. The vulnerability displayed isn't weakness; it's profound strength. It's an acknowledgement of one's humanity, a testament to the depth of feeling that defines our shared experience. For many men, that first moment of allowing tears to flow freely marks the beginning of a journey toward emotional wholeness.

In our sessions, we create a sanctuary where this transformation can occur. The power of having two supportive coaches present, offering different perspectives and complementary support, provides clients with the safety needed to access deeply buried emotions. When a male client finally allows himself to cry in our presence, we witness a profound shift, a breaking of emotional barriers that often leads to remarkable breakthroughs.

Partners frequently express frustration: 'He doesn't share what he's feeling'. 'He doesn't express any emotions'. Behind this complaint lies a yearning for connection that can only come through emotional transparency. When men embrace their capacity to cry, they often discover not only relief but a deeper connection with those they love.

Creating Safe Spaces for Emotional Release

For women, the struggle might manifest differently. While society may be more accepting of women's tears, they too face judgement, labelled as 'too emotional'

DOI: 10.4324/9781003752776-30

or 'unstable' for expressing their feelings openly. Creating environments where women can cry without fear of judgement validates their experiences and honours their emotional journeys.

Our approach excels in creating these essential safe spaces. The dynamic of two coaches working in harmony allows us to attentively hold space for clients as they navigate vulnerable emotional territory. We recognise that meaningful tears in therapy don't simply happen, they require careful facilitation, deep trust, and expert guidance. Through our complementary coaching styles, we help clients identify and release emotional blockages that may have been present for decades.

When someone, regardless of gender, feels safe enough to express their pain or unhappiness through tears, and has that expression acknowledged rather than dismissed, healing begins. The simple act of bearing witness to someone's tears, of saying 'I see your pain, and it matters', can be profoundly transformational. In our therapy sessions, these moments of emotional release often represent pivotal turning points in the client's journey.

The Full Spectrum: Tears of Joy and Hope

Tears aren't solely expressions of sorrow. Some of life's most beautiful moments are marked by tears of joy, gratitude, or overwhelming love. These tears of happiness represent the fullness of our emotional capacity, our ability to be so moved by goodness that we overflow.

We consider it equally important to facilitate positive emotional expression. Helping clients access tears of joy and hope is a vital component of our therapeutic approach. When clients who have struggled with emotional expression begin to shed tears not only in pain but in happiness, we celebrate this as a significant milestone in their emotional development.

When we liberate ourselves to cry tears of joy at births, weddings, accomplishments, reconnections, we embrace life's richness. These moments of emotional abundance point toward future possibilities, reminding us of our capacity for happiness and fulfilment. Our coaching sessions often become spaces where clients can practise experiencing and expressing the full spectrum of emotions, including the joyful ones they may have previously dampened.

The Physiological and Psychological Benefits

Beyond the emotional release, tears serve important physiological and psychological functions. Research suggests crying releases stress hormones and toxins from the body, while triggering the production of endorphins, our natural feel-good chemicals. The body, in its wisdom, has designed crying as a natural stress-relief mechanism.

In our coaching sessions, we educate clients about these benefits, helping them understand that tears are not just emotionally therapeutic but physically beneficial.

This knowledge often helps clients, especially men, reframe crying as a healthy, natural process rather than a sign of weakness.

Psychologically, tears help us process and integrate difficult experiences. They function as emotional punctuation, marking significant moments and helping us acknowledge important transitions and truths in our lives. Our approach creates carefully guided opportunities for this integration to occur in a supported environment.

Transformative Moments: Client Stories

Martin's Breakthrough

Martin, a fifty-two-year-old executive, came to our sessions initially to address work-related stress. During our third session, we gently explored his relationship with his father, who had passed away five years earlier. As we asked about unspoken words between them, Martin's voice began to quiver slightly.

'I never told him I was proud of him too', he whispered, his eyes glistening. We created space for this moment, both of us present but not rushing to fill the silence. When the first tear rolled down his cheek, Martin looked startled, almost apologetic. 'I haven't cried since I was twelve', he admitted.

We acknowledged his courage as more tears came. The dam had broken after forty years of emotional restraint. By the end of the session, Martin described feeling 'lighter, like I've put down a heavy rucksack I didn't know I was carrying'. In subsequent sessions, his wife reported a profound change in their relationship; he had begun sharing vulnerable feelings with her for the first time in their twenty-year marriage.

Melanie's Release

Melanie sought our help after a series of career disappointments left her feeling numb. 'I should be upset, but I can't feel anything', she explained in our initial consultation. A successful solicitor, Sarah prided herself on maintaining composure regardless of circumstances.

During our fifth session, I used guided imagery to help Melanie connect with her younger self. As she visualised speaking to herself as a hopeful law student, something shifted. 'She had such dreams', Melanie said, her voice catching. 'She believed she could make a difference'.

When we asked what she wanted to tell her younger self, Melanie's professional facade crumbled. 'I'm sorry', she sobbed, tears flowing freely. 'I'm so sorry I stopped fighting for what matters'. For nearly twenty minutes, Sarah cried deeply while we held space for this profound release.

Afterwards, she appeared transformed – her face softer, her body language more open. 'I haven't cried like that since my grandmother's funeral fifteen years ago', she told us. 'I thought I'd forgotten how'. In the weeks that followed, Melanie reported reconnecting with her passion for advocacy and experiencing a range of emotions she had long suppressed.

Embracing Our Full Humanity

Learning to express emotions openly through tears represents a journey toward wholeness. It's about reclaiming aspects of our humanity that cultural conditioning may have suppressed. The ability to cry, and to be present with others in their tears, enriches our relationships and deepens our experience of life.

Our way of working provides a uniquely effective framework for this journey. With two coaches present, we can simultaneously support the client experiencing emotional release while modelling healthy responses to tears. Our clients learn not only how to express emotions through tears but also how to be compassionately present with others who are crying, a skill they can carry into their personal relationships.

Whether you're working to overcome the 'big boys don't cry' programming, creating safe spaces for emotional expression, or celebrating tears of joy, remember that your tears are not signs of weakness. They are powerful expressions of your authentic humanity, markers of your courage to feel deeply and live fully.

In our therapy sessions, we witness this courage regularly, as clients allow themselves to cry meaningfully, often for the first time in decades. These moments of vulnerability become cornerstones of transformation.

In embracing tears, we don't diminish our strength, we amplify it, creating lives and relationships characterised by greater honesty, deeper connection, and more profound joy. As therapists, there is no greater privilege than facilitating this journey toward emotional wholeness through the healing power of tears.

Chapter 31

Barry and Edith – Breaking the Chains of Time

Healing after Decades

For thirty years, Barry and Edith had carried the weight of betrayal between them like an invisible wall. His single affair, confessed decades ago, had never been truly processed or healed – merely endured. They had built a life together, raised children, celebrated grandchildren, all while the wound festered untouched beneath the surface. At seventy and sixty-eight respectively, they sat in my therapy room asking the most painful question: was it too late to heal what time had calcified?

Our second session with Barry and Edith revealed deeper layers of their entrenched pattern. While they demonstrated willingness to engage with the exercises we'd provided, Edith's triggers remained unpredictable and powerful. During a particularly raw moment when Edith described being 'ambushed' by images of the affair while shopping in a department store, the same store where Barry had once bought a gift for the other woman, I recognised a quality in her response that suggested something beyond ordinary emotional reaction.

The visceral intensity of her physical symptoms, the way her present reality seemed to momentarily disappear, the inability to distinguish between past and present despite her obvious intelligence and self-awareness; all pointed to a trauma response that had become neurologically embedded over three decades of reinforcement. Her rational mind understood that thirty years had passed, but her emotional and physiological systems were responding as if the betrayal had just occurred.

After consulting with Maria, I suggested something we rarely offer in our standard approach: a solo session with Edith, focused specifically on addressing these trauma responses using more specialised techniques than our usual couples work allows.

'I think there might be benefit in working with just Edith for one session', I explained to them both. 'Not because Barry's perspective isn't equally important, but because the triggers Edith experiences have characteristics that might respond to specific approaches I'm trained in'.

Barry immediately agreed, his relief at any potential path forward evident in his quick response. Edith was more hesitant, perhaps concerned that this suggested she was 'the problem' rather than the affair itself.

'This isn't about assigning blame', I clarified, sensing her reservation. 'It's about recognising that you're experiencing genuine trauma responses that are causing

DOI: 10.4324/9781003752776-31

you significant distress. These responses have become neurologically embedded in ways that standard talking approaches sometimes struggle to address'.

With mutual agreement, we scheduled a solo session with Edith for the following week.

When Edith arrived for her individual appointment, she carried herself with the same composed dignity I'd observed previously, but there was a new quality of cautious hope in her demeanour. Alone, without Barry's presence, she allowed glimpses of vulnerability that had been carefully contained during our joint sessions.

'I want you to know that I don't enjoy feeling this way', she said almost immediately after settling into her seat. 'Barry sometimes thinks I cling to this anger because it gives me power over him. But it's the opposite. These feelings have power over me. I would give anything to be free of them'.

This simple admission created the perfect opening for the work I hoped to do with her. 'I believe you', I told her. 'And that's exactly why I think a different approach might help. What you're experiencing has characteristics of what we call emotional trauma; not because the affair wasn't genuinely traumatic, but because your nervous system has become locked in a particular response pattern that automatically reactivates when triggered'.

I explained how Timeline Therapy and clinical hypnotherapy might help address these deeply embedded patterns. These approaches access the subconscious processes where trauma responses are stored rather than relying solely on conscious processing.

'I'm not promising a miracle', I cautioned. 'But these techniques sometimes allow people to process experiences differently, to change their relationship with painful memories without erasing or minimising them'.

Edith listened with careful attention, asking thoughtful questions about the process. Her initial scepticism was evident but tempered by a willingness born of decades of suffering. 'At this point', she said simply, 'I have nothing to lose by trying'.

We began with Timeline Therapy, a technique that helps people work with their unconscious organisation of time and memory. I guided Edith to visualise her personal timeline, the way she internally represents her past, present, and future, and to locate the affair within this subjective landscape.

As expected, the affair occupied a disproportionately prominent position in her timeline, its emotional intensity undiminished by the thirty years of experiences that followed it. More tellingly, Edith described it as having tentacle-like connections to countless other points in her timeline, both before and after the actual events; explaining how seemingly unrelated triggers could instantly connect her to the pain of betrayal.

Working carefully with this visualisation, I helped Edith create a healthier perspective on these events; not dismissing their significance but allowing them to take a more proportional place in her long and complex life story. We worked to sever the automatic connections between neutral triggers and the intense emotional pain, to create space between stimulus and response where choice might live.

When Edith seemed ready, we transitioned to hypnotherapy. After guiding her into a relaxed, receptive state, I used specific techniques to help her subconscious mind reprocess the emotional trauma of the affair. This wasn't about forgetting what happened or minimising its importance, but rather about changing how these memories were stored and accessed, shifting them from raw, ever-present wounds to important but contained historical events.

Throughout the process, Edith remained deeply engaged, occasionally tearful but never overwhelmed. When we gradually brought the session to a close after more than two hours, the change in her was subtle but unmistakable: a certain lightness in her expression, a quality of relaxed awareness that hadn't been present before.

'I feel different', she said, sounding almost surprised. 'Not completely transformed, but ... it's as if something that was tightly knotted inside me has loosened. I can still see and feel everything, but there's a bit more space around it. Does that make sense?'

It made perfect sense. This was often how people described successful trauma processing: not a magical erasure of difficult experiences, but a shift in relationship to them that created room for new possibilities.

'This is just the beginning', I told her. 'Your mind will continue processing what we've done today. Pay attention to how you respond to things that would normally trigger you. Not with expectation, just with curiosity'.

Edith agreed to return for our third scheduled couples' session the following week. Before she left, she asked a question that revealed both her hope and her lingering uncertainty: 'Do you think Barry and I can actually move beyond this after all this time?'

'I believe meaningful change is possible at any age', I answered honestly. 'Not because the past can be erased, but because new chapters can always be written'.

The transformation that unfolded over the next week exceeded even my cautious optimism. When Barry and Edith arrived for what would be our final joint session, the change was immediately apparent. They entered the room together as always, but with a different quality of connection: a natural awareness of each other that hadn't been visible in previous meetings.

As they settled onto the couch, I noticed that the middle cushion no longer remained entirely vacant. They didn't sit pressed against each other; that would have felt forced and unnatural after decades of careful distance, but the space between them had diminished, filled now with a new quality of shared presence rather than emptiness.

'How have things been since our last meetings?' I ask, deliberately using the plural to acknowledge both our couples work and the individual session with Edith.

They exchange a glance that carries communication rather than assessment, a small but significant shift in their nonverbal language.

'Something has changed', Barry begins, wonder evident in his voice. 'Profoundly changed'.

Edith nods, her characteristic composure now complemented by a quality of ease that had been absent before. 'The work we did in the individual session', she says, turning to me, 'it was ... I don't have adequate words for it. Transformational, perhaps'.

'Can you share what's been different?' Maria asks.

Edith considers this thoughtfully. 'We were watching a film three days ago', she explains. 'There was a scene of infidelity; the kind of scene that would normally trigger hours of distress for me, intrusive thoughts, questions that Barry couldn't possibly answer to my satisfaction'.

She pauses, still seeming somewhat surprised by what she's about to describe. 'I felt a momentary tightness, an awareness of potential distress. But it was like ... like watching a wave approach but not being pulled under by it. I could see it, feel it, but remain separate from it. I was able to simply note it and return to the present moment, to the actual film we were watching together'.

'It was extraordinary', Barry adds, genuine awe in his tone. 'Edith turned to me and simply said, "That was a trigger, but it's passing". And then we continued watching. No hours of painful conversations, no retreating to separate rooms, no cloud hanging over us for days afterward'.

'That's happened several times now, in different situations', Edith continues. 'Not that the triggers have disappeared entirely, but my relationship to them has fundamentally shifted. They arise, I acknowledge them, but they no longer consume me or define what happens next'.

This description perfectly captures the intended outcome of the trauma work we had done: not eliminating legitimate emotional responses but creating space between stimulus and reaction where new choices become possible.

'And how has this affected things between you?' I ask.

Barry reaches across the diminished space between them, gently covering Edith's hand with his own; a gesture that would have seemed unimaginable in our first session. 'It feels like we've been released from a prison neither of us knew how to escape', he says quietly. 'Not that the past has been erased or forgotten, but that it's finally taking its proper place in our story rather than overwhelming everything else'.

'We're remembering aspects of our relationship that have been overshadowed for decades', Edith adds. 'Conversations that don't circle back to the affair, moments of simple pleasure in each other's company, the ability to truly listen to each other about present concerns rather than constantly revisiting past wounds'.

As our session continued, they share more evidence of transformation: a spontaneous decision to visit a garden centre together, something they hadn't done in years; an evening spent looking through old photographs of happy times they had almost forgotten existed; the first truly restful night's sleep Edith can remember having in years.

'The most profound change', Edith says thoughtfully, 'is that I no longer feel like a passive victim of my own responses. For thirty years, these triggers would ambush me, and then the pain and anger would simply take over, as if I had no choice in the matter. Now I can feel the initial response but choose what happens next. That space between feeling and action; it changes everything'.

Their progress has been so dramatic that we discuss whether they feel additional sessions would be beneficial. Both agree that while they remain open to further support if needed, they feel equipped now to continue their healing journey together.

'We've lost so much time already', Barry says, regret mixing with new determination in his voice. 'At our age, each day matters. We want to live whatever years we have left free from this shadow that's darkened so much of our life together'.

As we move toward the conclusion of our work together, I ask them the question that bookends our process: 'What have you gained from these sessions that you want to carry forward?'

Edith considers this thoughtfully. 'I've learned that being imprisoned by the past was not inevitable', she says finally. 'For thirty years, I believed my responses were simply fixed, that this pain was my permanent reality. I now understand that even patterns established over decades can shift, that new neural pathways can form even at our age'.

Barry nods in recognition. 'And I've learned that patience without hope is just endurance', he adds. 'I had resigned myself to simply weathering Edith's pain until the end of our days, believing nothing could ever really change. I now understand that meaningful transformation is possible even after decades of stasis, that our story didn't have to end as I feared it would'.

'What surprised you most about this process?' Maria asks.

'The speed of change once the right approach was found', Edith replies without hesitation. 'After thirty years of circling the same territory, to experience such profound shift in just weeks... it feels miraculous'.

'And that happiness could feel so unfamiliar', Barry adds with gentle wonder. 'I had forgotten what it felt like to simply enjoy Edith's company without bracing for the next storm. Rediscovering that at seventy-four feels like a gift I never expected to receive'.

They speak now with the quiet wisdom of people who have glimpsed a new possibility after decades of being stuck: not a perfect resolution or complete transformation, but a sustainable way forward that honours both the injury that occurred and the substantial marriage that contains it.

As our final minutes approach, I share my observations of their journey: the courage it took to try a different approach after so many years of being stuck, Edith's remarkable openness to addressing deeply embedded trauma patterns, the mutual commitment that kept them together long enough for healing to finally occur.

'You came to us as two people locked in positions that had calcified over thirty years', I tell them. 'What I see now are two people who have found a way forward that neither believed was still possible'.

'It feels like waking up', Barry says simply. 'As if we've been moving through life half-asleep for decades, and suddenly the world has colour and dimension again'.

'And freedom', Edith adds, the word clearly carrying profound meaning for her. 'Not from the past itself; that remains part of our history. But freedom from its power to dictate our present and future'.

As they prepare to leave for the last time, I observe the natural ease that has replaced their formerly careful coordination. There is an awareness between them now, a quality of attention that speaks to genuine reconnection. Barry helps Edith with her coat, and she turns toward him with a smile of acknowledgement that carries none of the guardedness I observed in our first meeting.

'Remember you can always reach out if you need additional support', Maria reminds them. 'Though I have a feeling you have what you need now to continue this journey together'.

At the door, they pause. 'Thank you', Edith says, genuine emotion warming her voice. 'For helping me find freedom I had stopped believing was possible'.

'And for not giving up on us when we had nearly given up on ourselves', Barry adds.

As they walk toward their car, I watch them from the window. Barry reaches for Edith's hand, and she accepts this gesture not out of obligation but with natural ease. Just before they reach the car, Edith says something that makes Barry laugh; a moment of simple, unguarded connection that would have seemed impossible just weeks ago.

Maria joins me at the window. 'I've rarely seen such dramatic transformation in such a short time', she observes quietly.

'Sometimes the right intervention at the right moment can shift patterns that years of conventional approaches couldn't touch', I reply. 'Particularly with trauma responses that have become neurologically embedded'.

In the quiet of our practice room, with the energy of their presence still lingering, I reflect on the privilege of witnessing such transformations. Barry and Edith haven't achieved a perfect resolution to their long struggle; the affair remains part of their history, some pain may still surface at times; but they have developed new capacities to respond to these challenges, to remain connected despite difficult emotions, to see their relationship as something larger and more complex than its most painful chapter.

Chapter 32

Unconscious Mind – Where Transformation Begins

As I sit in my therapy room, awaiting the arrival of my next couple, I often reflect on what makes relationship therapy so challenging yet so rewarding. After decades of working with hundreds of couples, I've come to understand that what unfolds in the therapy room is merely the visible tip of a much larger iceberg. The submerged mass, vast, powerful, and largely invisible, is the unconscious mind, where the true roots of relationship patterns reside.

The Dance of Two Minds

We humans exist in a fascinating duality. Our conscious mind, rational, analytical, and verbal, is what we typically identify as our 'self'. It's the narrator of our life story, the voice in our head that we hear as we move through the world. This is the mind that clients bring willingly into therapy, prepared to discuss their challenges and seek solutions.

Yet beneath this surface awareness lies the unconscious mind, a repository of memories, emotions, beliefs, and patterns that operate outside our immediate awareness. This second mind is far more powerful than most people realise, driving up to 95% of our behaviours and reactions. It works ceaselessly, processing millions of bits of information every second while our conscious mind handles merely forty bits per second. The unconscious holds our deepest fears, our earliest programming, our unprocessed traumas, and the templates for all our relationships.

In couples therapy, I'm not merely working with two people, I'm working with four minds: two conscious and two unconscious. The conscious minds

DOI: 10.4324/9781003752776-32

may genuinely want change, may sincerely love each other, may be committed to growth. But if their unconscious minds harbour unresolved wounds, limiting beliefs, or maladaptive patterns, these will undermine even the most genuine conscious intentions.

This is why so many couples express frustration that they 'keep having the same argument' despite their best efforts. Their conscious minds may resolve to communicate differently, but their unconscious minds continue running the same old programme, triggering the same emotional responses and behaviours that lead inevitably back to familiar territory.

Steven: The Pursuit of Unachievable Excellence

Let me share the story of Steven, a client whose external success masked a profound inner struggle. From the outside, Steven appeared to have everything: a successful career as a finance director, an attractive and loving wife, two healthy children, and a beautiful home. Yet he arrived in our therapy room alongside his wife Catherine, both exhausted and disconnected.

'I don't understand what's wrong with me', Steven confessed in our second session. 'We have everything I thought would make me happy. But I feel constantly anxious, like I'm always falling short. Catherine says I'm never present, even when I'm physically there'.

Catherine nodded sadly. 'It's like he's always chasing something just out of reach. He works until midnight, takes calls on weekends, and even when he does take time off, his mind is elsewhere: planning, worrying, strategising'.

As we explored Steven's history, two critical early experiences emerged. The first occurred when he was eight years old. Despite being of average weight, several classmates had begun calling him 'fatty' after he struggled during a physical education class. The memory still made him wince visibly decades later. 'I can still hear their laughter', he admitted.

The second formative experience involved his father, an accomplished academic. 'Dad was never unkind', Steven explained. 'But no achievement was ever quite enough. If I got an A, he'd say "That's good. Next time maybe you can get an A*". If I scored the winning goal, he'd point out how I could have played better'.

These experiences had planted toxic seeds in Steven's unconscious mind. From the schoolyard taunting, he had absorbed the belief that he was fundamentally inadequate and that others were always judging him harshly. From his father's well-intentioned but damaging pattern, he had internalised the message that love and approval were conditional upon achievement, and that 'good enough' was never truly good enough.

Steven's conscious mind knew these beliefs were irrational. He could acknowledge that he was successful by any objective measure, that Catherine loved him unconditionally, that his colleagues respected him. But his unconscious mind continued to run the old programming: 'You're inadequate. You must constantly prove your worth. If you rest, you'll be exposed as a fraud'.

To access these unconscious patterns, I used Timeline Therapy, asking Steven to imagine returning to those formative moments as his adult self. As he mentally revisited the schoolyard incident, powerful emotions surfaced: shame, humiliation, helplessness. Through the Timeline Therapy process, I guided him to observe how that eight-year-old boy had made sense of the experience, drawing conclusions that would shape his adult life.

'I decided I had to be perfect', Steven realised, tears streaming down his face. 'That if I achieved enough, no one could ever laugh at me again'.

The work with Steven's unconscious mind didn't end with awareness. Conscious insight alone rarely creates lasting change when patterns are deeply embedded in the emotional brain. We used several techniques to create what I call 'personal history modification': not changing what actually happened but changing how these experiences were neurologically encoded.

I guided Steven through a process of 'resource installation', helping him imagine his adult self providing his eight-year-old self with the support, perspective, and comfort that was missing in the original experience. We used bilateral stimulation techniques to help his brain reprocess these memories and store them differently. We created new neural pathways through repeated visualisations of responding to triggers with new, healthier patterns.

Over several sessions, Steven began to recognise how his unconscious programming was sabotaging his happiness and relationship. He began practising what he called 'good enough moments': deliberately leaving tasks incomplete, turning down optional projects, making small 'mistakes' and observing that the catastrophic consequences his unconscious mind predicted never materialised.

Two months later, the change in both Steven and his relationship was remarkable. 'I still work hard', he told me in our final session, 'but I've stopped trying to outrun my own shadow. I've realised that Catherine loves me, not my achievements. And I'm learning to do the same'.

Catherine reached for his hand. 'He's present now', she said simply. 'When he's home, he's really home'.

Sally: The Burden of Imagined Responsibility

Another client, Sally, presented with a different manifestation of unconscious programming. A bright, creative woman in her mid-thirties, Sally came to therapy with her partner Graham, who was frustrated by what he described as her 'constant state of worry'.

'It's exhausting', Graham explained during our first session. 'Sally stresses about everything; if I'm five minutes late, she imagines I've been in an accident. If her mother doesn't answer the phone, she's convinced something terrible has happened. She turns down job opportunities because she's certain she'll fail. I love her, but I'm running out of energy to constantly reassure her'.

Sally didn't disagree. 'I know my anxiety is irrational', she said, her fingers nervously twisting a tissue. 'I've tried meditation, breathing exercises, positive thinking. Nothing works for long. It feels like anxiety is just part of who I am'.

As we explored her history, Sally recalled a seemingly innocuous childhood moment that had taken root in her unconscious mind. When she was about six years old, her mother, who was raising Sally alone after her father's departure, had said during a minor illness, 'You know, Sally, I won't be around forever. You need to learn to take care of yourself'.

This comment, made during a vulnerable moment by a parent Sally adored and depended upon, had embedded itself deeply in her emotional brain. Her six-year-old self had interpreted it catastrophically: 'Mum is going to die, and it will be my fault if I don't prevent it'. This unconscious belief had spawned a hypervigilant approach to life, where Sally felt responsible for anticipating and preventing disasters of all kinds.

To access this unconscious material, I used a technique called Clean Language, asking questions that helped Sally explore her metaphorical landscape without contaminating it with my own assumptions. 'And when you feel anxious, that's like what?' I asked.

'It's like I'm standing on the edge of a cliff', Sally replied, 'and everyone I love is near the edge, and it's my job to make sure no one falls off'.

'And what happens just before you're standing on the edge of a cliff?'

Through this non-leading process, we uncovered the subtle triggers that activated Sally's anxiety and the unconscious logic that maintained it. She believed that her vigilance was all that stood between her loved ones and disaster; a tremendous burden she had carried since childhood.

To create change at the unconscious level, we used several approaches. Parts Work helped Sally recognise that her anxiety, while problematic in its current form, originated as an attempt to keep her and her loved ones safe. Rather than trying to eliminate this 'part' of herself, she learned to acknowledge its protective intention while updating its information and methods.

Through timelines, Sally revisited the moment with her mother, this time with her adult perspective. She was able to see how her six-year-old self had misinterpreted a simple statement, taking on a responsibility no child could possibly fulfil. In her imagination, she was able to have a conversation with her younger self, providing the reassurance and broader understanding that had been missing.

We also employed somatic techniques, recognising that anxiety is not merely a thought pattern but a bodily experience. Sally learned to identify the physical sensations that accompanied the activation of her anxiety programme and to interrupt this pattern through specific movements and postures that signalled safety to her nervous system.

The transformation wasn't immediate or linear. There were setbacks and difficult sessions. But gradually, Sally developed a new relationship with her anxiety. Rather than being consumed by it or fighting against it, she learned to recognise it as information, sometimes useful, sometimes distorted, that she could evaluate rather than automatically obey.

'Last week, Graham was late coming home, and my first thought was still that something terrible had happened', Sally reported in our final session. 'But it felt different. Like the thought was just passing through, not taking over. I noticed it, took a breath, and then just texted him instead of spiralling into panic'.

Graham nodded. 'She's still Sally; she still cares deeply about people, still thinks about what might go wrong sometimes. But she's not imprisoned by it anymore. There's a lightness to her that I haven't seen before'.

Accessing the Unconscious: Beyond Rational Conversation

These cases illustrate why traditional talk therapy, which engages primarily with the conscious mind, often falls short in creating lasting change. Steven could have intellectually understood for years that his worth wasn't dependent on achievement, but until we addressed the unconscious programming driving his behaviour, this insight remained impotent.

Similarly, Sally could have been told countless times not to worry, to think positively, to 'just relax'. Without accessing and transforming the unconscious beliefs driving her anxiety, such advice was as effective as telling someone with a broken leg to 'just walk normally'.

In my approach to relationship therapy, I employ a variety of techniques specifically designed to access and modify unconscious patterns:

Timeline Therapy allows clients to revisit formative experiences while maintaining the perspective and resources of their adult self, facilitating reprocessing of early programming.

Clean Language and Symbolic Modelling help clients explore their own metaphorical landscape without therapist contamination, revealing the structures of unconscious patterns.

Parts Work acknowledges the multiplicity of the psyche, allowing dialogue with aspects of self that may be operating outside conscious awareness.

Somatic Approaches recognise that patterns are encoded not just in thought but in the body itself, using physical awareness and movement to create change.

Bilateral Stimulation facilitates the reprocessing of emotionally charged material, similar to the natural processing that occurs during REM sleep.

Hypnotic Language Patterns bypass conscious resistance to speak directly to the unconscious mind, offering new possibilities and perspectives.

These approaches share a common understanding: lasting change requires engaging the emotional, experiential parts of the brain where unconscious patterns reside. It's not enough for clients to intellectually understand their patterns; they must have new experiences that contradict old programming at a visceral level.

The Ripple Effect in Relationships

In relationship therapy, this work with the unconscious mind creates profound ripple effects. When Steven released his driving need for external validation, not only did he experience greater peace, but Catherine no longer felt invisible and unimportant. When Sally's anxiety loosened its grip, Graham no longer felt responsible for managing her emotional state, allowing them both greater freedom and connection.

This is the true power of working with the unconscious mind in relationship therapy. Individual healing creates relationship healing, and relationship healing supports individual healing, in a virtuous cycle that transforms the entire system.

The conscious mind may bring couples to my therapy room, but it's engaging with the unconscious mind that creates the transformations they seek. When these deeper patterns shift, couples often report that problems they've struggled with for years suddenly become manageable, not because the problems themselves have changed, but because they're now approaching them from a fundamentally different place.

As a therapist, witnessing these transformations is profoundly moving. There is something almost magical about the moment when a person recognises the unconscious pattern that has been dictating their life and relationships, often for decades, and then discovers they have the power to choose differently. It's as if they suddenly find themselves in a larger room than they knew existed, with doors and windows they never noticed before.

The work is not always easy or comfortable. Accessing unconscious material often means confronting painful emotions that have been carefully avoided. But in the safety of the therapeutic space, with appropriate techniques and support, even the most entrenched patterns can shift, creating possibilities that once seemed unimaginable.

In the final analysis, this is why I remain passionate about relationship therapy after all these years. Each couple that walks through my door brings not just their conscious hopes and complaints, but the rich, complex territory of two unconscious minds that have been mapping the world since childhood. Helping them navigate this territory more consciously will help them chart a better future.

Chapter 33

Jon and Sophia – Beyond Sight

Seeing with the Heart

Sophia's progressive vision loss had arrived like a thief in the night, stealing not just her sight but her sense of self, independence, and nearly their marriage. When they first came to therapy, Sophia was exhausted from carrying both their emotional loads, while Jon retreated into anger and denial. They loved each other deeply – that had never been in question. What remained uncertain was whether love alone could survive the seismic shift that illness had forced upon them both.

Four months later, Jon and Sophia arrive for their final scheduled meeting. They enter the room with a synchronicity that speaks of newly established patterns: Jon still offering guidance but with a subtle difference in how they navigate together, Sophia accepting support without the reluctance that once characterised her movements. There is something more fluid in their coordination now, a dance of mutual adaptation rather than awkward accommodation.

They settle onto the couch differently too. The careful distance that once separated them has diminished considerably. Jon sits close enough that his arm rests naturally along the back of the couch behind Sophia, not as a conscious gesture but with the ease of habitual connection. Sophia's posture remains composed but carries less of the vigilant tension I observed in our first meeting.

'Welcome', I say as Maria offers them water. 'How have things been since our last session?'

They exchange a glance that carries communication despite Sophia's limited vision, a small but significant indication of their renewed connection.

'We've had what I'd call a breakthrough', Jon begins, his voice carrying an energy that was absent in our early sessions. 'It happened during that exercise you suggested about speaking memories to each other'.

'The one where we were supposed to describe meaningful places we'd experienced together', Sophia continues, building on his thought in a way that demonstrates their reestablished rhythm. 'Jon was describing a sunset we watched in New Zealand five years ago, and I realised something important'.

'What was that?' Maria asks.

'That even when I can no longer see such things with my eyes, I still hold them perfectly preserved in my memory', Sophia explains, a new quality of peace evident

DOI: 10.4324/9781003752776-33

beneath her words. 'Jon described that sunset in such vivid detail that I could see it again through his description: the exact colours, how the light played on the water, even the feeling of the wind. And I understood that while I'm losing one way of experiencing the world, other ways remain and can even deepen'.

'And I realised I'd been viewing Sophia's condition only as loss', Jon adds, his hand briefly touching hers in a gesture that seems both natural and meaningful. 'Cataloguing everything that was disappearing instead of recognising what remains. What continues to develop and strengthen even as her sight diminishes'.

This seemingly simple realisation represents profound progress; a shift from focusing exclusively on what is being lost to recognising what persists and even grows amid significant change.

As our final two-and-a-half-hour session unfolds, more evidence of transformation emerges. They speak of implementing a daily practice they call 'sensory sharing': deliberately experiencing the world through touch, sound, smell, and taste, developing a shared vocabulary beyond the visual. Jon describes his growing understanding that supporting Sophia doesn't mean solving her condition but being fully present with it, while Sophia acknowledges her recognition that accepting help doesn't diminish her essential strength and independence.

'The exercise on grief and growth was particularly important', Sophia says, referring to one of the tools we provided. 'I needed permission to genuinely mourn what I'm losing. Trying to be stoic all the time, to focus only on "staying positive", was actually preventing me from moving forward'.

'And I needed to understand that my technical problem-solving approach was partly a way of avoiding my own grief', Jon adds. 'Researching treatments and accessibility tools is necessary and helpful, but I was using it to escape the emotional reality we're facing'.

The way they discuss these insights shows how far they've come: speaking to each other as much as to us, building on each other's thoughts rather than presenting separate narratives, acknowledging their individual struggles within a framework of shared experience.

Perhaps most significantly, they've begun rebuilding their physical connection, approaching intimacy with new awareness and creativity rather than avoidance.

'We're learning different ways of being together', Sophia explains with dignified openness. 'At first, Jon was so afraid of hurting me or doing something wrong that he wouldn't touch me at all. Now we're discovering that physical connection can actually be deeper when it's not taken for granted, when it requires conscious attention and communication'.

'I was so focused on what had changed that I couldn't see what remained', Jon acknowledges. 'Sophia is still the woman I fell in love with: her intelligence, her strength, her particular way of seeing the world that goes far beyond physical vision. I was letting fear obscure that fundamental truth'.

This perspective, that essential connection can deepen rather than diminish through shared adversity, represents a profound shift from their initial positions of isolated struggle.

'Today, we'd like you both to share something you've been working on between sessions: your "I Am" poems'. This exercise, which invites each partner to reflect on the journey of their life through a series of 'I am' statements, often reveals deeper values and experiences that shape current patterns. Jon and Sophia have each crafted their poems independently and now will hear the other's for the first time.

'Who would like to begin?' Maria asks.

'I will', Sophia says, unfolding a sheet of paper that she holds close to her face, using her remaining vision. Her willingness to do this without embarrassment, to adapt rather than withdraw, itself demonstrates growth. She takes a measured breath and begins to read:

I am the girl who climbed trees to see horizons beyond our small town
I am the child who treasured books like windows to countless worlds
I am the student who found refuge in the precise lines of architectural drawings
I am the woman who once defined herself through achievements and adventures
I am the wife whose independence was a point of pride and identity
I am the professional whose vision created spaces for others to inhabit
I am now the woman learning to navigate by touch what once came through sight
I am the architect reimagining my own life's structure as foundations shift
I am the wife discovering vulnerability can strengthen rather than weaken bonds
I am the friend finding unexpected depth in voices once overshadowed by appearances
I am learning that weakness and strength are not opposites but companions
I am discovering that vision exists in many forms beyond the physical
I am beginning to accept that some losses make room for unexpected gains
I am finding courage to face darkness without being defined by it
I am creating memories that transcend the merely visual
I am still curious, still creating, still wholly myself
I am more than what I see or don't see; I am how I live.

Her voice remains steady throughout, though emotion colours the final lines. Jon watches her with undisguised tenderness, his attention complete and focused in a way that itself demonstrates their renewed connection.

After a moment, Jon unfolds his own paper and begins, his voice carrying a new quality of openness:

I am the boy who dismantled clocks to understand their workings
I am the child who believed every problem had a solution if approached correctly

I am the student who found clarity in the elegant logic of computer code
I am the man who built his identity on capability and certainty
I am the husband who promised protection without understanding its limits
I am the professional whose confidence came from mastering complexity
I am now the man confronting problems that cannot be solved, only lived with
I am the technician learning that not all solutions are technical
I am the husband discovering that true partnership transcends rescue
I am the companion finding strength in shared vulnerability, not just competence
I am learning that helplessness need not mean hopelessness
I am discovering that acceptance creates possibility where resistance creates despair
I am beginning to trust processes I cannot control or predict
I am finding courage to face fears I once refused to name
I am creating connection that relies on presence more than performance
I am still problem-solving, still protecting, but with deeper understanding
I am more than what I can fix or control; I am how I love.

The parallels between their independent poems are striking: both acknowledge the identities that once defined them, the painful process of releasing those definitions, and the discovery of deeper connection through shared vulnerability rather than mutual strength.

Their final statements, with their emphasis on being defined by how they live and love rather than by circumstance or ability, suggest a shared vision for their future together; not as a return to what was, but as an evolution into something new and potentially more profound.

As we move toward the conclusion of our work together, I ask them: 'What have you gained from these sessions that you want to carry forward?'

Sophia considers this with characteristic thoughtfulness. 'I've learned that independence and interdependence aren't mutually exclusive', she says finally. 'For so long, I viewed accepting help as a form of defeat, as giving up essential parts of myself. I'm learning that true strength sometimes means allowing others to support you; not because you're incapable, but because connection itself has value'.

Jon nods in recognition. 'And I've realised that my need to fix things was often more about managing my own discomfort than actually supporting Sophia', he adds. 'When I stopped trying to solve her vision loss and started being fully present with our experience of it, everything shifted. There's a different kind of strength in bearing witness without trying to change what can't be changed'.

'What has surprised you most about this process?' Maria asks.

'That intimacy could actually deepen through this challenge', Sophia replies. 'I expected loss upon loss: vision, independence, connection. Instead, I'm discovering new dimensions of relationship that weren't accessible when everything came easily'.

'And that acceptance isn't the same as resignation', Jon adds. 'I thought accepting Sophia's progressive vision loss meant giving up, surrendering to defeat. Instead, it's been the opposite: acceptance has freed us to focus our energy on creating the best possible life within our new reality, rather than exhausting ourselves fighting against it'.

They speak now with the quiet wisdom of people who have discovered unexpected strength through confronting profound vulnerability; not denying the genuine loss and grief that accompanies Sophia's condition but finding a way to integrate these challenges into a relationship that remains vital and evolving.

As our final minutes approach, I share my observations of their journey: their courage in examining patterns established over years of capability and independence, their willingness to develop new forms of connection as circumstances change, the small brave steps they've taken toward a different but potentially deeper intimacy.

'You came to us as two people facing a significant challenge primarily as individuals', I tell them. 'What I see now are two people who have learned to turn toward rather than away from each other in difficulty, to create meaning and connection even within circumstances neither would have chosen'.

'It feels like we're creating something new', Sophia says, the words carrying both acknowledgement of loss and genuine hope. 'Not a replacement for what we're losing, but a different kind of partnership that wouldn't have been possible without this challenge'.

'We're still grieving what's changing', Jon adds with honesty that no longer carries despair. 'But we're also discovering what can grow in the space that grief creates'.

As they prepare to leave for the last time, I observe how differently they navigate together compared to that first session. Jon's guidance is neither controlling nor reluctant now but offered with natural attention to Sophia's needs. Sophia accepts his support without the tension of someone fighting to maintain independence at all costs. There is a fluid coordination between them that speaks of new patterns consciously developed and gradually embodied.

'Remember you can always reach out if you need additional support', Maria reminds them. 'Though I believe you have what you need now to continue this journey together'.

At the door, they pause. 'Thank you', Jon says, genuine emotion in his voice. 'For helping us find each other again in the midst of everything changing'.

'And for showing us possibilities we couldn't see on our own', Sophia adds, the metaphor carrying special resonance given her circumstances.

As they walk toward their car, I watch them from the window. The physical coordination between them now appears both practical and intimate; Jon guiding Sophia with subtle cues that respect her autonomy while providing necessary support. Just before they reach the car, they stop and hug, a long moment of genuine connection that transcends the serious challenges they continue to face.

Maria joins me at the window. 'They've found a different way forward, haven't they?' she asks softly.

'Yes', I reply, watching as they drive away. 'Not the future they planned, but one that still holds meaning and connection. That's the work that matters'.

Chapter 34

Richard and Kaye – Finding the Roar Within

Richard had described Kaye as 'the beautiful dormouse' – caged, comfortable, and quietly suffocating in a relationship where Richard's need for control left no room for her authentic self to breathe. Their fundamental differences ran deep: his rigidity met her need for freedom, his certainty clashed with her spontaneity, his carefully ordered world felt like imprisonment to her wilder spirit. They had come to therapy hoping to bridge the unbridgeable, but some chasms, I had learned, are too wide for any bridge to span.

The next morning, I received an email from Richard. The tone was coolly professional, the content unsurprising: our session had not been helpful to him, he saw no value in continuing, and they would not be booking additional appointments. There was a perfunctory thank you for our time, followed by his elaborately formal email signature listing his various professional credentials and accomplishments.

I forwarded the message to Maria with a single comment: 'Expected, but still disappointing'.

Her reply came quickly: 'For Kaye's sake, I almost hope this prompts her to make a decision. No therapy can create equality where one partner is fundamentally committed to maintaining dominance'.

In the weeks that followed, I found myself thinking about Kaye often. In our practice, we measure success by relationships healed, connections restored, new patterns established. But sometimes success takes a different form: perhaps a seed planted, a question raised, a possibility illuminated where before there seemed only resignation.

I hoped that our brief encounter had offered Kaye something valuable, even if it wasn't what she had initially sought. Not a way to transform her relationship with Richard, but perhaps a first step toward recognising that she deserved more than to be someone's 'beautiful dormouse'. That captivity, no matter how gilded the cage, is still captivity. That perhaps, despite Richard's confident assertion to the contrary, roaring might indeed be in her nature after all, if only she could find the courage to discover her true voice.

Some months later, I received a card in the post. Inside was a simple note, unsigned but immediately recognisable in its implication:

'I've found my roar. Thank you for helping me remember it was there'.

DOI: 10.4324/9781003752776-34

Enclosed was a small photograph – not of the sender, but of a dormouse, sitting not in a cage but at the bottom of a tree in what was clearly a wild woodland, looking toward the open sky.

I placed the card on my desk and smiled. Sometimes the seeds we plant bear fruit in unexpected ways. Sometimes the cages we help unlock aren't the ones we initially set out to open. And sometimes, the most successful therapy isn't about bringing people together, but about helping someone find the strength to walk away.

In a profession dedicated to healing relationships, it can be difficult to accept that not all relationships should be saved. Some patterns are too deeply entrenched, some imbalances too fundamental to correct when only one partner seeks change. In those cases, our responsibility shifts – not to preserve the relationship at all costs, but to support the individual's journey toward wholeness, even if that journey ultimately leads them along separate paths.

As I prepared for my next session, I looked at the photograph of the free dormouse – a small reminder that liberation sometimes takes unexpected forms, and that finding one's voice after years of silence might indeed feel as powerful as a roar.

Chapter 35

What Have I Learned?

As I sit in my therapy room, the afternoon sun casting long shadows across the floor, I find myself returning to a story I wrote years ago, hidden away in the appendices of my doctoral thesis. This story, 'The Wayfarer', is a metaphorical journey of a young man sailing through uncharted waters, seeking meaning and connection. Though fictional, it's deeply rooted in my own experiences and captures the essence of my journey through relationships, both personal and professional, in ways that academic language never could.

In this story, the young Wayfarer sets sail on a boat named Hope, leaving behind the expectations of others to chart his own course across unknown seas. He encounters various islands, each representing different relationship experiences, from Loneliness to Love, with many challenging stops between. This metaphorical voyage has become the compass by which I navigate my understanding of relationships and my own journey through them.

'What have I learned?' seems such a simple question. Yet like relationships themselves, the answer is layered with complexity, contradiction, and unexpected wisdom found in the most unlikely places.

I've learned that we are all Wayfarers. Each of us sets sail from harbours of our childhood, carrying maps drawn by our parents, teachers, and early experiences,

DOI: 10.4324/9781003752776-35

maps that are often incomplete or misleading. We navigate by stars we barely understand, seeking islands that may only exist in our imagination.

The Islands We Visit

Think of the islands the Wayfarer encountered: Lonely, Rejection, Disappointment, Compromise, Disconnection, Unfulfilled, Unhappiness, Betrayal, Loss, and finally, Love. How many of these islands have you visited in your own relationships? I certainly have anchored at every one of them, sometimes lingering longer than I should have, sometimes departing too quickly.

My first marriage took me to the Island of Compromise, where I thought contentment meant settling for less than what my heart truly desired. I remember sitting across from my first wife at dinner, both of us maintaining a polite conversation while our inner selves screamed in silence. We were like the Wayfarer and the girl on that island, close physically but separated by an uncrossable sea of misunderstanding.

Many clients come to me having spent years on the Island of Disconnection. Like the beautiful woman who couldn't understand the Wayfarer's words, these couples have lost their shared language. They sit before me, describing the same events with such wildly different perceptions that one might think they're speaking of entirely different relationships.

'She never listens to me', a husband might say. 'I've been screaming the same thing for twenty years, but he never hears me', his wife responds.

Both are speaking truths, their truths, yet neither can translate for the other. This is where my work begins: not by teaching a new language, but by helping them remember one they've forgotten.

The Sea of Reflection

Perhaps the most important lesson I've learned is the value of what the Wayfarer experienced in the Sea of Reflection. After losing his love on the Island of Loss, he was forced to confront himself, to recognise that before he could truly love another, he needed to love himself.

I recall a man I'll call Edward, who came to therapy after his third divorce. Successful in business but a disaster in relationships, Edward was convinced that he simply had 'terrible luck with women'. One memorable session, I asked him what he liked about himself.

The silence that followed was deafening.

'I'm good at making money', he finally offered.

'And as a human being?' I pressed. 'What do you value about your character, your heart?'

He looked at me as if I'd asked him to explain quantum physics in Swahili.

Like the Wayfarer, Edward had never paused in the Sea of Reflection. He had sailed from island to island, relationship to relationship, without questioning what he brought to each encounter. Our work together wasn't about finding him a better partner, it was about helping him become a better companion to himself.

The Weather of Relationships

Another lesson – relationships have their own weather patterns, and we must learn to navigate them all. The Wayfarer experienced calm seas and raging storms, blistering sun and cooling rain. So do all relationships.

Many couples enter therapy expecting fair weather forever after. They want to eliminate arguments, banish disagreements, ensure smooth sailing at all times. I've learned this is not only impossible but undesirable. It's in weathering storms together that relationships develop resilience and depth.

Martha and Carlos had been married for thirty-eight years when they came to see me. Their primary complaint? 'We fight too much'. But as we explored their relationship, I discovered something fascinating: their arguments, while sometimes fierce, were also rituals of connection. They fought passionately because they cared passionately. Their problem wasn't the fighting; it was their shared belief that fighting meant something was wrong.

'What if', I suggested, 'your arguments are actually signs of how deeply you care about each other and your relationship?'

They looked at me sceptically, then at each other. And something shifted, a recognition that what they had interpreted as stormy weather was actually part of their unique climate, neither good nor bad but simply theirs.

The Companions We Choose

The Wayfarer's journey teaches us about the companions we choose. Hope, his boat, was more than transportation, it was a constant presence, supporting him through all conditions, adapting to his needs while maintaining its own integrity.

Our most important relationships should offer this same quality: support without submission, connection without control, shared journeys while respecting individual paths.

Then there were the people he encountered on each island, some welcoming, some indifferent, some actively hostile. I've learned that we often focus so intently on finding 'the right person' that we neglect to consider the entire community that comes with them.

Stuart and Clare, whose story I shared earlier, demonstrated this vividly. Their relationship couldn't be understood in isolation from Clare's children from her previous marriage or Stuart's cultural background. The island they inhabited together was populated by other people whose influence shaped their connection in countless ways.

I've come to believe that when we choose a partner, we're also choosing their world, their friends, family, cultural context, values, and histories. The question isn't just 'Do I love this person?' but 'Can I thrive in the ecosystem of their life?'

The Maps We Draw

Perhaps the most profound lesson from the Wayfarer's journey is about the maps we create. As he sailed from island to island, he carefully charted each one, marking its location, features, and the emotions it evoked. These maps became not just navigation tools but a record of his growth.

In my work, I've developed maps of my own, the Relationship Paradigm with its six elements: Communication, Connection, Commitment, Fun, Growth, and Trust. These aren't abstract theories but charts drawn from countless voyages with couples through treacherous and beautiful relationship territories.

I remember Jane and Thomas, who came to therapy after twenty years of marriage, their relationship reduced to logistics and obligations. 'We've lost our way', Jane said simply.

Using the Relationship Paradigm as our map, we began to chart where they were and where they wanted to go. Communication had narrowed to household management. Connection had been sacrificed to busy schedules. Commitment remained but had calcified into habit rather than choice. Fun had become something they experienced separately, rarely together. Growth existed professionally but not personally. Trust was intact but untested for years.

With this map, they could see not just what was missing but how each element connected to the others. Improving communication created space for deeper connection. Rediscovering fun strengthened commitment. Their journey back to each other wasn't linear but a spiralling exploration of all six elements, each supporting the others.

The Unexpected Harbours

One of the most delightful lessons I've learned is that relationships often take us to harbours we never intended to visit, and these unexpected destinations can be the most rewarding.

The Wayfarer began his journey searching for something he couldn't even name. He thought he was seeking adventure, freedom, perhaps love in some abstract sense. What he ultimately found was both simpler and more profound: the capacity to love himself and therefore truly connect with another.

I've seen this with countless couples. They enter therapy seeking solutions to specific problems, communication breakdowns, sexual disconnection, parenting conflicts, only to discover that addressing these issues leads them to unexpected treasures: deeper self-awareness, forgotten parts of themselves, new ways of being together that they couldn't have imagined.

One couple came to me because they couldn't agree on where to live after retirement. He wanted the countryside; she preferred city life. As we explored this seemingly straightforward conflict, we uncovered layers of meaning neither had recognised. For him, the country represented a return to the freedom and simplicity of childhood. For her, the city offered cultural stimulation she'd sacrificed during years of raising children in suburbia.

What began as a logistical problem revealed itself as an opportunity for both to honour important aspects of themselves and each other. Their solution, dividing time between a small city apartment and a country cottage, wasn't just a compromise but a creative expansion of their relationship, leading to a renaissance neither had anticipated.

The Truth about Perception

If there's one lesson that underlies everything I've learned about relationships, it's this: *In a relationship, there is no reality; there is only perception. Two people can have very different perceptions of a shared experience, and they are both equally correct.*

This principle, which I repeat often to clients, reflects the philosophical insights of Merleau-Ponty's concept of 'flesh' and Sartre's ideas about 'being-for-others'. Our perceptions aren't just subjective filters of objective reality; they're actively creating the reality we experience, especially in relationships.

Consider Harriet and Ed, whose story I shared earlier. When Harriet discovered evidence of Ed's affair, her perception was one of complete betrayal, a rupture in trust that threatened everything they'd built together. From Ed's perspective, the affair represented not rejection of Harriet but an escape from his own intense feelings of inadequacy, triggered by his undisclosed dyslexia and professional insecurities.

Both perceptions were 'true', yet dramatically different. The healing began not when one perception conquered the other, but when both could coexist, be understood, and eventually form the foundation for a new shared reality.

This understanding of perception has revolutionary implications. It means that relationship problems aren't about determining who's right and who's wrong, but about creating bridges between different perceptual worlds. It means that empathy, the ability to temporarily inhabit another's perception without abandoning our own, is perhaps the most crucial relationship skill.

The Transdisciplinary Voyage

My journey as a relationship therapist has taught me the value of transdisciplinary thinking, of sailing beyond the boundaries of any single approach or theory. Like the Wayfarer who had to adapt to different cultures and conditions on each island, effective relationship work requires flexibility, creativity, and a willingness to integrate diverse perspectives.

The rigid maps of traditional therapeutic models often fail to capture the complex, dynamic nature of relationships. A couple isn't merely a system to be analysed, a set of behaviours to be modified, or unconscious patterns to be interpreted. They're all these things simultaneously, plus cultural narratives, biological impulses, philosophical questions, and spiritual longings.

This transdisciplinary approach isn't just theoretical; it's deeply practical. When Rebecca and James struggled with walls of silence, they needed psychological insights about emotional withdrawal, sociological understanding of gender expectations, communication theory, and existential questions about meaning and connection. No single discipline could have addressed all these dimensions.

With Stuart and Clare, the blended family dynamics required perspectives from family systems theory, while their cross-cultural backgrounds needed anthropological sensitivity. Their long-term patterns of interaction called for both behavioural and psychodynamic approaches.

This is why I believe relationship therapists must be intellectual adventurers, willing to sail beyond the safe harbours of their training into uncharted waters where disciplines intersect and new insights emerge.

The Journey, Not the Destination

Finally, I've learned that relationships are journeys, not destinations. The Wayfarer discovered this when he realised that finding love wasn't an endpoint but the beginning of a new voyage, not a conquest but an ongoing exploration.

Too often, couples approach relationships with destination thinking: 'Once we're married ...' 'When the children are grown ...' 'After we retire ...' They postpone joy, connection, and growth, believing these will somehow automatically arrive at some future milestone.

But relationships exist only in the present moment, in the daily choices to turn toward or away from each other, to listen deeply or dismiss quickly, to hold space for difference or demand conformity. The quality of a relationship isn't determined by reaching particular landmarks but by how partners navigate together day by day.

I think of Debbie and Michael, who postponed addressing their relationship problems for years because 'once the children are in college, we'll have time to focus on us'. When that long-awaited moment arrived, they discovered they had become strangers, with little foundation to build upon. Their journey together had been put on hold for so long that they'd forgotten how to travel as companions.

Contrast this with Rita and James, who entered therapy while expecting their first child. 'We don't have problems', they explained. 'We want to strengthen what already works before the challenges come'. Their proactive approach created resilience that served them through the inevitable difficulties ahead. They understood intuitively that their relationship was an ongoing journey that required attention at every stage, not just during crises.

A Final Reflection

As I look back on the Wayfarer's journey and my own parallel voyage as a therapist, husband, and human being, I'm struck by a delightful irony: the most valuable lessons about relationships often come from their failures rather than their successes.

Each island the Wayfarer visited, even those of Loneliness, Rejection, and Betrayal, offered wisdom he couldn't have gained elsewhere. Similarly, my own relationship disappointments, the painful therapy sessions where couples couldn't find their way back to each other, and the moments of profound disconnection have been as instructive as the joyful reconnections and transformative breakthroughs.

This might be the most hopeful lesson of all: nothing in our relationship journeys is wasted. Every storm navigated, every wrong turn, every painful parting contains the seeds of growth and understanding if we're willing to chart them honestly on our maps.

I think of my client Raymond, who at seventy-two came to me after his third divorce, feeling like a complete failure at relationships. 'What have I learned?' he asked bitterly. 'Apparently nothing'.

But as we explored his relationship history, the patterns, the perceptions, the choices, something remarkable happened. Raymond began to see that each relationship had taught him something essential about himself and others. His first marriage showed him the importance of shared values. His second taught him about his fear of vulnerability. His third revealed his tendency to prioritise harmony over authenticity.

'I've had three advanced degrees in relationships', he joked in our final session. 'Just took me a lifetime to earn them'.

This perspective transformed Raymond's past from a series of failures to a meaningful journey of growth. It allowed him to approach new relationships not with fear of repeating old patterns but with confidence in his hard-won wisdom.

And isn't this what all of us want? Not perfect relationships, which don't exist, but the ability to learn from each voyage we undertake, to draw ever more accurate and nuanced maps, to become more skilful and compassionate navigators of the complex waters of human connection.

The Wayfarer began his journey seeking something he couldn't name and discovered it was himself he needed to find first. Perhaps this is the ultimate lesson: relationships are mirrors reflecting our deepest selves back to us. They reveal our fears, our wounds, our capacity for love and healing. They show us who we are and who we might become.

As for me, I continue my own journey as both Wayfarer and guide to others. Each couple that enters our therapy room brings new territories to explore, new weather patterns to navigate, new islands to chart. The maps I've drawn, my Relationship Paradigm, my Duo Coaching framework, continue to evolve with each voyage.

And always, like the Wayfarer with his boat named Hope, I maintain that fundamental optimism about human connection. Despite all the evidence of relationship difficulties I encounter daily, I believe profoundly in our capacity to find our way to each other, to create connections that nurture rather than diminish, to build relationships that help us become more fully ourselves.

After all, if a naïve young man in a small boat can navigate unknown seas, survive storms and betrayals, and ultimately find love, both for himself and another, then surely there is hope for all of us on our relationship journeys.

The sea may be vast, the weather unpredictable, the maps incomplete. But with courage, compassion, and the wisdom gained from each island we visit, we can all become more skilful Wayfarers in the great adventure of human connection.

Chapter 36

Hope for Humanity

As I near the conclusion of this book, I find myself reflecting on a question I'm asked in interviews or after speaking engagements: 'After seeing so many troubled relationships, are you optimistic about the future of human connection?' People seem to expect that years of witnessing relationship distress might have left me cynical or discouraged.

Nothing could be further from the truth.

Despite the pain, disconnection, and conflict I've witnessed in our therapy room, I remain profoundly hopeful about our human capacity for meaningful connection. This hope isn't born of naivety but of evidence – evidence I've seen firsthand as couples transform their relationships from battlegrounds to sacred spaces of healing and growth.

This chapter is about that hope, and why I believe that fostering better relationships at all levels – from intimate partnerships to global cooperation – represents our greatest opportunity for creating a thriving future for humanity.

The Ripple Effect of Relationship Well-Being

Relationships are not separate from the fabric of society; they are its fundamental building blocks. When relationships flourish, everything built upon them becomes stronger, more resilient, and more capable of positive growth.

Consider the cascading effects of a single troubled relationship: the couple experiences chronic stress, diminished health, and reduced productivity. Their children absorb the tension, potentially developing behavioural issues or struggles with their own relationships later in life. Extended family members become entangled in the conflict. Friends feel forced to take sides. Workplaces suffer from decreased focus and increased absenteeism. Communities lose the contributions these individuals might otherwise make.

Now, reverse this cascade: a couple develops a strong, supportive partnership built on the principles of the Relationship Paradigm – healthy communication, deep connection, unwavering commitment, genuine fun, continuous growth, and mutual trust. This relationship becomes a secure base from which both partners can thrive personally and professionally. Their children witness healthy conflict resolution

DOI: 10.4324/9781003752776-36

and emotional intimacy, internalising these patterns for their own future relationships. Extended family members benefit from the couple's stability and generosity of spirit. Friends enjoy the couple's balanced, positive energy. Workplaces gain from their focus, creativity, and consistent contribution. Communities benefit from their engagement and support.

This ripple effect extends outward in ever-widening circles, from the most intimate partnership to the broadest societal structures. I've come to believe that relationship health isn't just a personal matter – it's a public health issue, an economic issue, an educational issue, and ultimately, a matter of our collective human future.

The Current State of Relationships

If we are honest with ourselves, we must acknowledge that the current state of relationships at all levels gives cause for concern.

At the individual level, loneliness has reached epidemic proportions. In the UK, over nine million people report feeling lonely always or often, with dramatic impacts on physical and mental health. Studies show that chronic loneliness can be as harmful to health as smoking fifteen cigarettes a day. Worldwide, similar trends emerge, with developed nations particularly affected despite – or perhaps because of – technological connectedness.

At the couple level, approximately 42% of marriages in the UK end in divorce. While divorce isn't inherently negative and can be the healthiest choice in some situations, the high rate suggests widespread relationship distress. More concerning is how many couples remain together in states of quiet desperation – emotionally disconnected, functioning as roommates rather than partners, modelling unhealthy relationship patterns for their children.

At the family level, intergenerational trauma continues to cycle through lineages, with unhealed relationship wounds from one generation manifesting in the next. Children who witness poor relationship models often struggle to form healthy attachments themselves, perpetuating patterns of disconnection.

At the community level, social cohesion has weakened in many areas. Neighbourhood connections have diminished as digital interactions have replaced physical ones. The social fabric that once provided support, particularly in times of hardship, has thinned considerably.

At the organisational level, workplace relationships suffer from hierarchical power structures, poor communication practices, and environments that prioritise productivity over human connection. The resulting disengagement costs businesses billions annually in lost productivity, higher turnover, and diminished innovation.

At the national and international levels, political polarisation has intensified, with opposing sides increasingly viewing each other not just as having different perspectives but as fundamentally threatening. Cooperation on critical global challenges – climate change, resource management, pandemic response – is hampered by relationship dysfunction at the highest levels.

This reality could indeed provoke pessimism. But I see it differently. I see unprecedented opportunity.

The Relationship Revolution

What if we were standing at the cusp of a relationship revolution – a fundamental shift in how we understand, prioritise, and nurture human connection at every level?

I believe we are, and that this revolution has already begun. Consider these emerging trends:

1. **Growing awareness of relationship importance**: Research from fields as diverse as neuroscience, economics, public health, and psychology increasingly confirms what relationship therapists have long known – healthy connections are fundamental to human flourishing. This research is gradually influencing public discourse and policy.
2. **Evolving relationship structures**: As society moves beyond rigid relationship templates, people are creating connections that better serve their authentic needs. Whether traditional marriage, blended families, chosen families, or other arrangements, there's growing acceptance that meaningful connection comes in many forms.
3. **Therapeutic advancements**: Approaches to relationship healing have evolved significantly, with evidence-based methods showing impressive results. Innovations like Duo Coaching demonstrate that even deeply troubled relationships can transform with the right support.
4. **Digital reconnection**: After the initial fascination with digital connection at the expense of physical presence, many people are seeking more balanced approaches – using technology to facilitate rather than replace in-person connection.
5. **Workplace transformation**: Forward-thinking organisations are recognising that workplace relationships significantly impact performance, innovation, and employee well-being. Models emphasising psychological safety, collaboration, and meaningful connection are gaining traction.
6. **Educational evolution**: Schools are increasingly incorporating social-emotional learning into curricula, helping children develop relationship skills alongside academic knowledge.

These trends suggest not just incremental improvement but the potential for transformative change in how we approach relationships across society. To realise this potential, however, requires intentional action across multiple domains.

A Systemic Approach to Relationship Flourishing

If we truly wish to create hope for humanity through better relationships, we need coordinated efforts across all levels of society. Here's what this might look like:

Individual Level: Relationship Literacy

Just as we consider literacy and numeracy essential skills, relationship literacy – the ability to form and maintain healthy connections – should be recognised as fundamental. This includes:

- **Self-awareness**: Understanding one's own attachment patterns, triggers, and relationship needs
- **Emotional regulation**: Managing emotions effectively, particularly during conflict
- **Communication skills**: Expressing oneself clearly and listening deeply
- **Boundary setting**: Knowing how to establish and respect healthy limits
- **Conflict resolution**: Approaching disagreements as opportunities for growth rather than threats

These skills aren't innate; they're learned. And currently, many people learn them haphazardly, often internalising dysfunctional patterns from their families of origin or media portrayals. Imagine if we approached relationship skills with the same seriousness we approach mathematics or language – with structured learning, practice, feedback, and continuous development.

Couple Level: Preventative Approach

Currently, most couples seek help only when their relationship is already in serious distress – the equivalent of waiting until a disease is advanced before seeking medical attention. A preventative approach would include:

- **Relationship education before problems emerge**: Courses for couples at all stages, particularly during transitions like moving in together, marriage, or becoming parents
- **Regular relationship check-ups**: Normalising periodic review of relationship health, similar to dental check-ups or vehicle maintenance
- **Early intervention resources**: Accessible support when minor issues arise, before they become entrenched patterns
- **Celebration of relationship milestones**: Cultural recognition of relationship achievements beyond the wedding day
- **Destigmatisation of relationship support**: Reframing therapy not as a sign of failure but as a commitment to growth

Duo Coaching is often the lifeboat service called out in an emergency. I would also love to offer regular MOTs and preventative maintenance.

Family Level: Intergenerational Healing

Families transmit relationship patterns across generations, for better or worse. Interrupting negative cycles requires:

- **Parenting education that emphasises relationship modelling**: Helping parents understand that how they relate to each other powerfully shapes their children's future relationships
- **Family therapy approaches that address systemic patterns**: Working with whole family systems rather than just individuals
- **Intergenerational dialogue facilitation**: Creating safe spaces for different generations to share experiences and heal historical wounds
- **Support for families in transition**: Specialised help during divorces, remarriages, bereavements, and other significant changes

When a couple learns to relate in healthier ways, they don't just improve their own lives – they potentially alter the trajectory of their entire family line, healing backward and forward across generations.

Educational Level: Relationship-Centred Learning

Schools have tremendous potential to build relationship capacity from early childhood. This requires:

- **Comprehensive relationship education**: Age-appropriate curricula from primary school through university that address all aspects of relationships, not just sexual health
- **Teacher training in relationship-centric approaches**: Equipping educators to model and teach healthy relationship skills
- **Peer-to-peer relationship programmes**: Student-led initiatives that normalise discussion of relationship challenges
- **Parent–school partnerships**: Collaborative approaches that reinforce relationship skills across contexts

Imagine children graduating not just with academic qualifications but with the ability to form and maintain healthy connections throughout their lives. The impact on mental health, productivity, and social cohesion would be immeasurable.

Organisational Level: Connection as Competitive Advantage

Workplaces that prioritise relationship health gain significant advantages:

- **Leadership development centred on relationship skills**: Training managers to create psychological safety and meaningful connection
- **Relationship-focused organisational structures**: Models that emphasise collaboration over competition
- **Conflict resolution systems**: Processes that transform workplace disagreements into opportunities for innovation

- **Mentoring and peer support programmes**: Structured opportunities for meaningful workplace connections
- **Work–relationship balance policies**: Recognition that supporting employees' personal relationships benefits organisational performance

The most successful organisations of the future will be those that recognise relationship health as a strategic priority, not an HR afterthought.

Community Level: Rebuilding Social Fabric

Strong communities are built on relationship networks:

- **Community spaces designed for connection**: Physical environments that facilitate meaningful interaction
- **Intergenerational community programmes**: Initiatives that connect younger and older community members
- **Relationship-centred community governance**: Decision-making processes that build connection while addressing challenges
- **Community relationship rituals**: Regular events that celebrate and strengthen local bonds
- **Support for community connectors**: Resources for individuals who naturally build bridges between different community groups

The social capital generated by these approaches pays dividends in community resilience, particularly during crises.

Policy Level: Relationship-Centred Governance

Finally, government policy should recognise relationship health as a fundamental public good:

- **Relationship impact assessments for policies**: Evaluating how proposed laws and regulations might affect relationship well-being
- **Investment in relationship support services**: Adequate funding for preventative and intervention services
- **Economic measures that value relationship work**: Recognition of care work and relationship building in economic indicators
- **Housing and urban planning with relationships in mind**: Designs that facilitate rather than hinder connection
- **Cross-department relationship strategies**: Coordinated approaches that recognise relationship health affects all policy areas

Policymakers who understand that social connection underpins economic prosperity, public health, and national well-being will make decisions that strengthen rather than undermine relationship networks.

The Path Forward: Challenges and Opportunities

This vision of a relationship revolution faces significant challenges:

1. **Cultural resistance**: Deeply ingrained beliefs that relationship skills are innate rather than learned, or that relationship struggles are purely private matters
2. **Economic pressures**: Systems that prioritise short-term productivity over long-term relationship health
3. **Digital disruption**: Technologies that sometimes substitute shallow connection for deep engagement
4. **Measurement difficulties**: The challenge of quantifying relationship well-being compared to more easily measured outcomes
5. **Resource inequalities**: Disparities in access to relationship education and support

Yet for each challenge, I see greater opportunity:

1. **Evolving cultural narratives**: Growing recognition of relationships as skills that can be developed
2. **Economic evidence**: Mounting research showing the economic cost of poor relationships and benefits of strong ones
3. **Technological potential**: New ways to facilitate meaningful connection across distances and differences
4. **Measurement innovation**: Developing more sophisticated approaches to assessing relationship health
5. **Democratising access**: Creating scalable, affordable relationship resources for all

The key to realising these opportunities lies in coordinated action across sectors, with relationship therapists playing a crucial role as advocates, educators, and innovators.

The Role of Relationship Therapists in Social Transformation

As relationship therapists, we have a responsibility that extends beyond our therapy rooms. Our unique understanding of relationship dynamics positions us to:

1. **Challenge orthodoxy**: Question traditional approaches that may no longer serve couples effectively, developing innovations like Duo Coaching that better address contemporary needs
2. **Bridge disciplines**: Connect relationship science with fields like economics, public health, education, and urban planning

3. **Advocate for policy change**: Use our expertise to inform decision-makers about the societal impact of relationship health
4. **Democratise knowledge**: Share relationship wisdom in accessible formats beyond the therapy setting
5. **Shift cultural narratives**: Help reframe relationship struggles from private failures to normal human experiences worthy of support

This expanded role requires us to think beyond individual clinical practice to consider how our knowledge might transform broader systems. It asks us to become not just healers but social innovators.

A Personal Commitment

This vision of relationship-centred social transformation isn't abstract theory for me – it's the driving purpose of my work. My mission to impact and improve ten million relationships worldwide this decade reflects my conviction that relationship healing is one of our most powerful levers for positive change.

I believe that every couple who heals their relationship creates ripples that extend far beyond their household. Every parent who models healthy connection shapes the relationship future of the next generation. Every organisation that prioritises relationship well-being influences countless lives. Every community that strengthens its relationship networks builds resilience against whatever challenges may come.

Conclusion: The Reason for Hope

When I look at the troubled state of our world – environmental degradation, political polarisation, economic inequality, persistent conflict – I don't see evidence that human connection is doomed. Rather, I see symptoms of what happens when we neglect the fundamental importance of relationships.

And in this recognition lies tremendous hope. If relationship dysfunction contributes to our greatest challenges, then relationship healing offers a path toward their resolution.

This isn't magical thinking. It's based on what I've witnessed countless times in my therapy room: the transformative power of connection. I've seen couples move from bitter enmity to profound understanding. I've watched decades-old patterns shift in moments of genuine meeting. I've witnessed the healing that flows when people feel truly seen and heard.

If such transformation is possible between two people who've hurt each other deeply, why couldn't similar healing occur between communities, organisations, or nations? The principles are the same, though the scale differs.

My hope for humanity rests on this simple but profound belief: we are wired for connection. Beneath our defences, projections, and fears lies an innate capacity for empathy, understanding, and collaboration. Our relationship struggles don't reflect our nature but our wounding, our misconceptions, and systems that often work against our relational well-being.

When we create conditions that support rather than hinder this innate capacity – from the intimacy of a therapy room to the breadth of international relations – we unleash perhaps the greatest untapped resource for addressing our shared challenges: our ability to form meaningful, productive, healing relationships.

So yes, I am hopeful. Not despite what I've witnessed in my years as a relationship therapist, but because of it. I've seen too many seemingly miraculous transformations to believe that any relationship – whether between individuals, groups, or nations – is beyond the possibility of healing.

This hope isn't passive; it's a call to action. To prioritise relationships in our personal lives, our professional endeavours, our community engagement, and our policy advocacy. To recognise that the quality of our connections fundamentally shapes the quality of our world.

As this book draws to a close, I invite you to join this relationship revolution, in whatever capacity suits your circumstances and talents. Whether by healing your own relationships, supporting others in theirs, advocating for relationship-centred approaches in your workplace or community, or simply spreading the message that better relationships are possible, you become part of this hope for humanity.

Because ultimately, the future of our species doesn't depend primarily on technological innovation or economic growth, important as these may be. It depends on our ability to connect: with ourselves, with each other, and with the living world we share. In nurturing these connections lies our greatest hope for creating a world where all can flourish.

Appendix

Bibliography

Attachment Theory and Research

Ainsworth, M.D.S., Blehar, M.C., Waters, E. and Wall, S. (1978) *Patterns of Attachment: A Psychological Study of the Strange Situation*. Hillsdale, NJ: Lawrence Erlbaum Associates.

Bowlby, J. (1969) *Attachment and Loss: Vol. 1. Attachment*. New York: Basic Books.

Bowlby, J. (1988) *A Secure Base: Parent-Child Attachment and Healthy Human Development*. New York: Basic Books.

Phenomenological Foundations

Merleau-Ponty, M. (1968) *The visible and the invisible*. Translated by A. Lingis. Evanston, IL: Northwestern University Press.

Sartre, J.-P. (1943) *Being and nothingness: An essay on phenomenological ontology*. Translated by H. Barnes. London: Methuen.

Relationship Therapy Approaches

Bateson, N. (2016) *Small Arcs of Larger Circles: Framing through Stories*. Axminster: Triarchy Press.

Campbell, J. (2008) *The Hero with a Thousand Faces* (3rd ed.). New World Library. (Original work published 1949).

Chapman, G. (1992) *The Five Love Languages: How to Express Heartfelt Commitment to Your Mate*. Chicago: Northfield Publishing.

Gottman, J.M. (1999) *The Seven Principles for Making Marriage Work*. New York: Crown Publishers.

Gottman, J.M. and Silver, N. (2012) *What Makes Love Last? How to Build Trust and Avoid Betrayal*. New York: Simon & Schuster.

Lee, J.A. (1973) *The Colors of Love: An Exploration of the Ways of Loving*. Don Mills, Ontario: New Press.

Perel, E. (2006) *Mating in Captivity: Unlocking Erotic Intelligence*. New York: Harper.

Perel, E. (2017) *The State of Affairs: Rethinking Infidelity*. New York: Harper.

Therapeutic Modalities

Bandler, R. and Grinder, J. (1975) *The Structure of Magic I: A Book about Language and Therapy*. Palo Alto, CA: Science and Behavior Books.

Berne, E. (1964) *Games People Play: The Psychology of Human Relationships*. New York: Grove Press.

Grove, D.J. and Panzer, B.I. (1989) *Resolving Traumatic Memories: Metaphors and Symbols in Psychotherapy*. New York: Irvington Publishers.

James, T. and Woodsmall, W. (1988) *Time Line Therapy and the Basis of Personality*. Capitola, CA: Meta Publications.

Perls, F., Hefferline, R.F. and Goodman, P. (1951) *Gestalt Therapy: Excitement and Growth in the Human Personality*. New York: Julian Press.

Rogers, C.R. (1951) *Client-Centered Therapy: Its Current Practice, Implications, and Theory*. Boston: Houghton Mifflin.

Satir, V. (1972) *Peoplemaking*. Palo Alto, CA: Science and Behavior Books.

Neuroscience and Biology of Connection

Zak, P.J. (2012) *The Moral Molecule: The Source of Love and Prosperity*. New York: Dutton.

Zak, P.J., Kurzban, R. and Matzner, W.T. (2005) 'Oxytocin is associated with human trustworthiness', *Hormones and Behavior*, 48(5), pp. 522–527.

Trauma and Recovery

Tedeschi, R.G. and Calhoun, L.G. (1996) 'The Posttraumatic Growth Inventory: Measuring the positive legacy of trauma', *Journal of Traumatic Stress*, 9(3), pp. 455–471.

Tedeschi, R.G. and Calhoun, L.G. (2004) 'Posttraumatic growth: Conceptual foundations and empirical evidence', *Psychological Inquiry*, 15(1), pp. 1–18.

Works by the Author

Wilkie, N. (2019) *Reset: The Relationship Paradigm*. Lymington, UK: Academy for Relationships.

Wilkie, N. (2021) *Recover: Rebuilding Trust after the Shock of Betrayal*. Lymington, UK: Academy for Relationships.

Wilkie, N. (2024) *The Phenomenology of Relationships*. Doctoral thesis. Middlesex University.

Index

For Product Safety Concerns and Information please contact our EU
representative GPSR@taylorandfrancis.com
Taylor & Francis Verlag GmbH, Kaufingerstraße 24, 80331 München, Germany

www.ingramcontent.com/pod-product-compliance
Ingram Content Group UK Ltd.
Pitfield, Milton Keynes, MK11 3LW, UK
UKHW020008200926
475702UK00015B/2532
* 9 7 8 1 0 4 1 2 7 1 2 2 2 *